The Bessies

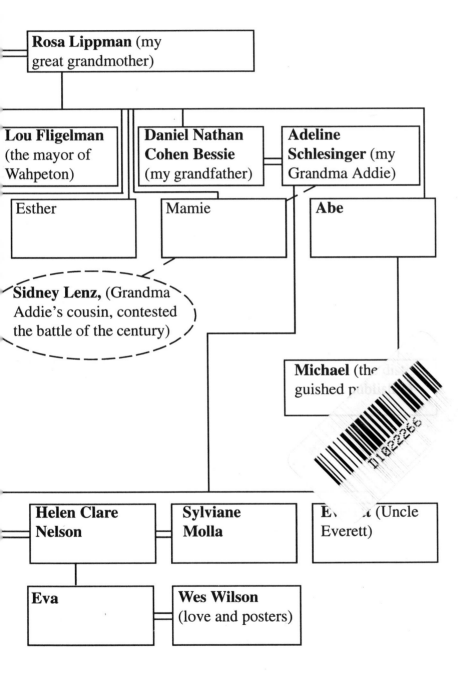

Rosa Lippman (my great grandmother)

Lou Fligelman (the mayor of Wahpeton)

Daniel Nathan Cohen Bessie (my grandfather)

Adeline Schlesinger (my Grandma Addie)

Esther

Mamie

Abe

Sidney Lenz, (Grandma Addie's cousin, contested the battle of the century)

Michael (the ~~distinguished~~ guished p~~ublic~~

Helen Clare Nelson

Sylviane Molla

E~~verett~~ (Uncle Everett)

Eva

Wes Wilson (love and posters)

rare
  birds

rare birds

an american family

Dan Bessie

THE UNIVERSITY PRESS OF KENTUCKY

Publication of this volume was made possible in part
by a grant from the National Endowment for the Humanities.

Editorial and Sales Offices: The University Press of Kentucky
663 South Limestone Street, Lexington, Kentucky 40508–4008

05 04 03 02 01   1 2 3 4 5

Frontispiece: Uncle Harry clowning around in 1940s Hollywood.

Library of Congress Cataloging-in-Publication Data

Bessie, Dan
Rare birds : an American family / Dan Bessie.
p. cm.
ISBN 0-8131-2179-5 (acid-free paper)
1. Bessie family. 2. Burnett family. 3. Bessie, Dan—Family.
4.Bessie, Alvah Cecil, 1904- I. Title.

CT274.B465 B47 2000
929'.2'0973—dc21   00-028312

for my sons, Joe and Tim Bessie,
and in memory of my daughter,
Lisa.

contents

stories: preface to a family

If you cannot get rid of the family skeleton, you may as well make it dance.

GEORGE BERNARD SHAW

Perhaps my concern with the diffusion of family life so routine in today's America helped to inspire this book. Time, distance, work pressures, and a steady stream of blows to our collective psyche seem to have created a nation only occasionally held together by strong family ties. We're partitioned into "eligible singles," "newly marrieds," or "young families." Many of us barely fifty have packed it in to Sun City or other "active retirement" reservations to bask in our "golden years."

While some manage to sustain family tradition, others, with little to hang on to, simply will their disfunctionality to the next generation. And even for many of those who *do* manage to ease through with a healthy equanimity, life nevertheless too often seems alienating.

True, religion and strict codes of conduct hold many families together—though some merely talk a good game in public while kicking the gilt-edged portrait under the bed as soon as the windows are shuttered. And though most families do the best they know how, our splintering into units of two, three, or five can disengage us from any larger purpose and force too many to take on the world alone.

Nor have we created, either within communities or nationally, a consistent quality of leadership working to unite us as a whole people, as a single family whose main reason for being might be to nourish the hopes and help achieve the possibilities inherent in each of its members.

So families plod along as best they can, and those without a family to plod along with tough it out on their own. Fortunately, many somehow manage, through friends and associates, to *create* family where none really exists.

Even without getting terribly sociological, examining "family" seems important. By taking a look at how one particular set of associated individuals slogged through to bring order and happiness out of chaos and despair (and sometimes fell far short of that goal), perhaps I can stir in those of you who scan these pages a notion or two about the value of family within your own lives and your own relationship to it. Why? Because I'm convinced that my family history contains, in microcosm, the similarities and peculiarities to be found, in one way or another, in most American families.

The threads I weave are common to us all. These just happen to be *my* rare birds—your own simply have a different plumage.

Some of us can "point with pride" to traditions reaching back across generations and which keep on sustaining. My own ties have been more tenuous. In addition to an exceptional woman as a mother, the one concrete thing I did have that helped me hold together a family whose hidden heritage I had to *discover* was stories.

Stories were something to hold on to if, like me, your brain rarely sat still for more than five seconds, was always whirling about like a fly trapped in a Mason jar, formulating, questioning, answering questions before anyone asked them, letting thoughts bump and crunch against one another or become hopelessly tangled—writing scripts that didn't have a beginning, a middle, or an end.

Fantasies became realities, free-floating, carrying me to distant shores, reinventing myself as the hero of thrilling adventures, or providing secret assurance of superhuman strength, even after the sixth-grade bully got finished beating me to a pulp. Stories were a life raft when the ship seemed ready to flounder.

Dan Bessie,
Vermont, 1934
(above) and
New York,
1936 (right)

At first, the great emptiness I felt was a lack of that big huggable American Family of cozy myth, profusely and colorfully illustrated in the *Saturday Evening Post.* You've seen the ads: portly grandparents with a dozen cheery offspring gathered around the Thanksgiving table; the rosy-cheeked aunt and uncle bundling up the walk in a Christmas snow, arms loaded with perfectly wrapped presents; Mom, Pop, a parcel of kids and a hyperactive collie headed for the beach in the new Ford "woodie." The images danced in my head. The record got stuck in an endless groove.

Stories were a kind of glue, helping me to mentally stick together a family that always seemed to be falling apart. Before I was five, we had moved half a dozen times and another half dozen before high school. My parents divorced when I was six, and Pop went off to fight in the Spanish Civil War. His brother, my Uncle

Dan Bessie, Brooklyn: 1938 (left) and 1941 (right).

Everett (a doctor), gave my brother David and me diphtheria shots, took us to Coney Island once, and came to visit a couple of times. Grandma Addie was a regular while we lived in New York. She took us to Macy's Thanksgiving Day parade and to meet her cousin Sidney, who captivated us with card tricks. And when a long day's work left Mom worn out, Grandma sometimes made dinner, rapidly stirring in her long Lucky Strike ash when it dropped into the tomato soup.

Mom had three brothers: Leo, Verne, and Harry. Uncle Leo, a legend in advertising, I didn't meet until my teens. In Connecticut we lived near my amiably formal Uncle Verne and Aunt Laura and stayed at their home one entire summer after Mom's nervous breakdown. Then, and later, while Mom recovered and looked for work, Verne paid for a series of private schools for David and me. We wrote weekly letters from those schools, and since houseparents censored them, we drew a rain cloud or a sun at the top as a "secret code" for Mom when we felt happy or sad. Mom's youngest brother, my astonishing Uncle Harry, materialized now and again without the slightest warning.

Before my eighth birthday, we moved to Pennsylvania, where Mom married Harold, an uneducated farmhand who rode us around on the hay baler or the harrow and filled our heads with fantasies of his own. One night, after we'd come home from a long ride in a new Buick that Harold had mysteriously acquired, two men waiting on the front porch took him away. David and I never saw Harold again.

Like many divorced, weekend fathers, Pop, busy with his own life, visited when he could. Soon after we moved to California in 1946, his name was splashed across the headlines as a dangerous Hollywood Red. In 1950, he went to prison for a year.

So it was mostly Mom and David and me—and the stories: *The Wind in the Willows, Alice in Wonderland, The Wizard of Oz,* and a dozen other books that parents of the 1930s (and since) read to their kids. Safety meant curling up next to Mom and dozing off halfway through one of Toad's remarkable adventures.

Even with a large portion of emotional security, held in place by Mom's gentle awareness, reality somehow never lived up to the magazine images. Never mind that these were media creations; the bridge between logic and feeling seldom got crossed. Sometimes the images dimmed, but in harder times they came roaring back.

As I grew older I heard other stories, but these were more immediate and grounded in reality. They concerned the family— Harold and Mom; Pop and the Spanish Civil War; Uncle Harry and Uncle Leo; Grandma Addie's cousin Sidney; and Pop's Dutch grandfather, who, around 1854, stowed away on a boat for America. Pop's stories were headlines, splashes of color, natural for a writer. Mom's were often deeper and usually more personal.

Except when Pop or Mom became nostalgic, life was too crowded to pay much attention to these stories or to the folks who populated them. Then I'd remember that I'd heard all of this before, nod, feign interest, then promptly forget and go back to whatever occupied the moment. With time, with the gradual ability to separate fact from fancy, and with a lingering need to recreate that friendly circle of family that never really existed, I began to explore the stories, to discover these people.

Leaves on the ancestral tree had been blown away long before I appeared. Some people never met. Others didn't like one another or simply didn't care. Except with Mom, there was rarely time to draw close, to get to know each other, to feel comfortable enough to share ideas, experience differences, or spend a lazy summer afternoon trolling for bass (another cozy image).

If there are sad pages in my stories, there is also a lot of fun—and a few surprises, for in the sorting-out process, some of the important things I thought I'd lost have been rediscovered.

While I haven't been able to gather all of my relatives around the table or share special time with every one of them, I have with some. With others, that restless, wandering mind got in the way. Habit is a sticky demon. Still, I've learned that each of them was there for me all the time, even those who died long before I showed up. As I've found out more about them, I've come to understand how each has touched me and helped form a part of who I've become. They return bearing gifts. Each has left something of his or her self behind. This isn't always tangible (I do have Great-Grandpa Adolphe's tiny gold-plated cigar cutter). Most often it's a simple recognition of kinship, of belonging. If there is an occasional plodding bumpkin in the crowd, I've also found that far from being a flock of stuffy nobodies, they've been an often exciting, occasionally peculiar, but always fascinating bunch.

These lives are only sketches. Still, I've tried to paint in colors rich enough to provide a general history while highlighting what made each of them special. Though I pose an occasional question or offer an opinion, I've tried not to pass judgment or muck about with psychology. Better that they speak for themselves.

They blanket the political landscape—from Karl Marx to Barry Goldwater. There are sixties hippies and a small-town grocer, gay puppeteers, a dynamic publisher, and the leading "birder" in the entire world. I've come to care about each one and to respect them all. Their histories often merge with the sweeping (but also particular) aspects of the history of our nation. My people have been witness to a considerable chunk of what we call "the American experience."

Through writing, I recreate them. Writing brings them closer. Not in the Norman Rockwell sense, for with some of them in attendance the festive board would be less than festive (Mom liked to say that each family has its share of preachers and horse thieves), but certainly with a growing awareness that, like every person who gets to pass this way, I play a small part in a larger drama. That comprehension helps me to better understand my own humanity— which may be the finest thing family has to offer. I'm convinced that every family harbors within it the seeds of this discovery, and such discovery is vital, because it helps us to more fully understand who we are, individually and collectively.

In recreating family, I've also learned that the restless mind that troubled me for so long may not be so special after all; many of the people whose stories I retell seem to share the same quality. Against long odds, each has hacked his or her own path through the forest, heard the "different drummer." If they exercised caution in one area, they took chances in another. For a time I thought it was genetic, that we were all just an outrageously creative bunch. But maybe not; perhaps the restive disquiet is simply a by-product of life in a nervous America.

Sometimes I wish my ancestors had been less unconventional, more settled. Sometimes I wish they'd passed on those solid, middle-class virtues mirroring the comfortable ads. On the other hand, if I *had* inherited those traits, I wouldn't have this wonderfully wise, foolish, quirky, and all-too-human collection of characters to tell you about.

ONE

the old gentleman

*He went off to fight the Indians. Only one story returns
to mind: the sense of humor the Indians displayed when
they caught him and other troupers swimming in a
stream. When they came out they found that the Indians
had tied knots in their clothes, soaked them in a stream
(higher up, where they couldn't be seen by the troupers),
then shat on them! After they had washed them off in the
stream, they took hours to untie them—or have you ever
tried to untie a knot in a wet piece of cloth?*

ALVAH BESSIE
IN AN UNPUBLISHED LETTER RECALLING FAMILY STORIES

Ever since Pop began to intrigue me with the exploits of a
mysterious great-grandfather who had gone off "to fight the Indians
under General Custer," I had lusted after his dress sword, tradi-
tionally passed down to the eldest Bessie son. Two years after Pop's
brother, my Uncle Everett, died in 1965, the famous relic finally
arrived. Its luster had long since been conquered by rust. Insignia
and fancy braiding were no more. I stuck it into a closet. There it sat
for fifteen years, until my son Tim—then sixteen and slighted, I
suspect, because his older brother Joe would eventually inherit the
sword—borrowed it, promising to "polish it up nice." Well, he made
a mess of it (a polished mess), so now it's back in the closet, keeping
its secrets, though Tim threatens to "restore it" one of these days.

Still, my interest in this celebrated ancestor was piqued. But
discovering enough about him to report accurately proved as knotty
a problem as Great-Grandpa had in untying those knots after the
Indians had exacted their earthy revenge. Never having met the man,
I had only Pop's fragmentary tales to go by. So I began reinventing my

great-grandfather in my mind's eye—first on some dilapidated Dutch schooner riding out a fierce Atlantic gale:

> *"Hello. Terrible wind, isn't it? My name is Greta Schuster. And who are you?" inquires a fetching young lass. After an embarrassingly long pause, the fifteen-year-old boy manages a weak, "Adolphe Bessie."*
>
> *"Aren't you the shy one?" she responds, "Where are you going in America?" Adolphe shrugs. "I'm going to meet my uncle in a place called Pennsylvania," adds Greta.*
>
> *Adolphe nods dumbly. Greta giggles, starts away, then turns back and waves a delicate hand. "Well, I hope I see you sometime." Then she disappears down a stair.*
>
> *Adolphe, green around the gills, heads for the railing to heave his lunch.*

In my version, Adolphe regains his sea legs, carries on a torrid shipboard romance with Greta, is married by the captain, and then, after arriving in New York, rises to enormous wealth and lives out his days in flamboyant splendor on a rococo estate overlooking the Hudson River.

So much for adolescent fancy. In reality, Adolphe, apprenticed to an uncle who was a grocer (or maybe a butcher), was loafing outside the shop in Amsterdam one day in early spring, catching drops from melting icicles on the end of his tongue. Convinced that Adolphe was sassing him, the uncle, cursing and screaming, stormed out with a broom and chased the terrified kid down the cobbled street. Adolphe, ashamed to return home, sneaked up a gangplank and ducked into the hold of a ship transporting cattle to America. Pop reports that "he spent most of his time trying to keep the cattle on their feet in the heavy weather and arrived in New York exhausted."

Immigration restrictions being lax in those days (1854), the boy came ashore, crawled into a wagon, and fell asleep. When he woke he was far out in the country, around what is now 125th Street in Manhattan, on a farm owned by a Dutchman, who promptly put him to work.

It's hard to sort out the facts from Pop's gift as a raconteur (for these were not always the same). Adolphe had learned a little English, including "sure," and when he was sent off one morning on a trip downtown, hauling vegetables to the Fulton Market in lower

Manhattan, he became intrigued by an Army recruiting poster and by the dashing blue uniform of a sergeant who stood nearby:

> *"Hey, kid, wanna join the Army?"*
> *Adolphe looks around, but since there is no one else in the immediate vicinity, he decides the sergeant must be addressing him. He beams enthusiastically. "Sure," he replies.*

3

What the Dutch farmer thought when neither his apprentice nor his horse and wagon reappeared, Pop didn't say. But after this he has Adolphe fighting the Indian Wars along with General Custer, then the Civil War under Grant, including the Battle of the Wilderness, "where conditions were so dreadful and they were so thirsty at one point and unable to get water, that they would have died if they had not drunk their own urine."

The stories became more elaborate as Pop got older. Following the war, Adolphe married Rosa Lippmann, one of three (or four) sisters in a family originally from Germany by way of England. They moved "to Virginia—or maybe it was one of the Carolinas" and opened a general store. It took the rebels about six weeks to discover that Adolphe had been a Yankee soldier—whereupon, they burned down his store. Adolphe took off on foot for New York (a long walk, if true), where he found employment as a law clerk.

After working a year to raise the money to bring his wife and one or two kids to New York, he sent it to her. In cash! Pop says that the letter was opened by Rosa's parents, who took it and moved to New York themselves.

What can I say? Following this lapse of financial judgment, Adolphe saved for another year to bring the family north as well as enough to launch himself into real estate. (My Uncle Everett recalled that his grandfather had "once owned half of Brownsville," a section of Brooklyn.) Later, Rosa's delicate health (tuberculosis) required an arid climate, so in 1884, Adolphe packed the family off to Wahpeton, a town studded with tall grain elevators rising above the rich black soil of North Dakota's Red River Valley. An official publication of 1887 called the air, "dry, pure, and full of invigoration."

The nineteenth-century midwestern air certainly invigorated Adolphe, for he sired nine children (not the nice round ten Pop claimed) by Rosa. More than enough to exhaust any woman. She died at forty-seven, leaving daughter Helena to manage the household and raise the smaller kids. But since none of these good people bothered to jot down their exploits for a remote great-grandson-to-be, filling in the blanks has been a tricky assignment. Still, slowly connecting the dots adds color to the old sepia photos. And that's exciting, for you never know what vivid eccentricity you'll uncover.

Adolphe is supposed to have always bought ten pairs of every item needed for the ten children (again, it was actually nine). Ten pairs of shoes, ten sets of underwear, and so forth. The kids then sat down and tried them on, and whoever got something that fit kept it:

> *"These are bloomers, father!"*
> *"Do they fit, Abraham?"*
> *"Uh, yes, but—"*
> *"We must make do, my son. Next year, perhaps you'll be more fortunate."*

There is also the story about a brother serving as a musician in the Court of Maximilian of Austria (later, Emperor of Mexico). Adolphe was certain that after Maximilian's three-year reign was terminated by Benito Juárez in 1867, his brother would have found his way north. Adolphe made several futile trips to New Orleans searching for him.

Tradition recalls a sister who, at fourteen, ran away from home, converted to Catholicism (the Bessies are Jewish), and joined a cloistered order in Paris. Adolphe once visited her there after she'd become a Mother Superior "by special dispensation from the Pope!" Lacking evidence, I let my imagination ramble:

> *"When are you and the rest of the family going to give up that barbaric faith, brother?"*
> *"I've never been much of a practicing Jew," Adolphe replies.*
> *"That's hardly a receptive answer."*
> *Adolphe shrugs. The good Sister rises, smiles indulgently and takes her leave with a whispered, "I'll pray for you."*

All this running away from home at an early age leads me to suspect some less-than-harmonious goings-on in the ancestral Bessie household.

Another Dan Bessie (Pop's cousin) claimed the original family

4

name was de Bessie and that Adolphe's father, a French diamond cutter living in Belgium, did a big job for the Czar of Russia and spent back-wrenching months hunched over his workbench under the scrutiny of hawkeyed guards. Adolphe, says Dan, took off to see the world along with a disgruntled Russian soldier. The Russian was caught and sent back. Adolphe hopped ship for America. (Pop confirms his cousin's story but says it was a different Bessie who cut the gem, the famous Kohinoor Diamond, which is now part of the British Crown Jewels.)

My search for Adolphe continued. My father, along with Adolphe's obituary, had identified Adolphe's birthplace as Amsterdam. Others said Belgium or maybe Paris. I searched for verification. Many letters of inquiry later, I discovered evidence in the National Archives, in Adolphe's own hand, of his birth in Lille, France (May 11, 1839), and relayed this to Pop. I awaited his response a bit smugly but wasn't at all surprised, even given his affection for things French, that he'd reply in his usual curmudgeonly fashion:

18 October 1983.

I will go to my GRAVE knowing DAMNED WELL that there never was a DE BESSIE family from which you and I are far-descended DOWN. THAT MAN WAS DUTCH. I FEEL DUTCH. Sylviane [his third wife and widow] SAYS I am Dutch, i.e., STUBBORN. I do NOT feel French though I have an affinity for the French, as you may have noticed. I ALSO have an affinity for the Spanish and PREFER to believe we came from a Spanish family named Besse, which left Spain at the time of the Inquisition, as THOUSANDS OF JEWS DID—and migrated to Holland.

There was a stubborn streak in Adolphe, too. On trips to New York, my grandfather Daniel would take him to swanky uptown restaurants like Delmonico's, or Rector's, or The Bucket of Blood. At one of these places, a bottle of Tabasco was put on the table, and Adolphe said, "What a cute little bottle of ketchup." His son told him it was not ketchup but a sauce that was very hot, and he shouldn't use more than a drop or two. "Don't josh me," replied Adolphe, arching a bushy brow, "I know a bottle of ketchup when I see it!" He doused his steak and ate every bit of it, sweat pouring down his face and refusing to admit he was wrong.

While I treasured all these stories, the one that first got me scratching my genealogical itch was Pop's often-repeated tale of Adolphe's last hours. The year was 1907. January. From his home in Wahpeton, Adolphe sent identical telegrams to his by-then far-flung children: "Am dying," it said, "Come at once. Will not die until everyone arrives. Love, Papa."

It took days for everyone to reach Wahpeton, and son Daniel was last to arrive, chugging into town just before dawn on the local milk train. As Dan entered the sickroom, the Old Gentleman mustered his feeble strength, rose slightly from his pillow, looked around at the assembly of six daughters and three sons—and some of their husbands and wives and children—and said, "You're all here. Now I can go."

And that is precisely what he did.

The rusting sword was my first concrete link to this shadowy great-grandfather. Later, more items appeared: a memorial notice from the "Loyal Legion of the United States," listing Adolphe's military record; a 1906 letter on stationery of "The Adolphe Bessie Real Estate and Investment Company," thanking grandson Everett for a birthday letter; and a treasured photo of a distinguished looking fellow in a rakish Stetson, pince-nez glasses, and a Buffalo Bill goatee—the Old Gentleman himself.

But I wanted more. (Stubborn. Maybe Pop's insistence on our Dutch bloodline was accurate?) I started pestering relatives I'd never met, perused Amsterdam's city archives, sneezed through dusty registers in Lille going back to the 1500s for Bessies, Besses, and de Bessies. At the LDS Genealogical Center in Salt Lake, where the Mormons are cataloging the world, I plunged into their microfilm. No trace of Adolphe.

Finally, I got around to the 1880 New York Census, which locates Adolphe in Brooklyn. And he *does* list his birthplace (and that of his parents) as Holland. Shortly after, a distant cousin uncovered an old family bible noting the death of a Helena Bessie (nee, Van Gelder) in Antwerp in 1880. So, a letter to Antwerp and in return, a copy of her death certificate, confirming her birthplace as Amsterdam and her husband's name (Adolphe's father) as Daniel Nathan Cohen Bessie.

Great-grandfather Adolphe Bessie, the "Old Gentleman,"
about 1906.

Still, the record was confused; there was the *French* origin, in
Adolphe's own hand, from the National Archives.

I now suspect that the Bessies were sprinkled up and down the
Flemish corridor, from Amsterdam, through Belgium, and into
northern France. Possibly Adolphe's mother was visiting relatives
in Lille when it was time for her to deliver? Or maybe there was a
quota on Dutch immigrants when he enlisted in the U.S. Army, and
listing France as his birthplace made better sense?

Military records added to the mix. James Buchanan was president in 1856 when Adolphe signed up for a five-year hitch and was shipped "out west." He must have seen the immense buffalo herds then roaming the plains, though what "Indian Wars" he fought in Minnesota remain a mystery; the great Sioux uprising came a year after he left. But he did take part in the "campaign against the Mormons" in Utah in 1857.

Washington, responding to its dislike of an "un-American priesthood" running the territory, and popular clamor demanding that "something be done" about polygamy sent an armed expedition in to put down the "rebellion." An impetuous decision, for the Saints had a virtual private army, the Nauvoo Legion, whose guerrillas drove off the army's stock, burned their supply wagons, and generally made their lives miserable until a compromise could be worked out. A shaky beginning to Great-Grandpa's military career.

No trace of the headstrong General Custer turns up in my ancestor's record. Their outfits were hundreds of miles apart during Adolphe's Civil War service, and by 1876, while the Old Gentleman was gobbling up Brooklyn real estate, Custer was busy getting himself and 265 of his men slaughtered at Little Big Horn. Still, there were plenty of Native Americans on Adolphe's frontier, even if his one memorable encounter had to do with a band of Indians soaking his clothes, tying them in knots, and then defecating on them.

Maybe Adolphe took to army life, for at the start of the Civil War he reenlisted. Pop has him "commanding a battalion of blacks." Although Adolphe spent most of his time with the Fifty-fifth Pennsylvania Volunteers, he concluded his service as a lieutenant-adjutant with the Twenty-first U.S. Colored Troops (black units were staffed by white officers). While "serving under Grant in the Battle of the Wilderness" makes for engaging copy, Abe Lincoln plucked Grant from his western command and put him in charge of the Union Army only two months before Adolphe resigned in May, 1864, so I'm not comfortable fueling rumors about a personal meeting. Still, why not speculate:

> *The crusty general approaches a line of recruits strung out along a*
> *dry creekbed. They are hot, filthy, and dog-tired after a three-day*
> *retreat through tangled underbrush. Cook has scraped together what he*
> *can: beans, mainly, with a sliver of fatback and a moldy biscuit. Grant*

stops next to a short lieutenant of about twenty-one with round, gentle features and thick black hair, who has somehow managed to stay neater than the rest.

"What's your name, soldier?"

The lieutenant jumps up and snaps to attention—spilling his mess kit down his coat in the process.

"Adolphe Bessie, sir."

"The accent. It's . . . French? Belgian?"

"Uh . . . Dutch, your honor."

"Umm. Good to have you with us. Marvelous cause we're fighting for. Getting along all right, are you? No complaints?"

"Oh, no sir, none at all."

"Very good, Bessie. As you were."

As Bessie holds the salute, Grant starts off. Then he turns back: "By the way—a lieutenant with gravy on his tunic—now, that's not a good example for the men."

When I saw the motion picture *Glory*, my heart skipped a beat, for I knew that Adolphe's unit had played some part in the famous assault on Fort Wagner, South Carolina. Alas, when I rushed home to check, I discovered that the Twenty-first was not on hand to storm the Confederate bastion along with the heroic Fifty-fourth Massachusetts Colored Infantry but arrived months later as part of a mopping-up operation. And when I found the roster of Adolphe's company in a book listing Civil War units, my balloon was completely deflated; he's listed as a regimental clerk.

His military record does, however, include an assault of another kind, one more suited to a clerk—a protracted paper bombardment of the war department, producing a flood of documents attesting that he had contracted "swamp fever" while on active duty in and around Hilton Head, South Carolina. Attempting a cure, he had ingested "large quantities of quinine, becoming partially deaf and suffering from constant headaches thereafter." Federal bureaucracy (and the Bessie stubbornness) being what it is, Adolphe's petition for a disability pension was granted only after he'd exhausted reams of stationery and tubs of ink tracking down and securing affidavits from army doctors and men who had served with him who could testify to his infirmities.

Although there's no honorable way to conjure greatness out of mediocrity, surprises do occur. By chance, I discovered an article in

Great-grandfather
Adolphe cuts a dashing
figure in his Civil War
uniform, about 1862.

American Heritage chronicling the trial of a black soldier in Adolphe's unit, Sergeant William Walker. Walker, protesting the army's policy of paying black recruits ten dollars a month (less three dollars more deducted for clothing, which whites did not have deducted) instead of the thirteen dollars paid white soldiers, got into a tiff with a Lieutenant Wood, threatened to shoot him, then

> did unlawfully take command of his Company "A," and march the same with others of the Regiment in front of his Command-ing Officer's tent, and there ordered them to stack arms; and when his Commanding Officer . . . inquired of the Regiment what all this meant, he, the said Sergeant Walker, replied, "We will not do duty any longer for seven dollars per month"—and when remonstrated with, and ordered by their Commanding Officer . . . to take their arms and return to duty, he, the said Sergeant Walker, did order his Company "A" to let their arms alone and go to their quarters, which they did—thereby exciting and joining in a general mutiny.

Testifying for the prosecution, Great-Grandpa nevertheless made it appear that it was Lieutenant Wood who had started the argument by threatening Walker. More interesting is that Sergeant Walker and other blacks, attempting to redress their grievance, came first to Adolphe's tent for a sympathetic ear. Adolphe, who was sick at the time, told Walker, "I [will] see about it."

For his courage in standing up for equality, the United States Army executed Sergeant Walker.

All this adds legitimacy to another of Pop's stories—that Adolphe initially went south to open his store (the one the rebs burned down) at the behest of black soldiers in his company, who told him it was a good place to live and that blacks would patronize his business because he was an honorable man.

Adolphe and Rosa probably moved to Georgia (not Pop's "Virginia—or maybe it was one of the Carolinas") after the Civil War, since the 1880 Census records list that state as the birthplace of their first child, Henrietta. And other scraps of information began falling into place. Although no musical brother has turned up at the Court of Maximilian, on the deaths of two of Pop's cousins, a number of photos began coming my way. Among them was an old sepia-tint taken in Brussels. From within a flowered oval, a placid young woman in the habit of a Catholic nun peers out. She holds a bible. Prayer beads dangle from her sash. On the back of the photo is a notation: "*A mon cher frére Adolphe* [to my dear brother Adolphe]. Alice—Sister Marie Xavier. April 1899."

I was closing in. Mediocre as he may have been, intriguing as he seemed, large as life (or small as life, take your choice), the puzzle pieces were beginning to fit.

But one big problem remained: what kind of *person* was this tenacious, distinguished–looking French/Belgian/Dutchman with the Buffalo-Bill goatee and the pince-nez glasses?

THE MOST UNFORGETFUL [*sic*] CHARACTER
I HAVE EVER KNOWN,
by Mrs. Ed Rena Baldwin.

The town was small, on the North Dakota prairies. It is one of the richest farming centers in Richland County. Three railroads ran through the town. Huge grain elevators dotted the tracks. The man was Adolphe Bessie, a Jew. We were Catholics.

This appeared in my father's mail during the late 1950s, following a *Time* magazine article catching up on the "Hollywood 10" a decade later. The memoir was that of an old woman who had grown up across the street from the Bessies in Wahpeton. She'd written her story at the behest of a social worker doing battle against the ravages of time on some elderly minds.

Aside from Pop's cousin Jessie's memory about schoolmates pulling her pigtails because she was Jewish, no hint of anti-Semitism has turned up during Adolphe's life on the prairie. When he's mentioned as a Jew, it's always as an incidental part of an account, signifying the utmost respect.

But why choose Wahpeton? Well, there's a logic: seeking clean air for Rosa and refuge from the teeming streets of Brooklyn, Adolphe returned to the familiar ground of his first military service, settling not far from the Yellow Medicine Indian Agency, Fort Snelling in Minnesota, and Fort Abercrombie in North Dakota— places where he'd been stationed years before.

The Great Dakota Boom was on. The Northern Pacific was running ads in two hundred newspapers in 1884 (the year Adolphe arrived), offering surplus railroad land for as little as $2.50 an acre. Government land was even cheaper, as low as $1.25 each for up to 160 acres. From 1878 to 1890, the North Dakota population increased from 16,000 to 191,000. Sixty-nine percent were foreign-born or children of the foreign-born. Although the boom slacked off within two years, dozens of towns, thousands of farms, schools, and churches popped up on what had been empty grassland. Millions of bushels of wheat were being produced for the flour mills of Minneapolis. Here was an ideal place for a man with a clerk's mindset (and a little cash) to make a killing.

But if Mrs. Ed Rena Baldwin's account is to be trusted, Great-Grandpa was not only a speculator. He was, she says, "a man of short stature, but a giant in good deeds. His immediate family was nine children, though in his big, generous heart, he raised eleven orphaned children of his relatives."

An infamous scoundrel and "soldier of fortune," Albert Sunderhauf, married Adolphe's daughter Henrietta, who died at thirty-two after bearing seven little Sunderhaufs. Albert then skipped town, leaving the kids with a friend. Adolphe hired detectives, who located the brood in a dingy hotel in a small town in Minnesota and bundled them all back to Wahpeton.

Great-Grandma, gone by now, was spared this unpleasantness. Mrs. Baldwin's letter depicts her in a wheelchair, remembers Rosa and Adolphe addressing one another as "Papa Dear" and "Mama Dear," and recalls a one-story building with the sign, "A. Bessie & Sons, Insurance & Mortgages."

Adolphe seems to have made an excellent living in Red River Valley real estate. He must have, in order to support all those kids, grandkids, and "orphaned children of his relatives." Apparently, he loved it. My great-uncle Abe passed on the story to his own son, Mike, that Adolphe was "unhappy at the dinner table if he looked around and there were less than a dozen people present; if so, he would go out and drag strangers in from the street."

A white picket fence surrounded the Bessie home, a large "southern structure . . . spread out on half a block of green, beautifully tended velvety lawn." Inside was a combination dining room and library running the length of the house. "Papa Dear" would sit in a leather chair next to a large window and watch his neighbors. Mrs. Baldwin recalls him rushing out in velvet smoking jacket and slippers one rainy morning to lead "old Blind Joe Forman" safely across a muddy street. She also remembers him pulling her out of "mire almost up to my knees" and losing one of his slippers in the process.

"He came to the family rescue again and again," she says. During their most profound sorrow, her brother Johnny, attempting to save the mayor's son from a swirling eddy in the Red River, drowned along with his friend, and Adolphe hired men and boats to drag the river for days until Johnny's body turned up. A double funeral was held, one across the street from the other, the mayor's son in a hearse, Johnny in a delivery truck. "It was Papa Bessie who footed all the expenses."

Fourth of July celebrations began with a cannon, shot off at sunrise, then nighttime fireworks displays to the accompaniment of "Ohh's and Aah's" from the large group of children invited, and "after the celebration an immense freezer of home-made ice cream was set out on the lawn and each went home happy with a full stomach and a fist full of skyrockets and Roman candles and a laughing, happy regard for the most unforgetful [sic] person I have ever known."

A cozy testament. But what of the provocative notices in the *New York Times* for June 7 and 8, 1881? In these we learn that Adolphe Bessie, "the . . . notorious straw bail bondsman," was locked up for representing himself as owning a home and two lots that he didn't own, and that he had "several times used [these] as surety in obtaining the release of various criminally included individuals."

There is little more. We're left hanging with the unquiet news that "he will be taken to court tomorrow."

So far, I've uncovered no outcome to these curious dealings. In Wahpeton at least, Adolphe was a solid citizen and was even elected justice of the peace. (His grumpy side came out, too, as we shall see in the next chapter.)

Not much interested in the history of the "very dull Bessie family," Pop deliberately lost contact with most of his cousins and had a low opinion of his grandfather, who he dimly remembered "putting my teddy-bear near the window to give it a sun bath." To Pop he was "this dopey Adolphe Bessie" for sticking his tongue out in Amsterdam, for being a Yankee who opened a store in the South, and for moving his tubercular wife to North Dakota (where winters are sub-zero).

Perhaps. But I harbor a soft spot for the Old Gentleman. It must have taken real strength of character to run away from home at fifteen, brave three thousand miles of ocean, enlist for duty on the sparsely populated and hostile plains, endure four years of civil war, then end up in a dusty frontier town supporting an enormous family and half the neighborhood. If my reconstruction takes him down a peg, leaving him less than the noble figure of youthful imagination, that seems OK. If he didn't charge across the prairie savaging the Sioux with General Custer, more power to his memory. The reality feels better than the myth.

Those who knew him clearly loved him. Following long paragraphs of glowing obsequies for Adolphe, the *Wahpeton Times* for January 17, 1907 went on to report: "The remains were escorted to the Milwaukee station by members of the Grand Army of the Republic," from there to be transported to New York for burial in Brooklyn's Cypress Hill Cemetery—where he lies today, no doubt awaiting a visit from his inquisitive great-grandson:

"Hello, Great-Grandpa. I hope your days were as rich and full and as happy as these gleanings indicate."

I wait, but there is no response. I continue: "Any sage advice? A few words of wisdom?"

The Old Gentleman doesn't answer. Maybe he's peeved about Tim messing up his dress sword? Maybe he's still suffering the effects of that Tabasco sauce at Delmonico's? More likely he's simply not going to butt in. He's lived his life. Time to rest.

And he understands that I have my own journey to complete.

TWO

odd birds

Albert Sunderhauf was a tall Prussian with a Kaiser Wilhelm mustache. He kept his wife pregnant with a dozen kids or less, and when she was in bed almost ready to give birth, or ill, he would bring women home and screw them on the couch in the living room, first hanging a mirror in such a way that his bed-ridden wife could see them. [Henrietta, Albert's wife, was Adolphe Bessie's eldest daughter.]

From a letter from Alvah Bessie to the author.

Everyone has a skeleton in the closet. While rumor and innuendo add flesh to the bones, opening the closet door lets you see them dance.

Those who followed in Adolphe's wake were a quirky lot. If they lived less colorful lives than did the Old Gentleman, nevertheless, they had their moments. As a collection, they seem rarer still. Albert Sunderhauf's son Floyd, Pop's favorite cousin, grew up so handsome that the Marine Corps posed him for a celebrated poster featuring a young blonde recruit in summer uniform sitting atop a low stone wall in the tropics, his rifle across his thighs. Floyd won medals for marksmanship in the Corps, and in teaching Pop to shoot told him that the end of his rifle was "moving so much you could stir cake with it."

Floyd's father was another story. Pop met his Uncle Albert only once, in a New York apartment cluttered with trophies from the Gold Rush in California and Alaska (he had been to both): walrus tusks, sealskins, spears, bows and arrows, old guns, pistols, and swords. Pop was visiting his cousin Floyd one day when Albert appeared. "An apparition is the exact word," said Pop. "Well over six feet tall, erect, wearing a red silk cummerbund . . . and thigh-high mosquito boots of fine, thin, soft leather. He said, 'Wer ist das?' and Floyd said, 'Dan Bessie's Sohn,' and the old man said, 'So?' which sounds like Zo, turned on his heel and left the room."

Here was the same gallant who abandoned his seven motherless kids in a Minnesota hotel. Pop says that his father Dan once called on Albert Sunderhauf in his office with a horsewhip and because of his ill treatment of Dan's sister, told him to stand and he would whip him. Albert did so; Dan whipped him "until his arm gave out (a likely story)," and the Prussian never flinched. Albert told Dan that he let him do it "because he liked him."

Legend has it that Sunderhauf couldn't sleep on a bed, because he had asthma and started to suffocate the moment he lay down. "This, my parents said, was God's punishment for his evil life and mistreatment of the sister and many other unfortunate women."

Adolphe's second daughter, Helena, had better luck, for when Louis Fligelman, an itinerant Rumanian peddler—and the only eligible Jew in a hundred miles—meandered into town one day, Adolphe saw his opportunity and quickly arranged a match.

Helena, a "dear, good woman, generous to her family," according to daughter Rosa, took on the job of raising the seven abandoned Sunderhaufs, in addition to her own three daughters, and "kept a wonderfully clean, efficiently managed household at a time of no technological advances."

Maybe Lou Fligelman had something to do with this, because a flyer issued during his second term (as mayor of Wahpeton, North Dakota) demands, in 120-point type, that the city "CLEAN UP!"

> The Children of Israel spent 40 years in the wilderness, yet we have no record of any single death from typhoid nor cholera nor other plagues during that time. Why? Because every day was clean-up day.

With Adolphe as a justice and with Fligelman exhorting them to exterminate flies and "remove all manure, tin cans, paper and other unsightly filth and rubbish," the good Wahpetoniens had daily reminders of the Children of Israel. But perhaps Lou was no neatness freak. Maybe he was simply ahead of his time, for what city

Adolphe with his wife, Rosa Lippmann Bessie
(pregnant with their first child), about 1867.

wouldn't thrill to a mayor who admonishes, "If a city is dirty and suffers from filth and disease, it is not the fault of the laws but of its citizens. A community is like a mirror; it reflects the people. If the people are clean in mind, they will be clean in person and their premises will be clean. Do not wait for your neighbor to start things moving—be the first one yourself."

If one can believe the funeral oratory, Lou Fligelman, who became Adolphe's real estate partner, was a saint among men.

When Lou died at age fifty, Grandpa Dan imported Helena, her three daughters, and the Sunderhauf kids to New York (as he had his other widowed sisters). Every Sunday he made the rounds with Pop in tow, bringing to each sister either a box of candy or a dozen

19

Lou Fleigelman, the Rumanian peddler
who married Helena Bessie.

American Beauty roses. "It was on one of these Sundays," said Pop,
"which I came to hate, that, when I was sixteen and 'dating' Jessie
Fligelman" (Helena's youngest), his father stopped on the corner of
157th and Broadway and demanded, "What's going on between you
and Jessie?"

I said, "What do you mean?" knowing very well what he
meant. I was scared because I was afraid she had told her mother
Lena [Helena] who had told her brother Daniel that one night
she pretended to be asleep on the living room couch and let me
feel her up. He then explained what he meant, and I said nothing
was going on.

Aaron Bessie (*left*), Adolphe (the "Old Gentleman"), and Grandpa Dan Bessie, about 1904.

Said he, "brilliant" man and graduate attorney from the University of Michigan, "If I ever hear that anything is going on between you and Jessie, I will kill you both—and then I will kill myself!"

Pop remembered her as "an ugly bowlegged girl with sex-appeal," but her youthful photos betray his sour image. In her eighties, Jessie, still a charmer, continued to treasure an early volume by Edna St. Vincent Millay with a poetic dedication from Pop. Though he wrote her mash notes and took her to the movies, she found him "too young"; and he *was* a cousin. When I told Pop (himself then approaching eighty) that I was in touch with Jessie, he frowned and said, "Don't give her my address."

Following Adolphe's death, the birds began flying the nest. Two daughters took husbands with dependable midwestern names and melted into the American outback. Another stampeded across the prairie in the Great Oklahoma Land Rush. The Sunderhaufs, after years of Helena's mothering, left for Montana.

Like so many hoping to carve a bigger slice of the national pie, Daniel and Aaron worked with Adolphe for a time then went their separate ways. By the mid-1930s, few second-generation connections remained. And so I, of the fourth generation, had only the vaguest notion that other Bessies existed. As with so many families, the little heritage that remained had to be sorted out from among fading photos, scanty records, and dusty memories.

Pop's maternal grandmother, Amelia, arrived from Budapest, packing with her recipes for such exotic concoctions as goulash, kreplach, and halushken. My grandma Addie inherited them, and when she was in the mood, Mom, David, and I inherited the delicious results.

Addie's father, Bernard Schlesinger, came from Vienna, where he'd been a brewer. Following the trade for a time in New York, with a partner, he discovered a method for preserving brewer's yeast by compressing it. This made it last much longer than ever before. The partner thought Bernard had come up with a great idea and offered to buy it from him. Shocked, Bernard replied that as his partner the idea belonged to the both of them. Six months later, the partner (his name was Fleischmann) bought him out for five hundred dollars. True? Perhaps. And this version of the "rise" of Fleischmann's Yeast seems typical of the foggy business sense of my entrepreneurial ancestors.

Bernard then went on the road as a commissary man, following the railroads west, supplying little towns along the line with beer, liquor, and food. For a time, the Schlesingers lived in Butte, Montana. By then (about 1880), Native Americans had become impoverished outsiders, and Grandma Addie recalled them coming to the house begging for food, which her mother, "being afraid of them, would put outside the door, if they would go away."

Later, in New York, Addie was part of a circle that included the great comedienne Fanny Brice and Addie's own cousin, Daisy, "one of the original *Florodora* Sextet." (*Florodora* was the runaway Broadway hit of 1900.) Pop must have inherited his gift as a raconteur from Grandma, for I recall her keeping me spellbound with stories: how, as a child, she had watched in horror as a skyrocket launched from a Manhattan rooftop (legal in those days) came down and killed a young cousin; the time she and her mother were in the reception line greeting President William McKinley when Leon Czolgosz gunned him down in 1901; and her claim of a relative who "played the cello

Grandma Addie in her salad days, 1890s.

before the crowned heads of Europe"—though a fuzzy recollection may have garbled this tale with the one about Adolphe's brother playing with Maximilian's orchestra in Mexico. Addie's own adored brother, Cornelius (Corny), took a Christian surname, sold baubles at Tiffany's, and died young.

Before marrying my grandfather, Dan Bessie, Addie, who had once won a contest as the "prettiest shop-girl in New York," had been propositioned by madams of New York's ubiquitous houses of ill fame, who brought their girls into the store where Addie worked to buy gowns, hose, hats, or gloves. When asked to join their stable, she would (says Pop) demurely decline. When Dan, fresh from the University of Michigan, law degree in hand, arrived in New York, met Addie, and proposed, she is also supposed to have demurely declined—for she was sought after by a string of young men, including the wealthy Ed Timmons, tugboat king of New York Harbor. When she couldn't decide, Grandpa, dejected and being an admirer of the Great Imperialist Cecil Rhodes (Pop got stuck with Cecil as a middle name), took ship for Africa to hunt for gold or diamonds. On the way from New York to Boston, "first port of call, Dan got *so* seasick that he got off in Boston, took the train back to New York and proposed again—and was accepted."

Her wedding imminent, Addie and two or three other brides-to-be pooled their money to buy a "100% sure contraceptive, sent in a plain package." When the envelope arrived, inside was a simple slip of paper with the admonition, "Keep the damned thing out."

She didn't. So with son Everett soon on the way, Dan applied for a clerk's job with a Manhattan law firm. The firm offered twenty-five dollars a month. "That won't pay carfare and lunches," said Dan, who lived in Brooklyn. "Move closer to the office," the firm suggested. Instead, he took a job tacking up Bull Durham signs in the country— anything above 110th Street in those days. It led nowhere; neither did a job selling soap. A year later, he entered business with his sister Carrie's husband, Dan Jacobs—a "nebbish," according to Pop. (Others concur.)

Family lore has Grandpa Dan inventing the folding paper box, ancestor to the takeout carton for Chinese food. Then, it was used for butter or pot cheese. The partners were known as the "two Dans," and Dan Jacobs mostly ran their factory in a loft on Rector Street in the Bowery, while Dan Bessie was mostly on the road.

Those butter-boxes came back to haunt Pop. Years later, when he and my mother were living in Vermont, he entered a store in Manchester to buy a pound of butter. The man behind the counter produced one of the little folding boxes, on the bottom of which was stamped the company name, "Bessie & Jacobs."

"Where did you get this thing?" I asked the storekeeper, and he said, "Twenty years ago, some smart Jew came in here and sold me a million of them."

"A *million*!?"

"That's right," the store man said. "I've still got a couple hundred thousand."

"That smart Jew," I said most undiplomatically, for in Vermont in 1935 Jews were alien creatures who wore black beards and lived in Boston (a neighbor's son assured me), "that smart Jew," I said, "was my father."

"*No!*" said the storekeeper, looking at me with added distaste.
I owed him about $76.00 at the time.

⌣

Forty-five years later I stopped in another Vermont store in the village of Peru, three miles from where my parents had lived. When I told Pop about it he looked worried. "I hope you didn't tell them where I live," he said, "I still owe them fifteen dollars."

⌣

The world was racing at locomotive speed from 1903, when the Wrights flew at Kitty Hawk, until women won the vote in 1920. The first workers' soviet was established in St. Petersburg; sailors on the battleship *Potemkin* mutinied; San Francisco was torn apart by a ruinous earthquake; Peary reached the North Pole; the Mexican Revolution began; World War I engulfed Europe; immigrants crowded into America; and Agatha Christie's first mystery was published.

Dan and Addie prospered in the new century. He taught her to play poker and how to bet on the races. They could afford a maid and had moved to a classy brownstone in East Harlem, "when it was a respectable neighborhood" (Grandma's words). Here, near the corner of 120th Street and Lennox Avenue, my father Alvah was born on June 4, 1904. His first year, he survived pneumonia, rickets, and marasmus (caused by the body's difficulty assimilating food). Neighbors said he looked like "starving Cuba."

Grandpa Dan's youngest brother, Abe, came to live with them. Adolphe had planned a military career for his son; and though I'm dubious about an obscure North Dakota Jew and former regimental clerk mustered out for headache being able to pull it off, the Old Gentleman is supposed to have arranged a commission at West Point. But Abe had other ideas; deeply impressed by a family doctor in Wahpeton, he'd decided on medicine. Adolphe, aggrieved and with his stubbornness at full tilt, refused to pay for Abe's studies— so Grandpa Dan put him through medical school at Columbia.

Great-Uncle Abe gets my vote; how many people follow their dreams instead of bowing to family pressure?

Abe's training was of little help, however, when less than a year

Grandma Addie with Alvah (Pop) and Everett (*right*).

after he graduated, his brother Aaron came east seeking a cure for an advanced case of Hodgkin's disease. As a teen, Aaron had been a daredevil bareback rider, who could, galloping like mad, "shoot the head off a prairie-chicken perched on a barbed-wire fence, with a rifle or revolver." Pop saw his uncle for the first (and last) time, "just wasting away," on his return home from Maine's Camp Cabbossee in the summer of 1914.

Pop idolized his Uncle Abe and wanted to follow in his footsteps. Dan Bessie decided otherwise, just as he had decreed that Pop, at age six, would play the violin and Everett, the piano. "Everett will be the doctor," he said, "You will be a lawyer." Though Pop bit his tongue, he got even by swiping bottles of rye whiskey from his father, and Melachrino cigarettes. And he became "very sick indeed" when he later smoked them in the balcony of the John Bunny Theater on Broadway. This was surely punishment for sin, he decided. Clearly, the lesson didn't stick, for when his father hung his

Great Uncle Abe and Great Aunt Ella.

trousers inside the bedroom closet before bathing, Pop, lying in wait, sneaked into the bedroom, lifted his wallet, "and deftly exchanged a one-dollar bill he had given me for a two- or a five-dollar bill, and once even for a ten."

Some recall Grandpa Dan as warmhearted and giving, "charming and gregarious, always dapper in spats and a cane." Everett adored him. Pop had a different view, "disliking my father and everything he believed in, and liking everything of which he disapproved." Dan "washed his hands at *least* fifty times a day and changed his clothes, inside and out, twice a day." He tipped his hat to pregnant women in the streets and when asked why, replied, "Because she's going to be a mother." He was lavish with Addie,

Alvah (*center*) with brother Everett and their father, Daniel
Nathan Cohen Bessie, in New York, 1909.

showering her with rings, pendants, diamond brooches, and wrist-
watches, along with candy and roses every Friday night—something Pop may well have resented.

One of Pop's few recollections of his mother ever showing
affection occurred when she "lost" a five thousand dollar diamond
lavalliere and ran into the street yelling for the police. Not more than
five or six years old then, Pop found the lavalliere under the living
room sofa. Seeing her coming toward the house with a policeman, he
ran to her shouting, "Mama, mama, I found it!" Whereupon she
lifted him in her arms, hugging and kissing him, tears streaming
down her face. (Years later, a psychiatrist suggested that, starved for
Addie's love, he must have hidden it there, because she never took
it out of its velvet-lined box unless she was going out on the town.)

The gifts kept coming, in spite of (or maybe because of) the late
night arguments Pop heard coming from his parents' bedroom. "I
understood those midnight quarrels. He wanted her; she didn't
want him." Then he'd hear a suitcase being pulled from a closet, his
father stomping down the hall, slamming the door—only to return
before dawn, quietly. Years later Addie confessed to Pop that she

Alvah (Pop), in a "Most Beautiful Baby" contest at
Asbury Park, New Jersey, 1907.

never cared for sex. She had gone to her cousin Daisy (she of the
Florodora Sextet), who told her, "You mustn't leave Dan. He's a good
provider, a good father, and a good husband. Men are like that."

It was Grandpa Dan she didn't care for sex with. While he was
away, Addie would sometimes peek into the boys' room then open
the front door and whisper, "They're asleep" to someone. "Someone"
was a traveling salesman named Kohne, who traveled at different
times than Dan. Then Pop heard giggling and the sound of bed-
springs, and the next morning, in his mother's room there would
always be two whiskey glasses behind the curtains on the windowsill.

For Pop, childhood seems to have been one long endurance test;
in addition to sickness, he tolerated being dressed as a cherub for

"beautiful baby" contests during summers on the beach at Asbury Park; suffered morning immersions ("for your health") in a tub of cold water, while his father counted slowly to ten; put up with Sundays at his aunts' and the hated violin lessons until he was twelve. But by then, he had discovered what quickly became an all-consuming passion—snakes.

Pop's Uncle Abe encouraged this interest in natural history, answering his youthful questions without a hint of patronizing. By his teens, Pop was writing indignant letters to the *New York Times* protesting the slaughter of native birds, rooting out reptiles on New Jersey's Hackensack Meadows, and seeking the elusive painted turtle in Van Cortland Park.

For a time, Dan indulged this "rich man's hobby." Pop spelled it all out in a fictionalized novella about his youth, *The Serpent Was More Subtil:*

> "Blockheads," my mother called us all when I insisted I had a "right" to keep the snake and my father and my brother backed me up.
> "I don't want the thing around the house."
> "*Father* sent me a baby alligator when he was traveling on the road in Florida," I said plaintively. "Selling butter-boxes."
> "You think I don't remember?" cried my mother. "It got out and I stepped on it in the dark in my bare feet."
> "You squashed it dead," I said accusingly. (Maybe it was that alligator—*Alligator mississippiensis*—that sparked my original interest in *reptilia* after all!)

By the time he reached Dewitt Clinton High School, Pop was volunteering his weekends in the Amphibian Department of the American Museum of Natural History and daydreaming of a glamorous career in the slippery world of ophidia (snakes). This bubble was eventually burst when Dr. R. Maple Foss, curator of herpetology, "discovered that I did not have a scientific mind."

Early on, Pop had been assigned the task of scrubbing jars and bottles (until he dropped and smashed a huge aquarium), or dispatching painted turtles by injecting the creatures with formaldehyde. Dr. Foss's judgment was confirmed after Pop had labored for weeks identifying and categorizing (by sex) 675 pickled specimens of a tiny Southwestern snake. This information he wrote down neatly and carefully and, marching into Foss's office, presented it with an appropriate flourish. Foss looked up from a paper he was writing and said, "What's this?" "The beast," replied Pop. (Beast was Foss's favorite word for his little charges, whatever their sizes.) "What beast?" inquired Foss. A month had passed since he had set Pop to this task, "and no doubt, as he had not seen me in that length of time, he had forgotten the problem, if not the youth he had set to it."

Then, remembering, Foss giggled nervously, said he knew this was the answer Pop would come up with, but that it was incorrect, and directed that he do the work all over again. "To be a scientist," he added, "one must work slowly, patiently, and accurately. There's no glamour in it."

While Pop classified snakes and salamanders, Grandpa Dan, whose folding butter-box factory had folded (priced out by automatic packaging), explored other opportunities. In the process, he decided to teach his young ophidiaphile a lesson in "the value of a dollar." Appearing before his son one morning, holding a metal cylinder of painted brass with a huge cork in one end and a ring through the cork, he announced that he had invented a fire extinguisher that would put all the other extinguishers out of business. (Dan had also come up with an automatically flushing toilet, which never caught on, and a perpetual motion machine activated by seawater. It sank.)

"But it has no . . . what do you call it?" said Alvah.

"Plunger?" said Dan, "Of course not. That's the beauty. Eliminating the plunger eliminates all moving parts, and makes it cost about one-fifth of what ordinary extinguishers cost."

"Then how does it work?"

Producing a hook from his pocket, his father demonstrated how the extinguisher would hang from it. Then, when a fire started, one simply pulled down on the extinguisher, the cork came out, and the contents were poured on the fire. A dim-witted invention, thought Pop, to whom squirting the fire from a distance seemed much more fun—and certainly safer.

Convinced it would make him rich, Grandpa produced a

Saturday Evening Post bag stuffed with the first installment of fifty thousand expensive yellow flyers he'd had printed, and told Alvah he'd pay fifty cents a day if he'd distribute them after school to every apartment in upper Manhattan.

Alvah was soon exhausted from trudging up endless stairways with the heavy sack, so late one afternoon, he made his way to the end of a jetty and began floating the remaining flyers down the Hudson River. Printed on heavy coated stock, they quickly sank.

Dan's butter-box bust, his undistinguished extinguisher, and the automatic toilet failure finally led to a painful spell of gastric ulcers, followed by a serious operation with a portion of his stomach removed. This in turn, says Pop, "was followed by my father's determination to become a millionaire, again."

So Grandpa became a stockbroker. Following tips from a young man who had taken a liking to him, he raked in a tidy bundle in just a few months. One day in December of 1922, this young man advised Dan to take everything he could beg, borrow, or steal and buy cotton futures. He'd be filthy rich by the end of the week.

On Tuesday of that week, Grandpa had $500,000 (on paper). By Thursday, he had $750,000. On Friday, the bottom fell out of cotton futures, and Dan Bessie was wiped out. On Saturday at 3 A.M., he awoke with violent pains in his chest that ran down his left arm to the tips of his fingers. Everett, in medical school by now, applied his brand new stethoscope to his father's chest and then called his Uncle Abe, who arrived in pajamas and an overcoat.

As they sat and watched, Dan, slightly out of his head, started to babble about "the flower of our young manhood" being killed off in the war. Then tears came to his eyes, and he began to sing, "The old oaken bucket . . . the iron-bound bucket . . . the moss-covered bucket . . . that hung in the well. . . ."

My grandfather came to his senses long enough to notice Alvah snickering at his singing. He castigated him for that, then he complained that the injection Abe had given him had worn off.

In Pop's narrative, Nathaniel Leonard is Grandpa Dan. Abe is Uncle Sidney:

> "Now, Nate," said our uncle, "It hasn't had a chance to work. Give it time."

My father closed his eyes. Then he opened them wide and took a deep breath. His mouth stayed open. We watched him and Uncle Sidney said, "Stop holding your breath, Nate. Let your breath out."

Dutifully, Nathaniel Leonard let out his breath and was still. Uncle Sidney sat looking at him for a few moments, then he applied his stethoscope. He glanced at my brother and my brother got the signal and ran downstairs, returning almost immediately with a neighbor, Dr. Weidenbaum, in *his* pajamas.

Weidenbaum listened too, took the stethoscope from his ears and said, "I'm sorry. He's gone."

"But doctor," said our Uncle Sidney. "I just heard his heart beating."

"You heard your own heart," Dr. Weidenbaum replied.

After Grandpa died, the family relocated to less opulent quarters, where Pop's interest in reptiles continued. By then, Addie was used to living with snakes and lizards. She even let Pop remove the expensive encyclopedia from the fancy glass-fronted Globe-Wernecke bookcases to fill the cases with exotic species, borrowed for study from the snake house at the Bronx Zoo. And she didn't complain (too much) when a five-foot boa constrictor escaped— although Pop's Grandmother Amelia offered a ten-dollar reward for its capture, locked herself in her bedroom, and refused to come out until the creature was caught.

Pop kept at his hobby, lecturing on snakes and amphibians one summer at several Boy Scout camps in New Jersey. Installed in an office (with his name on the door), he sat back in a swivel chair, lit up a Lucky Strike, and tabulated his imposing titles: "*Julian Leonard,* I thought [Pop's other self in *The Serpent Was More Subtil*], Member: Audubon Society, Linnaean Society. Donor: New York Zoological Society. Staff member: Herpetological Department, Natural History Museum. Staff Naturalist: Trailside Museum, Palisades Interstate Park."

He seems to have enjoyed ministering to sick rattlers, a mother raccoon and her baby, and an infant skunk. And he gave talks at a nearby Girl Scout camp, "where it was possible for the girls to observe the living snakes and it was possible for me to observe the living girls."

But at seventeen, Pop was a bit of a snob. A few days after

The young naturalist (*left*) and a friend, 1920.

swimming a string of lakes (to impress a girl a fellow staffer was attempting to bed), he was awakened from feverish sleep by voices. Bound and gagged, he was carried, terrified, to a lake. Then, discovering he was ill, the rowdies hauled him back to the Trailside Museum, where, accompanied by such endearing jeers as "circumcised prick," "Jew bastard," and "swim, Jewboy, swim," they poured rancid water from the botanical specimens over him, cut off most of his hair—what Grandma Addie called his "natural Marcel wave"—and smeared his face with iodine. It burned. Then he was being untied, and he heard running feet and the door slam. Then silence. He lay there shaking until he was certain the coast was clear.

Then he tore off the blindfold, got up, and groped his way to his office door. He went inside and switched on the light.

"*Jew* Leonard," he thought. It was his first real taste of anti-Semitism; but many telling experiences lay ahead before Pop came to terms with the defensive arrogance he nurtured, an arrogance that had certainly contributed to the incident.

And it was soon after this that Dr. R. Maple Foss discovered that Pop "didn't have a scientific mind." So Pop bundled the snake collection into pillow cases and took them back to the zoo. Grandpa Dan would have approved.

Long before the event, Dan told Addie that the day after he died she would get phone calls from men who would say they were Wall Street friends, who would offer condolences, and tell her that her future and that of her sons would be secure if she would only invest in some stocks they had in mind.

"*Hang up the phone!*" he warned her.

She didn't hang up. And though Pop and Everett were left money for college, most of Dan's $150,000 insurance was flushed into the market or lavished on one summerlong binge in Atlantic City, where Grandma threw endless parties and lost heavily on poker and the ponies, in company with such notorious mobsters as Jack "Legs" Diamond and Arnold Rothstein, both of whom, she told me (at least five times), "always treated me like perfect gentlemen."

I never knew my grandfather; he died ten years before I was born. But Grandma Addie constantly came to our rescue during the long, lean years, lending Mom a few dollars or a sympathetic ear, taking David and me to Prospect Park or to Macy's Thanksgiving Day parade, or cooking up one of her mother's Hungarian recipes.

She never understood money, and she never had any job skills. For the rest of her life she lived in a tiny flat on East 81st Street, supported by Uncle Everett. She stayed up till 3 or 4 A.M. playing solitaire, smoking, working crosswords in the *Daily News,* and listening to the radio—all at the same time. Then she'd sleep for two or three hours and wake completely refreshed.

When I stayed with her during youthful trips to New York, the stories she told got mixed up in her head, so it took me a long time to sort out the facts. She was a gentle heart, and I have a vivid picture of the last time I saw her, standing in her doorway at the end of a long hall, wearing scruffy slippers and a ratty kimono, a Chesterfield dangling from her lips, like one of Dorothy Parker's lonely old women who shuffle through ancient hotels in *Ladies of the Corridor*. On my last visit, she smiled as I was leaving, waved to me cheerfully, and said, "Good-bye, Alvah."

By the time Pop finished college, Everett was interning at Gouverner's Hospital in the New York slums and supporting his mother and grandmother. My great uncle, Dr. Abraham Bessie, who attended his brothers and most of his nearby sisters in their final hours, had become the family patriarch—and what little Jewish heritage the Bessies brought with them from Europe, was, like their thirty-five years in North Dakota, a fading memory.

THREE

turnabout

*I was hooked. No, that's not strong enough. I fell
completely in love with the theater, the way it was built,
the way it was written, and the grand way in which it
was acted . . . how special were those nights and how
dear those performers.*

RAY BRADBURY

*It's about puppets. You may think you won't like it, but
you will.*

CLIFTON FADIMAN

I was almost twelve before I learned that my uncle Harry and
his partners in the Yale Puppeteers were celebrated entertainers.
Nobody had mentioned that Robert Frost had tromped through a
New Hampshire cloudburst to see them perform, that Albert
Einstein had chuckled at a puppet Harry had made of him, or that
they'd entertained everyone from John Barrymore and Amelia
Earhart, to Marlene Dietrich, Groucho Marx, and Tennessee
Williams. I wasn't aware that my uncle had created marionettes of
most of the important personalities of his day, or that Charlie
Chaplin, intrigued by Harry's artistry, had lingered long after a
show to carry on an animated discussion about puppetry and
pantomime.

In my earliest memory, Uncle Harry always materialized out of
thin air, announcing his visits in a singular way: nickels and dimes
(and an occasional treasured quarter) suddenly came tumbling
through the front door keyhole. My brother David and I dropped
what we were doing, stared at one another, then scrambled for the
loot, screeching, "Uncle Harry's here!" The door opened and there

he stood—a mop of unruly hair and a grin like that of a small boy who's caught a wet frog. The short jackets and striped shirts he wore made me think he was a sailor. He never stayed long—fifteen minutes, half an hour, but the moments were magic. He'd produce a pickle jar filled with pennies, and then he'd flourish a handkerchief and turn it into a dancer or a flop-eared mouse. The dancer spun around and kicked out a cotton leg, or the mouse bounced up Harry's arm, unraveled, and transformed back into a handkerchief. I recall nonstop chatter punctuated by shy, nervous laughter. Then he'd slip Mom five or ten dollars, because times were hard in the thirties, and after that he'd vanish. Early in 1941, Mom told us that Harry had moved to Hollywood to start a puppet theater, so another visit seemed unlikely. But like most nine-year-olds, I was too busy to care.

By the summer of 1944, Pop was also in Hollywood, on staff at Warner Brothers, writing scripts that found Errol Flynn putting the kibosh on Nazi saboteurs in Canada or parachuting into Burma to wipe out an entire Japanese regiment. A fat raise in salary allowed him to bring David and me out to "The Coast" for a month-long vacation.

One evening a week or so after we arrived, we left his home on Coldwater Canyon and drove through the Hollywood Hills in his bulky 1940 Hudson. We turned off Sunset, drove down La Cienega, past a hot dog stand shaped like an enormous hot dog, and pulled up next to where a big white banner announcing *"Turnabout Theater"* danced above the street. Along the way there had been snide little comments from Pop about Uncle Harry and his partners. The words have faded but he implied an "oddness" about them, something not quite right. Maybe I heard "queer," more likely "fairy," for that was current, and Pop used the term liberally. I hadn't the foggiest notion what he was talking about.

Turnabout Theater was unique. We entered through a patio fragrant with flowers and blossoming olive trees and picked up our tickets at the box office, above which hung a naked cherub with a "no refunds" sign suspended from an unexpected part of his anatomy. David and I giggled. Inside, the rich maroon walls were autographed, as I later told friends, "by every famous person in the world." Shirley

David and Dan Bessie at the Turnabout Theatre, 1944.

Temple had signed next to Theodore Dreiser. Thomas Mann had signed, along with Bruno Walter and Arnold Schönberg. (Turnabout was a favorite with expatriate Germans.) Rows of streetcar seats, salvaged from the old Pacific Electric yards, ran the length of the house. Seatbacks were reversible so that audiences could face in either direction, because after the puppet show, a live revue took place on another stage at the opposite end of the theater. Instead of numbers, the seats had names: "Pyramus n' Thisbe," "Rise n' Shine," or "Peaches n' Cream." High stools at the back accommodated the overflow.

I looked around. Uncle Harry was nowhere in sight. I fretted. But moments later the doors were closed, the house lights dimmed, and a spotlight picked up and followed three debonair, tuxedo-clad gentlemen marching down an aisle. In the lead, our fabulous uncle, followed by his partners, Roddy and Forman—the Yale Puppeteers! They vanished through a curtained alcove.

The show, *Tom and Jerry*, spoofed the *Horatio Alger* stories Harry had grown up with. In them, the poor but honest lad conquers grim adversity, gets rich, and wins the girl of his dreams. But in Harry's version the poor boy becomes poorer, the rich boy becomes richer, and after tramping the world, they return to Frumpington, Maine, to find the girl they both adore married, fat, and frantic as she tries to corral three screeching toddlers.

As the play ended—and with no warning—Harry, in velvet smock, flowing tie, and big floppy beret, dropped onto the stage and spread his arms, enveloping his little wooden children. The sudden appearance of a giant astonished everyone and drew suitably gigantic gasps, followed by delighted applause.

The hour went by too fast. A rich coffee aroma was drifting in, and as the lights came up, Forman appeared and invited everyone to the patio for a cup. "And don't forget," he reminded, "when you come back, the show continues at the opposite end of the theater. Please take the same seats you were in before, so if you've been in front for one show, you'll be in back for the other. That is, if you've been sitting in 'Pure n' Simple,' don't try to get in 'Hot n' Bothered.' Turnabout is fair play."

A mini-version of musical chairs followed the intermission. Theatergoers banged their seatbacks about, and those who had been facing in one direction stood around scratching their heads and trying to figure out what was what.

As the lights went down again, a disjointed clash of drum, kazoo, violin, and calliope could be heard. Parting curtains then revealed a motley troupe reminiscent of a Salvation Army band. In turn, each member stepped forward to testify to a litany of vices from which Turnabout had saved him. Uncle Harry sang: "I used to forge initials on many a shady scheme. To the post office officials, I was pinup boy supreme. But my life of crime I quit it, and I'm happy to admit it, when I heard the magic word, 'Turnabout.'"

At his Steinway next to the stage, Forman introduced the acts, accompanied most numbers, and kept up a snappy repartee between curtains, while in back, the actors hurriedly changed costume. The hour-long revue included songs, sketches, and dancing—mainly comic, but sometimes risqué or lightly political. Though I was captivated, this was *clearly* no theater for kids.

Elsa Lanchester got the loudest applause. In one number, she appeared in a sleazy dress, mop in hand, hair pulled into a knot, feet encased in a disreputable pair of husband Charles Laughton's bedroom slippers, and sang "If You Can't Get in the Corners," a title borrowed from a cleaning woman working for the Laughtons:

If you can't get in the corners, you might as well give up.
　　Me, I do agree—
For a thing that sucks and blows, through a nozzle or a hose,
　　Just ain't for me.

Pop didn't try to explain the double-entendres.

In addition to Elsa, I was impressed by a short, intense woman wearing a bulbous red nose on a stoically comical face, who clomped about the stage in a pair of hilarious dances.

But Uncle Harry was special. He won me over as a melancholy poodle at the end of a long leash, then surprised me when he reappeared in another scene as a gentle old man reminiscing with his wife, played by Dorothy Neumann. He showed up again in the finale, sweeping the stage and closing up, as the company sang their sentimental, "Goodnight Again."

Afterward, Forman invited everyone backstage to Harry's workshop. Another fantasy—rows of gaudy marionettes hung from the high ceiling. Carefully labeled boxes lined the shelves: "Matches (virgin and spent)," "Silverware (honestly acquired)," and on and on. Most held puppet parts: "Bosoms (male)," "Bosoms (female)," "Bottoms (weeny)," or "Thighs (wooden, no use to peek.)" I peeked. A sign above the workbench said, "Costume Department—we outfit no one over 30 inches." My uncle had traded in his stage manager's outfit for a tux. Perched on a narrow stair leading to an upper gallery, he sat smoking and anxiously fingering a curtain-pull as curious patrons milled about. He greeted us briefly then went back to answering questions about how he made the puppets and how they worked.

In the Green Room, guests inspected marionettes of FDR, Toscanini, and other celebrities. Coffee was served again. (Regular fans had their own mugs with names engraved.) David and I had Cokes and finally got a chance to chat with our uncle, along with Forman, gracious and charming, and with Roddy, who fussed about, playing host. They asked if we were enjoying the summer and how Mom was, and Harry arranged with Pop to pick us up several days later to take us on a tour of Hollywood.

On the way back to the Valley, David fell asleep in the Hudson, and I remember staying awake longer than usual that night, reliving an evening of pure enchantment.

Harry in his Hollywood workshop, 1941.

My uncle Harry Burnett, his second cousin, Forman Brown, and Richard (Roddy) Brandon, Forman's lover and lifelong companion, had organized other theaters, but Turnabout was the grandest and most successful. From 1941 until the mid-1950s, Turnabout was written up in magazines such as *Colliers* and *Holiday* and became a "must" for tourists, attracting patrons from around the world who "heard about you in Paris," or in Rome, Lisbon, or Elmira. The boys—Harry, Forman, and Roddy were always "the boys"—and their theater had also become *de rigueur* in the movie colony.

Writer Ray Bradbury, who contributed a forward to *Small Wonder*, Forman's affectionate memoir of the Yale Puppeteers, came to Turnabout thirty-five or forty times—his first ticket purchased from the ten dollars a week he made selling newspapers on a Los Angeles street corner.

The puppet shows were vest-pocket musical comedies, parodies of well-known stories. Forman created all the material (including the music and lyrics) and played piano backstage, while Harry and Roddy, with an assistant or two, manipulated the puppets. Everyone did voices. In some shows, my uncle interacted with the puppets. In *Gullible's Travels*, a tiny marionette was smitten with Lilly Putia, a winsome giantess played by Harry. The puppet sat on her lap and crooned a love song, and at the final curtain, gazed up at Lilly and declared, "Acres and acres and all mine!"

Forman's lyrics ideally complemented Harry's marionettes. In *Caesar Julius*, likenesses of Hedda Hopper and Louella Parsons, gossip columnists who regularly dropped by the theater to dig up dirt on the stars, were puppet reporters covering the chariot races in Rome. Their duet, Forman's pithy comment on their work, concluded,

> Now, Louella has a cellar stocked with cyanide,
> And Hedda has a bed'a coals where souls are fried.
> We're just a sweet old pair, whose smiles will never dim;
> Who will never turn a hair as we tear you limb from limb.
>
> Louella has a telephone that's acid proof,
> And Hedda has been fed upon a serpent's tooth.
> If we ever have a secret, we must tell it or we'll burst,
> For the glory of the syndicate, and William Randolph Hearst!

Forman and Roddy served the intermission coffee. (Bette Davis kept urging them to install a bar.) Roddy also sold tickets as well as managing the entire operation. Turnabout was a family affair, with Harry, Forman, and Roddy taking turns selling programs and ushering, while Elsa Lanchester and the others pitched in to mop or dust when things got hectic.

Elsa, best remembered as the monster's mate in *The Bride of Frankenstein*, came to Turnabout on a two-week trial and stayed twelve years; her only payment, the rights to more than fifty songs Forman wrote for her. Charles Laughton thought of her as a *diseuse* (in the manner of Yvette Guilbert, immortalized by Toulouse Lautrec). Elsa could, in the course of an hour, become an obnoxious brat, a Cockney charwoman, and a beautifully gowned creature of astonishing beauty.

Forman told me that when he first submitted a song to Elsa, she'd look it over, humming it quietly and without comment. Then she'd tuck it in her bag, and nothing more would be heard. But when she appeared for the first rehearsal, she had choreographed the number all the way to the lift of an eyebrow, with every gesture so meticulously worked out that once the song was done on stage, it never changed. Berthold Brecht—Elsa remembered the great dramatist as "a man who did not wash and who stank up my house with his inferior cigars"—said that she was the only performer he'd ever seen who, alone on the stage, had the capacity to fill in the frame of a proscenium arch the same way the Japanese did in a woodblock print. One old-time fan nostalgically told Forman that he remembered Elsa singing a ballad under a rose arbor in a small garden behind a white picket fence. Recalling the number, Forman pointed out to me that except for Elsa and a chair, the stage was empty.

Lotte Goslar, the dancing clown with the red nose who impressed me that summer night in 1944, was also featured. Lotte, world famous before Marcel Marceau rose to stardom, combined mime with bursts of explosive energy, charging across the stage in an orgy of peevish foot-stomping and waving of arms. In "Disgruntled" and "So What" she brought a light, funny interpretation to negative emotions. Her "Life of a Flower" and "Grandma Always Danced," in which she dies then reappears in heaven clad in a long nightie (dancing), were classics. The puppets and most of the revue were highly verbal, so Lotte's mute, mobile interludes provided welcome contrast. Once seen, she was hard to forget—and at eighty, she was still dancing!

Everything and everybody about the theater was special. Its 160 seats were sold out weeks in advance, until business started falling off with the arrival of television (and Elsa's departure). The lights went down for the last time in 1956, after 4,535 performances. In its fifteen years, the theater attracted a flock of enthusiastic fans, who showed up over and over.

Ray Bradbury remembers it as "the fastest love-at-first-sight that any theater-prone fan ever experienced." He dragged friends and relatives along to see Forman's "fabulous take-off on *Die Valkyrie*," or Harry, "lost on a desert island, holding a telephone directory . . . and gloomily singing 'Look at the Book That I Took.' It was all grand, it was warm, it was all fun, and they were, though they did not know it, my family."

And it felt good to claim them as a part of mine. After 1946, when Mom found a job directing a nursery school and moved us from Poughkeepsie, New York, to Santa Monica, I saw the show another dozen times, two or three of them with some high school heartthrob I wanted desperately to impress. (The girls were invariably more impressed with the marionettes than with me.)

The years 1947 through 1950 coincided with my father's appearance before the House Committee on Un-American Activities, the "Hollywood 10" case, and his subsequent year in jail. Few classmates were sympathetic, and my own understanding was confused, so showing off Uncle Harry helped to deflect the barbs and provided a safe harbor from turbulent seas. Once again, it was an attempt at trying to piece family back together.

Since being gay was rarely talked about openly, Harry's sexual preference was never mentioned. And I wasn't about to raise the issue. Though family loyalty was strong, in my teens I was as likely as anyone to pass along the latest "homo" joke.

Still, I loved to brag about my famous uncle. His acting was as skillful as his puppetry. Along with his melancholy poodle, I remember him as the hind end of a horse, a triangle player waiting to strike his one note, and dancing a lopsided polka with Lotte. There wasn't a dry eye in the house during his "Last Show," an old circus clown getting ready for his farewell performance.

After the final curtain, I took friends back to his workshop, where Harry, perched on the stairs as usual, sat biting his nails as he answered questions. At the time, Forman shared a home with his aged mother, but Roddy, who lived above the theater (as did Harry), let me show off his room. The walls, alive with old circus posters, surrounded a bed resembling a ticket wagon. A nearby storage gallery housed scores of marionettes from shows not then on the boards. The largest, a brontosaurus six feet long, hung next to a six-inch-high ballerina, who danced in a miniature show within one of the regular puppet shows. Harry's astonishing creations included a voodoo witch doctor, a cigarette-smoking hippo, a dozen rats in tutus, Roman puppets (senators, gladiators, charioteers), and a line of busty chorines with big lavender letters on their hot pink panties

Uncle Harry as the dashing, romantic figure I remember.

spelling T-U-R-N-A-B-O-U-T, which glowed in the dark when my uncle turned off the lights, switched on an ultra-violet lamp, and had them bend over and raise their skirts.

It was as much a marvel as Ray Bradbury remembers:

> If I were to have one wish at this time in my life, it would be to have someone put me in some sort of backward-turn backward slipstream device and mail me off to 1946 or thereabouts, to sing the magic word "Turnabout" and see my old friends pull strings

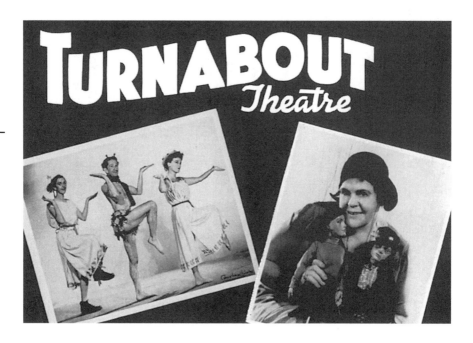

A Turnabout Theatre postcard from the 1950s.

or hear Elsa lilt her way through "If You Peek in My Gazebo," or "I'm Glad to See You're Back Elaine." For an evening like that, I think I would pay just about any price, and to hell with reason.

This pleasant madness began in the fall of 1919, when Forman arrived from Otsego, Michigan, to room with the Burnetts while attending the University of Michigan. He found a moody second cousin in Harry. Given to strange depressive spells, Harry often retreated to the roof, refusing to come down for hours. Photos show twelve-year-old Harry as Chaplin's tramp or clowning in women's clothes. He was the class cutup and a trial to his mother. Amateur magic and his crystal radio set were simply not enough of an outlet for his restless energy.

One day, Tony Sarg's traveling marionette show came to town. Forman bought two tickets and took Harry. Forman's ignorance of puppets until then had been complete, and he "labored under the illusion that they were somehow worked by electricity." Harry was bewitched; he'd found his calling. Too shy to speak with the

TURNABOUT

An Occasional Bulletin of Turnabout Theatre

VOLUME IV   APRIL, 1945   NUMBER 5

ELSA LANCHESTER

The "New Yorker" prints each week a list of film revivals currently playing in Manhattan. They are memorable pictures, and it is a rare week indeed when Elsa Lanchester fails to be represented in one or more of their casts. Everyone remembers her fine characterizations in "Henry VIII," "Rembrandt", "The Beachcomber", "The Ghost Goes West", "Naughty Marietta', "Lassie Come Home", "Ladies in Retirement" and many others. In England she is also remembered for her Peter Pan, and her many roles at the Old Vic and other London theatres. In London, too, she operated her own theatre club with great success, but Turnabout Theatre has offered her her first opportunity in America to appear as a revue artist. She came to the theatre shortly after it opened in July, 1941, where she discovered in Forman Brown a writer who could tailor songs to her special needs, and a stage where she could display a facet of her talent hitherto unsuspected by American admirers of her film portrayals.

. . .

Non Sequitur Dept.: "Is Elsa Lanchester married to Charles Laughton?" a gentleman asked one evening not long ago. On being assured that she was, he remarked, "My, she must be a busy woman!"

CONCERNING TURNABOUT THEATRE

Turnabout Theatre was built in 1941, and opened in July of that year. The idea was conceived and put into execution by The Yale Puppeteers (Harry Burnett, Forman Brown, Richard Brandon) who, with Dorothy Neumann, comprise the four owners and directors of the enterprise. The theatre to a remarkable extent is the result of their cooperation. Miss Neumann costumes and directs the revues, and performs notably as an actress. Mr. Brandon is general director and business manager, doubling as puppeteer. Harry Burnett designs and makes the puppets, directs the puppet productions, and appears also in the revues. Forman Brown writes all the material, both words and music, plays the piano, operates puppets, and acts as master of ceremonies.

. . .

Larry Stevens, the new singer on the Jack Benny show, was a Turnabout discovery. He auditioned and became a member of the Turnabout troupe in the early days of the theatre, and appeared here as singer and puppeteer for more than a year. He has just signed a contract for a series of Victor recordings. Turnabout wishes him deserved success in his promising career.

. . .

Lotte Goslar recently turned down an offer to appear in a forthcoming Broadway musical show. It would have been her fourth appearance in such productions. She plans to continue at Turnabout Theatre.

. . .

A new puppet show is in the making, and will be coming along some time this Spring. Tentatively called "Tom and Jerry," it pokes a bit of fun at the Alger books and the Gold Rush days. Forman Brown's script promises an evening of smiles, with a round dozen of new songs in his brightest vein, and the Flamboyant Fifties offer Harry Burnett a fine opportunity for colorful puppets and settings.

. . .

Turnabout audiences are fooled nightly regarding the size of the puppets. Their apparent increase in stature is purely an optical illusion. The puppet stage and entire *mise en scene* are so carefully adjusted to the dimensions of the puppet actors that, with no normal-sized objects for comparison, the figures seem gradually to become much larger than they actually are. If you are still unconvinced, take a trip back-stage at the end of the performance. The puppet workshop is well worth a visit. "It has revolutionized my whole kitchen!" exclaimed one enthusiastic lady.

The Turnabout Theatre's occasional bulletin, signed by Elsa Lanchester.

puppeteers, he raced home, vanished into his basement shop, and didn't surface until he'd fashioned a rough candle-wax puppet, with a doll's head, and strung it to a tennis racket. Dubbed "Hamlet," it quickly became the talk of the neighborhood.

Harry and Forman were soon performing at high schools and house parties in and around Ann Arbor. Mom sewed costumes and contributed a funny bit as an asthmatic grandmother in their first offering, *Little Red Riding Hood.*

Beginning in 1921, summers were spent touring, in an ancient Model T, to the huge, gabled resort hotels (Otis Skinner called them "The Great Inflammables") along Lake Michigan, through towns such as Saugatuck, Petoskey, and Cheboygan. Forman and Harry were simply, "The Puppeteers—Students of the University of Michigan." Crude at first, the marionettes were stowed in an old telescope bag; uprights and braces were wrapped in a tarpaulin held together with straps. These were packed into a pair of oblong boxes, which, placed end-to-end, served as their first stage.

As Forman titles his memoir, they were a *Small Wonder.* Locals would spot the Model T, packed with show biz apparatus, point and whisper, and the boys became "for a splendid moment that most romantic of all romantic things—an arriving theatrical troupe, freighted with a glamor of footlights and unreality, a glamor mysterious and slightly suspect."

In 1926, Yale's drama school offered Harry a scholarship. At Yale, he met Brandon Rhodehamel (Roddy Brandon, later Forman's lover, who died in 1985). Harry, a churning dynamo, pulled Roddy and Forman along with his enthusiasm. Neither gave it much thought. Harry needed plays written? Forman wrote them, just as he'd ghosted Harry's English compositions to help him through college. Harry needed another puppeteer? Roddy was available.

Their programs, up to and including those at Turnabout, were always lampoons of popular stories or fables. Preceded by an overture featuring the "Hayden Trio," there might follow a play such as *The Pie-Eyed Piper,* or *Uncle Tom's Hebb'n.* Like most early performers whose humor was molded by popular culture, the boys caricatured blacks (and farmers, opera singers, "shrewish" women and other "types"). Roaming north from Boston to Bar Harbor and back down through the White and Green Mountains to Lake George, a typical early program featured "a Hindu sketch by Mr. Brown," along with "a mock duet and a dance suite showing a negro crap-shooting ballet." (*The New York Times,* June 12, 1927)

Mom chided them about the stereotypes, but few others took them to task. And I was too much in awe of my uncle to notice. Absorbed with theater and its demands, the puppeteers rarely examined their own clichés. Still, democratic sensibilities creeping into American life brought changes, for in 1950 they retired *Uncle Tom's Hebb'n.* On the other hand, no color barrier existed in who they employed, and at Turnabout, Roddy became testy with more than one customer put off because the theater admitted blacks.

Personal life was equally colorblind. For a time, Roddy's infatuation with a black entertainer caused a temporary rift with Forman. As with most troupers who show up for a single night then fold their tents and move on, there was seldom time for developing close relationships. Forman and Roddy had one another, but Harry was consumed with his puppets. Lovers appeared then vanished, but there was never a long-term companion. Harry was simply too busy.

Older brothers Leo and Verne were helpful if Harry needed anything, but if they were aware of the boys' lifestyle, they didn't let on, though Forman felt that Verne "had suspicions" and "looked askance" at their relationship.

Sticking pins into the pompous and self-important afforded special pleasure for the puppeteers, but except for topical jibes such as the Hedda Hopper–Louella Parsons number, the boys were seldom political by design. The world was simply raw material for sport, and they as comfortably wove Al Capone, "Legs" Diamond, or Gertrude Stein into an evening as they did Noah's Ark coming to rest atop Southern California's Mt. Wilson, where it was greeted by members of the Los Angeles Chamber of Commerce.

At Yale and beyond, Roddy took over the business end, booking them into resort hotels, colleges, and private schools. They played for lumberjacks and millionaires, performed by candlelight in rustic hotels, and used a billiard table as a stage. A day's take (after expenses) might find them flush at twenty dollars or leave just enough lonely coins in the hat for coffee and donuts.

Memorable moments filled those barnstorming days: there was a private performance one night in Kennebunkport at the home of Booth Tarkington (*Seventeen, The Magnificent Ambersons*), "with the wise and gracious novelist holding a lantern in the garden while we stowed away our bags and cases, and waving us Godspeed with it, a tall, thin figure showing dim behind the arc of swaying light"; there was a Gloucester fisherman, who, in return for tickets, took the puppeteers sailing; there was a certain matron, living alone in forty luxurious rooms with thirty or more servants, and in whose music room they played for a suburban garden club. The woman had eight footmen in scarlet livery and during World War I had lodged complaint with the government because of her inability to secure eight six-foot footmen who "matched."

They spent "pleasant hours in the pine-circled cottage of Robert Frost, listening to his dry yet vibrant voice in anecdote after anecdote concerning his contemporaries." (Forman and Frost had met at the University of Michigan while Frost was poet in residence.) Playing Franconia, New Hampshire, in 1927, Forman discovered a badly weathered house in need of repair on fifty rustic acres. He drove out to meet Frost. "Robert came down, and together we tramped over it, pacing out its boundaries, flailing through the thickets for its spring." If Frost said it was a bargain, it was a bargain. Forman bought the property. Reflecting on his purchase, he thought of the woods, the meadow, and the spring as "mine;" absurd, childish ideas "when we consider the dignity and immortality of trees and earth and water, yet ideas peculiarly gratifying to humankind."

Summers found them on the road (Mom joined them for a season while Forman was abroad), the winters often in separate activity. After returning from Europe, Forman left for Michigan to fulfill a teaching assignment. Roddy went to Texas to recover his sometimes-delicate health, while Harry set out to track down the great marionette maestros of France, Czechoslovakia, and Italy.

Bumping his way from theater to theater in third-class carriages, and inspired by a magnificent puppet extravaganza in Turnin that included twirling ballet dancers, airplanes roaring across the stage, and puppet spectators in sidewalk cafes waving flags and applauding a puppet military parade, Harry landed back in New York with a daring plan. Oblivious to a lack of funds, and with

Harry bound for Europe, 1929.

"nothing but gall," he approached Norman Bel Geddes, the biggest designer in New York. "You know," said Bel Geddes, "I've always wanted to show up Tony Sarg." So for two hundred dollars a set, Bel Geddes designed two complete puppet shows, *Bluebeard* and *Hansel and Gretel.*

Harry found a studio on Bank Street, shoehorned in between stables where horses peered placidly in from second-story windows and whinnied in the middle of the night. Working feverishly, they put the show together with two or three volunteers and my mother, who, "surrounded by mountains of colored rags, yarn, crepe hair, braid and ribbons, sewed and fitted and tacked, sketches and color charts propped before her, piles of gangling puppet bodies at her side."

As "Harry Burnett's Marionettes," the boys set off on tour in a dilapidated truck they'd bought for the occasion. Christened "Camille," because the engine kept dying so beautifully, they had to be towed into town after town; so, deciding to lighten the load, they began dropping off scenery. When word got back to Bel Geddes that the beautiful cave scenery he'd created for *Bluebeard* (for example), had been left by the side of the road, he sent a telegram telling them to "stop wrecking my reputation, or else take my name off your advertising."

Summer turned to fall, then to winter. The boys returned to visit family in Michigan, filled a booking in Indiana, then moved down through Missouri in driving rains and along muddy Oklahoma roads toward the fulfillment of a longtime dream—California.

The bucolic landscape of the twenties no longer existed; the place had been "discovered." But they located a modest house in a secluded canyon not far off Hollywood Boulevard and opened their first theater, Club Guignol (capacity, thirty-five), in Harry's basement shop.

In a city ever impatient for a new diversion, Club Guignol was an instant success. And by the time a meddlesome neighbor (objecting to the traffic) succeeded in having it closed as a fire hazard, Olvera Street, a decaying alley leading off Los Angeles' old Plaza, was being refurbished. So on that now-famous byway, Harry, Roddy, and Forman opened Theatro Torito, "AMERICA'S SMALLEST AND SMARTEST THEATER—ONLY EIGHTY SEATS—ALL ONE DOLLAR."

Small Wonder is alive with infectious recollections of those who flocked to their door: Marie Dressler, who always brought her chauffeur in to see the show; John Barrymore, entranced by the fact that it was real theater and who "could almost smell the grease paint;" Gloria Swanson; Dolores del Rio; Oscar Klemperer (he loved the puppet orchestra); Marlene Dietrich (she went unrecognized); Greta Garbo. "The audience struggled to keep its mind on the play— as did, it must be admitted, the puppeteers," and the then-celebrated cartoonist, Don Herold, who "always thought a puppet was the exhaust-pipe on a motorcycle."

Harry, who had been creating remarkably accurate portrait puppets for some time, immediately set to work on miniature versions of stars scheduled to appear, or whom the boys *hoped* would appear. Gary Cooper was caricatured, as well as Ramon Navarro, Martha Graham (with whom Harry studied dance), Aimee

Semple McPherson (the evangelist), and Albert Einstein, who attended a private performance one memorable afternoon. A rumpled figure in a broad-brimmed uncomfortable hat, the great physicist bowed stiffly, smiled, and laughed through *Mister Noah*, to which Forman had added syntactically muddled German. Then, when Einstein's own puppet appeared, an entrance he had not expected, "for a moment it was met with surprised silence, and then by a truly Olympian guffaw."

Einstein stayed for some time after the performance, nibbling cookies, asking questions, examining the puppet, and chuckling at the blue-smocked replica of himself. "He viewed it critically. 'Gut!' he said. '*Gut, gut! Aber zu schmachtig, zu schlank!*' ("Good, but not fat enough"), whereupon, fumbling in his pocket, he drew out a page of a letter, crumpled it carefully into a ball, and poked it up beneath the smock. He viewed the augmented embonpoint with approval, thanked us all, and smiling, took his way down the street, mingling with the Sunday throng, who, to his great satisfaction, paid him no notice."

The puppet has vanished into a collection, but Einstein's letter, written to him by a colleague—and with equations scribbled on the envelope—is on display at Caltech in Pasadena.

Ever restless, the boys closed up on Olvera Street after two years and returned for a summer season in a refurbished barn at Forman's New Hampshire farm. But the year was 1931. The Depression was on. Homes were shuttered, lawns a tangled wilderness. Hotels they had always found bustling with vacationers were either not open at all or "haunted by a pathetic few who seemed to sulk in the shadows, ashamed to flaunt their prosperity in the face of an impoverished society."

Nothing worked. Not even dressing Harry "as a clown and driving over the hills and through the valleys, hurdy-gurdy wheezing, tossing out handbills to gaping children and amused or suspicious adults." So on to New York for a modestly successful winter season. Then, like so much in their lucky lives, an urgent call came from the Coast: would the boys return to California to create two hundred dancing marionettes for a fantasy film, *I Am Suzanne*?

You bet they would!

Typically, the movie fell far behind schedule and mangled the

(Left) Harry with Helen Hayes as Queen Victoria and his puppet of her, 1930s.

Albert Einstein in 1930 with Uncle Harry's portrait puppet of him, California Institute of Technology, Pasadena, California.

The puppeteers in New Hampshire, 1933.

budget. In the midst of the boys' mass-producing puppets, Rome's Teatro dei Piccoli, originally hired for the job, arrived from Rome in "a flurry of baggage and staccato Italian." Clearly resented by the newcomers, Forman was certain the producers had an even greater fear "that if we met, dead puppeteers would strew the studio floor and litter the beautifully symmetrical geranium beds."

Teatro dei Piccoli departed in a snit, leaving Harry and his assistants to finish the job.

In New York again (my first memories of Harry date from this period, for by 1936 we had moved to Brooklyn), the adventure went merrily on. They played the Nora Bayes Theater, the Lyceum, and Manhattan's posh Barbizon Plaza with a revue, *Sunday Nights at Nine.* All along, Forman had been creating a variety of rich material, far beyond what the puppets could absorb. And Harry yearned to do more acting. So out of the Barbizon Plaza experience the idea of combining a live revue with the puppet shows began to emerge. But how to accomplish this in a natural manner? The shows had become elaborate, with dozens of figures, lights, scene changes, and complicated paraphernalia. How could they dispose of it all quickly enough to make room for live actors? Then, too, California was beckoning again.

On the way west, someone (Roddy, perhaps) came up with the idea for a playhouse with a stage at both ends. Soon after they arrived, a congenial developer who remembered the boys from Olvera Street, because Teatro Torito was sold out whenever he tried to get tickets, built a theater to their specifications.

Turnabout Theater was born.

Once again the boys, along with a fourth partner, director and actress Dorothy Neumann, threw themselves into a frenzy of activity, and their welcoming little establishment on La Cienega opened for business on July 10, 1941. Once again this unique theatrical experience became obligatory for the Hollywood crowd. Once again the famous crowded in to autograph the walls, and drink the coffee, and marvel at Harry's carved creations and Forman's wonderful songs—all of this designed, I like to believe, for the arrival of my brother David and me that unforgettable summer evening in 1944.

～

The early fifties brought Tommy Turnabout's Circus, an imaginative children's show that was Roddy's dream and on which he spent his life's savings. Roddy was the ringmaster; Harry, the chief clown. A trained horse spelled out words, and the stars were a black and an Anglo boy alternating as "Tommy Turnabout," who fell asleep then woke to find himself in the circus. Fine notices didn't rescue it financially.

The acclaimed folksinger Odetta was one of Turnabout's big discoveries. Initially tagging along on Saturdays to help out her mother, Turnabout's cleaning woman, she'd often neglect her assigned dusting to just sit, quietly mooning over the Puccini, Verdi, or Wagner Uncle Harry always played. When Harry and Forman discovered her "lovely, natural singing voice" (she was sixteen at the time), and when they learned that her mother couldn't afford a vocal coach, Harry paid for lessons. After starting in Turnabout's circus, Odetta soon graduated to the theater's main stage, where her spirituals and work ballads were an immediate hit.

Life found me too preoccupied to see much of the puppeteers after Turnabout closed. But I learned of brief revivals in San Francisco and in San Diego and was aware that for the next twenty years Harry taught puppetry to children and adults, and that they were receiving honors of all kinds from their fellow entertainers— including the first Lifetime Achievement Award from the Los Angeles Drama Critics Circle.

By 1985, both Mom and Pop had died. Uncle Harry was one of the last connections to a river of memory I didn't want to let dry up. Even if he hadn't been a gregarious bundle of energy and charm, this was reason enough to maintain the tie.

Since the mid-1970s, I'd been attending Harry and Forman's annual birthday party or dragging friends to performances they presented for longtime fans on the small stage of a big, ramshackle Hollywood home they shared. Turnabout House was almost as enchanting as the theater itself. Leaving today's decaying Hollywood, one stepped back into 1927, to a world crowded with dusty photos of mostly forgotten stars, posters, and memorabilia from the puppeteers' touring days, and pictures of the artists who populated their several theaters. Like most old troupers, whose real terror is that nobody will ask, Forman played the shy schoolboy then quickly let himself be talked into plunking down at the piano to sing three or four of his hundreds of songs.

Before a heart condition forced him to spend his last months on the living room couch, Roddy was the busy mother hen, cooking, cleaning, and continuing to organize things as he'd done for more than fifty years.

Harry kept manufacturing puppets in his garage workshop, until at eighty-five he tired of them. Then I'd usually find him in a favorite tattered chair, knitting little woolen hats that he gave to anyone who dropped by. He donated hundreds of them to a children's hospital. Until his eyesight began to fail, he insisted on working his favorite puppet, Simon Legree, or he'd flourish a soiled handkerchief and do the same tricks for guests that he did for David and me on those distant yesterdays when we were kids.

While their times necessarily kept Harry, Forman, and Roddy circumspect about their homosexuality, they pretty much lived the lives they wanted to live, busy and content in their work, with a legion of friends, young and old, who popped in at Turnabout House on a regular basis. For those who didn't know they were gay (or didn't care to let on), it didn't matter. Being "artistic" was quite acceptable.

As I got to know Harry and Forman better after Roddy's death, I started to develop an understanding of the part being gay had played in their lives, an understanding I'd had only a glimmer of until I finally read *Better Angel*, the pioneering novel Forman wrote back in 1933. Pioneering, because it was perhaps the first gay American novel with a happy ending.

Uncle Harry finally "came out of the closet" (sort of) in his mid-eighties; though a year or two earlier, when Forman began talking openly with me, Harry became a bit upset. Possibly because the subject hadn't been discussed, he wasn't sure what I knew or didn't know, or what I thought about him, and I think that among straight people he still felt embarrassed. But until he slowly began tuning out to life around him a year or so later, he sat knitting his hats or shuffled out to feed the portly pigeons (each one had a name) under the banana tree on his funky California patio. And I think he was not only reassured that I loved him, he seemed to genuinely look forward to my visits.

We'd come full circle. True, I didn't suddenly materialize in the way *he* did when I was five, slipping coins through chinks in the door, but I was family—and I believe that was enough.

FOUR

dwell in the wilderness

*Why I became so interested in family history when I was
a kid is probably because Grandma Clark kept telling me
she thought none of the young Burnetts would ever
amount to anything much—that we would always be
poor, etc. So I thought if I looked back a ways there
might be some ray of hope. The whole genealogy was
written out in pencil on the back of a large Bissel carpet
sweeper poster.*

VERNE BURNETT, IN A LETTER TO HIS BROTHER, LEO

If Uncle Harry was the big attraction in the mid-1940s, it was
because his infrequent visits and impish antics were in huge contrast
to the behavior of his brothers, Leo and Verne. Even as a kid, I saw
them as kindly and generous uncles, but stuffy. Harry, by comparison, was a three-ring circus.

Mom's oldest brother, Leo, owned a big farm north of Chicago.
Here, he spent part of each weekend overseeing improvements to
the land and the rest plotting ideas for campaigns his advertising
agency was involved with. He'd try them out on his perpetually
patient wife, my Aunt Naomi, and anyone else who would listen.
Leo and I didn't meet until 1948, when I was sixteen.

Earlier in the 1940s, when Mom, David, and I spent a lot of time
at Uncle Verne and Aunt Laura's in Connecticut, I didn't know that
my uncle had been exploring the Burnett family roots. Visiting the
Verne Burnetts had more to do with dressing for dinner, waiting for
Laura to ring a little silver bell summoning Cook to bring on the
main course, or listening to Verne expound on the next great
consumer convenience—frozen, dehydrated vegetables—which his

company, General Foods, was then developing. (He had a tall wooden rack on the sunporch, where kernels of corn and rows of peas shriveled before my eyes.)

By the time I got around to considering family history, Leo, Verne, and both of my aunts had died, and with them, what little they might have remembered. Except for Verne's brief interest, their lives were too busy for this curious nonsense. Who their ancestors were or what they accomplished would be left to a nosy nephew.

Uncle Verne lost that Bissel carpet sweeper poster and so boxed me into a genealogical corner. I'm still picking up memory scraps from his explorations, still trying to link tidbits of fact with misty legends of a Scottish king, an illustrious general, and a buckskin-clad explorer pushing west to Oregon and the Pacific.

"The family thought he was a descendant of George Rogers Clark of Revolutionary War fame," said Verne of his grandfather Mortimer in a letter to Leo. Given the snide comment about the young Burnetts, it's small wonder the Clarks cultivated a famous ancestor. But even if tales of the general who scuttled the British-Indian alliance in the West, and of his brother William, of the Lewis and Clark expedition, prove as trumped-up as Adolphe Bessie's stint with Custer, they are heroic images to conjure. At least until some genealogical archer punctures the balloon.

I like the one about the Scottish king even better. It calls up the rugged Highlands, skirling bagpipes, and mountain tribesmen sweeping out of the heathery hills to skewer the British again and again until the land is safe and free. Alexander Bernard or Burnet "of Leys" is another of those obscure patriarchs. Attached in some way to the fortunes of Robert the Bruce (who plotted strategy by watching a spider spin its web), in 1324 he received from that king charters of land in Aberdeenshire. His lineage traces on to Bishop Gilbert Burnet, acting prime minister of England under William and Mary, and to his son William, last British colonial governor of New York State. It hardly matters if this data in *Burke's Peerage* turns out to be a wild goose chase. At least I know that Mom's grandparents, George Burnett and Susan Acheson, made their way west along the Erie Canal during the mid-1800s to help carve out a colony in central Michigan.

Wilderness they had. In abundance. They cleared the land for crops, and if Uncle Verne's report that George was killed when his ax slipped while he was chopping down trees is more exotic than his actual death from a strangulated hernia, the aura of bulging muscles and sweaty corduroy nevertheless hangs in the air. It is Lincoln-esque to the core, even if the clear-cutting lumbermen did leave in their wake fields mostly unsuitable for agriculture and decimated the cover for fur-bearing animals. Wild turkey, the grayling trout, and that most famous of now-extinct American birds, the passenger pigeon, quickly vanished.

61

They followed northern trails, these hardy Protestant folk— Scotland, Canada, upper New York State, maybe Holland. Achesons, Van Husens, and Formans married Clarks and Burnetts, and most of them wound up smack in the middle of the state. They called their homestead, Rochester Colony, Duplain Township—later, St. Johns.

Soon after they met, Pop began quizzing Mom for stories about her family. He was a careful listener, for a richly textured portrait survives in what I've always considered his finest novel, *Dwell in the Wilderness.*

As Mom's parents prepare for their wedding night, her father-to-be wonders what he is expected to do, as his bride, her voice strained and harsh, sobs, "Put out the light, I'm undressing." Fear and anxiety engulf each of them. As he slips in between the sheets, he can hear her "heavy breathing and a stifled sob, and a word or so that sounded like *Our Father . . .*"

Mom's plump, self-pitying mother, Rosa Belle Clark, contrasts with her handsome, gangly, good-natured father, Noble Israel Burnett. In an agonizing parallel to her own experience, the book version of Rosa Belle's own mother warns that "men are beasts," but that "it is God's will that we suffer this martyrdom for our souls' sake." Counseling her daughter about sex, she says, "*That* is intended for the purposes of procreation, and perhaps this contrast is intended to keep the world in balance. I cannot know; it is all too bewildering for my poor brain, but you will find it the better part of Christian wisdom to suffer the base carnality of your future husband, rather than kick against the thorns, and your salvation will be that much more assured."

If sexual repression was a part of the conditioning, not everyone in the family got the message. When Grandma's sister May Belle married the lively Will Parsons, he flatly refused to give up the girlfriend he already had. According to Mom, they slept three in a bed, and it became quite an amicable arrangement (though I have no report from either of the women).

When his father died, Noble Burnett left school to take a job in a dry goods store to support his mother. He put himself through high school and at the same time saved enough to take a two-year business course, then return to St. Johns, where he opened his own small emporium: Noble Burnett.

Dwell in the Wilderness has him teaching himself geography as he inventories the stock, noting "vanilla beans from Mexico, woven cloth from Great Britain . . . pineapples, bolts of French silk (kept under lock and key), whale oil from the far Pacific" and other goods from the world beyond St. Johns.

My grandmother Rosa had also left school early. After her father's death, she took a job in a local button factory and kept it until she married. After that, she cooked and cleaned and put up with her mother-in-law, "an obstinate, cranky old woman." She didn't take much lightly—not the old woman, not her husband's neglect in failing to wrap a gift he was sure would please.

Mom's recollections and Pop's novel both paint the same vivid family portrait: meals passed with scarcely a word, Rosa's pouting because Noble had forgotten their anniversary "till the very last minute and then grabbed up any old thing that was lying around the store, and you dump it in my arms [a pair of red garters, unwrapped] and expect me to be delighted with it!"

The withdrawn silences continued. Grandma sniffed and set her jaw. And she suffered the "base carnality" her mother warned her about for enough years to produce four children. Leo came first, in 1891, then Verne, then my mother, Gladys May. Mom hated the name and after leaving home began calling herself Mary. In 1901, Harry was born. Each would contradict Great-Grandma Clark's prediction that they "would never amount to anything much."

A hundred years later, it's difficult to judge what kind of people these actually were. Legend is often one-sided and spiced with personal bias; memories are fuzzy, and facts become twisted. But as with the Bessies, a rock-hard independence comes through. Even the most profound tragedy reflects this stoicism. When Mom's

Noble Israel Burnett, grandfather of Dan Bessie, about 1890.

young cousin Leon, son of her aunt Lilly Belle, tried to crawl under a freight train on his way home from school, the train started and both his legs were cut off. Leon pulled himself home by his arms, up onto the porch, and asked his mother for a drink of water before he died.

Religion and cold climates seem to forge that "rugged individualism" so dear to the preindustrial ideal. At the same time, they foster an often-sterile emotionalism, like those in an American version of an early Ingmar Bergman film. These were people who didn't talk to one another much about what bothered them. They bottled it up. Their reward would not be of this earth.

⌒

Mom's early life was alive with contradiction. Periods of cloudy alienation were mixed with bursts of energy and happiness. She remembered the time her mother threw a carving knife at fourteen-year-old Leo; she remembered the cross her mother always bore, the drooping mouth, the sulks, and the hurt little girl feelings she would affect at real or imagined wrongs. Mom recorded many of these in her diaries:

> "Aren't you going to eat, Mother?"
> "I'm not hungry now."
> There would be no conversation except when my father would ask about our day or about any plans we had. Then I would help Mama clear the table and go out in the kitchen to do the dishes. And while we were there I would see her eating endlessly as she moved around the kitchen, but I hadn't as yet put much together in my head.

Rosa had a trunk full of pithy sayings: "Pretty is as pretty does;" "Every fox smells his own hole first;" "Beauty is only skin deep." When Mom first saw herself naked in a mirror and ran into her mother's bedroom to announce, "Look Mama, I'm beautiful," there was a shocked reprimand and, "Pride comes before a fall." When she sobbed out her frustration over her mother's refusal to let Charlie Britton, her eighth grade graduation date, take her on a sleigh ride, out came, "There are lots of pebbles on the beach."

But if Rosa inspired Pop's title ("It is better to dwell in the wilderness, than with a contentious and an angry woman." Proverbs 21:19), she was also the mother who nursed her daughter through a case of pneumonia the doctor had given up on. If her slumbering frustrations led her to rip off her own clothing and tear it to shreds more than once, something Mom learned of years later, she was also a mother who stayed up long nights sewing a black vellum jacket with pink borders for a Christmas doll. If a Puritan and provincial childhood created in Rosa a lifelong fear of sex and prohibitions that

⌒

often made no sense to her children, she was also a woman with a desperate drive to educate them, to see that her sons "made men of themselves and became well-to-do citizens."

Mom saw her first ten or twelve years as rich for growth. Small-town impressions flood her diaries: the old barn, Daisy the cow, the corn patch, piano lessons, elocution lessons, the drive to climb trees and play ball like Leo and Verne. ("That's not ladylike.") There were her mother's occasional outbursts of gaiety, breaking into a sudden recitation: "Said Briar Rose's mother to the naughty Briar Rose, 'What will become of you my child, the Lord A'mighty knows.'" There was fudge and popcorn on Sundays and the smell of coffee from the tall granite coffee pot, brought to a boil with eggshells for settling. She remembered learning to do "girl things," and "the wonderful feeling of bare feet in mud, of running games of tag until we all dropped breathless on the grass." She recalled cutting the long hair growing from her Grandmother Clark's chin after she died, as she had in life, the elaborate death rituals then in vogue: front doors draped in black crepe, mourners filing into somber sitting rooms. Then later, she and Harry and neighbor kids retreating to the backyard to play out funerals and cemeteries with little graves off in a corner near the grape vines.

From their father, a man who cared for a simple life, his work, a happy family, and a few close friends, Mom and her brothers learned a love of nature, a basic honesty, and consideration in relationships. Noble took Verne on long walks in the woods on Sundays or holidays. He knew the name of every tree, every tiniest plant, every weed. And his children inherited these sensibilities; Leo and Verne were always planting flower and vegetable gardens, and Harry developed a passion for hiking.

Again, it filters down. My brother David is never so content as when he's tending his five acres in the Sierra foothills.

My mother, whose world was never financially comfortable but was filled with raising David and me, found an outlet in her writing, in an ability to treasure the smallest things: a friendly windowsill plant, the sound of country crickets, or a fat water bug scuttling under the sink when she'd surprise it by flicking on the light.

A "theater in the round" is how Mom described her childhood, one directed by a hardworking, kind, and loving father, a basically

The Burnetts of St. Johns, Michigan, about 1905. *Top,* Rosa and Leo. *Bottom,* Mary (Mom), Verne, Harry, and Noble.

kind and loving (and ambitious and difficult) mother. Even with the sulks, if Mom or her brothers complained, Noble would admonish, "I don't want you children to say things against your mother. She works hard and gets tired sometimes." That was that. They kept their feelings buried. "Keep your own counsel," was the rule. Like most people of that time (and since), the Burnetts were too busy making a living and raising kids to spend time in subjective speculation about what they were doing. They just did.

Mom, Leo, and Verne grew up with the acceptable personalities of most middle-class midwestern children. Harry was different, an oddity. He vexed his family, Rosa in particular. Mom's great empathy, developed early, helped her to understand him. Gradually, they broke the family code of silence by sharing more intimate feelings. This led to a closeness lasting all their lives.

Verne turned out his own neighborhood paper on a hand press, sold the homemade potato chips Rosa made, or peddled the *Ladies' Home Journal* and *McCall's* door-to-door.

Leo developed a knack for art, looked over his dad's shoulder as he laid out ads for the store on big pieces of wrapping paper, then took a correspondence course and learned to letter show cards himself. By age twelve, he was working summers as a printer's devil and reporter on the *Clinton Democrat.* He wrote obituaries and met the local train to interview townsfolk leaving or returning home. The Protestant work ethic saw him through high school and into the University of Michigan.

In spite of my grandfather's hard work and long hours, that same ethic did little for the store. Over the years he'd extended so much long-term credit to customers having a hard time that finally Noble Burnett couldn't pay its accounts. Rosa, blunt with her feelings, refused to allow him to mortgage the house. Without mortgaging the house, he told her, the store would fail.

"Then let it fail," replies the Rosa character in *Dwell in the Wilderness,* "if you're not man enough to keep it going." Noble let his last two clerks go, and with Rosa working in the store part time, did his best to rescue the business. Perhaps Leo helped with the advertising:

NEW SPRING GOODS AT NOBLE BURNETT

A smart collection of Embroideries, Flouncings, Bands, Yokings, Laces, Newest Patterns in Wool Dress Goods, Suitings, Waistings, White Goods, Welts, Poplins, Linens, Chambrays, Madras, Batiste, Flaxon.

Newest Creations in Muslin Underwear at Popular Prices

Special bargains to close balance of season's goods in Cloaks, Suits, Skirts, Dresses, Robes, Waists, Sweaters, Shawls, Outings, Gowns, Caps, Knit Goods, Hosiery, Underwear. Rock bottom prices on Sheetings, Muslins, Crashes, Ginghams, Prints.

Free Library Votes, Fish Trading Stamps or Premium Coupons with every Purchase.
We need the money, let us fill your orders.

St. Johns, Mich.   **Noble Burnett**   St. Johns, Mich.

But it wasn't enough. Soon after, Noble was injured in a train wreck en route to Detroit to try to secure a loan. Rosa ran the store during his long recuperation and worked with him for months after he returned. Mom was eleven or twelve then and would decades later remember what she would call an irrepressible break in whatever loving relationship her mother and father may once have had. "They still slept in the same bed, still worked hard, and the family pictures were still taken, but there was a droopy expression on my mother's mouth, and a turning away of the head when my father tried to kiss her on the cheek."

Sundays were Rosa's "headache days," and the Congregational Church saw the Burnetts less often. Gradually, Rosa began taking over financial responsibilities. But the income never met all the bills, and Noble Burnett was forced into bankruptcy. The store with all its finery and fixtures was sold at auction.

Because her own schooling had been cut off in the eighth grade, Rosa was determined the children would complete their education. Leo would graduate from Michigan in another year, and Verne was getting ready to enter; so in 1913, she sold the house in St. Johns and moved everyone to Ann Arbor, to a smaller place, but large enough to take in a border or two. This would also cut down on expenses for the boys.

Noble simply went along. The breach between him and Rosa was wider than ever. He still carried his head high and tried to help around the roominghouse. But his wife had taken over. "Whether she knew it or not," writes Mom, "she was on her way."

Rosa got into real estate, showing property on foot. Then she'd come home exhausted, take pail and brush, drop to her knees and scrub down the porch. Later, her employers bought her a big, boxy Ford. She'd become stout by then, like the clubwomen in the *New Yorker* cartoons of the 1940s, so the car helped. And she'd developed a sideline: maneuvering her way into marketable homes before other realtors, she would often discover valuable relics, buy them at a fraction of their value, then resell to a list of contacts for whom antiques were becoming quite the fashion.

The failure of the store, the strain of leaving behind good friends and his hometown—these had taken their toll on Noble. He could find no decent-paying job in Ann Arbor, and none were of a station that pleased Rosa. The accident had slowed his body but had left a mind still eager to be out and doing. He was loved by his sons, but by 1916 they were on their own, moving into the business world. He had failed at business; what advice could a failure possibly offer?

Seen too as a failure by his wife, he also saw himself as a failure in the eyes of society—for this was a society in which the man was supposed to be the breadwinner, and if not, he wasn't much of a man. His daughter seemed to be getting along. His youngest son, a clown, secretive, he loved but didn't understand. Noble wanted to be of use, but how? What road was open to him?

According to Mom, the letter in *Dwell in the Wilderness* from Eben (Noble) to Amelia (Rosa) accurately reflects the kind of man her father was.

Dear Amelia,

I am going now. I think that it is best. Until further notice, please address me care of General Delivery, Detroit. I will let you know where I am as soon as I am settled. I will try to find work and will send you every penny I can spare.

Please, Amelia, try to understand what I am doing. I know that I have not been a very satisfactory husband to you, but we have lived together so long—twenty-eight years—that there should be no secrets between us at this time. If I have been a burden to you, as I know well I have, I am sorry. Believe me, I have tried to do the best I could to provide for you and the children, and I really feel that by making this move I will be better able to help you with the expenses of their education and their remaining time in school. There is more work to be found in the city than in Wolverine [Ann Arbor].

If ever I have hurt you, please forgive me. If ever I have failed to understand, forgive me. I find that there is little I can say now, except good-bye, and that you will no longer be troubled by my illness and my "touchiness." I take all responsibility for what I am about to do, and if there is ever a question of blame to be placed, I cheerfully assume it. You have done the best you knew how, but it now occurs to me that maybe we are simply not suited to each other, and maybe we have not made a strong enough effort to understand each other's little peculiarities. No two people are alike; it would be a strange world if they were.

But although we have lived so long together, I find that I still do not understand you, and I know I irritate you at times beyond your endurance. I love you, Amelia, but I cannot help what I am going to do.

I am confident that there will be something in the city that I can

competently do, and that I will be able to help you make both ends meet
. . . Good-bye, my dear, I know I am a failure, but I have been faithful.
Be careful of yourself and when I have an address, do not fail to call on
me if there is anything that I can do.

Your devoted husband,
Eben Morris

By the time General Pershing led American troops into France in 1917, Leo had graduated, worked as a reporter on the *Peoria Journal,* and was now in the navy. On active duty at the Great Lakes Training Center, he spent most of the war building a cement breakwater and stacking bodies from the 1918 flu epidemic. Verne went through college, where he worked on the *Michigan Daily,* then joined the army's Motor Transport Corps and was shipped overseas. Harry's status as a detached loner began to change when cousin Forman Brown arrived in 1919 to room with the Burnetts and attend the university. Forman was a kindred spirit, though if Rosa had known just *how* kindred, he and Harry wouldn't have been permitted to share the same bedroom—or the same *house.*

Mom was caught up in poetry and drama through high school (she played Hero in *Much Ado About Nothing*), and this continued at the university. She majored in English and education, because in those days well-bred young ladies became nurses, teachers, or secretaries. She studied Chaucer and until she was past eighty could still rattle off much of his prologue to *The Canterbury Tales* (in Middle English). After her first term at Michigan, she took a year off to teach in a one room rural school:

> It had started during the noon hour. I was still a big kid at nineteen, with one year of college behind me. The October sunshine, the thrill of autumn leaves that sparkled and danced over the countryside, the thought of tomorrow being Friday when I would take the ten-mile ride by interurban back to Ann Arbor for a weekend date, the war, the thoughts of one brother overseas and the confident desire to conquer the world; all these churned and swirled as I sat on the stoop and took the last bite of an apple. The children were playing in the gravel, selecting pretty leaves to wax, and it seemed to me all at once that it was silly to go inside.
>
> from one of Mom's unpublished stories

Instead of continuing with lessons, she got into a game of hide-and-seek with the kids, only to be discovered by a frowning County Superintendent of Schools who arrived on a surprise inspection. She bustled the children inside and plunged into addition, but the superintendent didn't approve of the way she was teaching. What these country children needed, he lectured, was a practical mathematics, drawn from the daily cycle of farming life: how many yards in an acre, how many pigs in an average litter, how many quarts of milk an average dairy cow gave. "Finished with the speech, he wiped his pince-nez, smiled at me with his little cat smile, and walked out the door."

By her last year at Michigan, a fellow student had come into Mom's life: Melvin Dick. Weekends at home they dated. Recalling the winter of 1918–1919, she writes, "We had been to the ice skating rink the night before. You in white turtle neck and knitted cap. Sure on the ice (learned from childhood on the lakes of northern Michigan). I in long sweater, scotch plaid skirt and knitted tam. My weak ankles turning. You laughed at me in joyful mood and caught me by the arm whenever it seemed that I might fall. So we walked the mile home on snow-packed sidewalks, swinging our skates and laughing of such silly things."

But there was an even stronger pull on her affections, a young man with deep-set eyes, wide forehead, dark hair, a "mouth full of poetry and a heart full of song;" a man whose sensitivity, she had learned, meshed with her own—her cousin, Forman Brown. Mom's attraction to Forman was clouded by something neither of them knew how to deal with. Though increasingly aware of his homosexuality by now, Forman didn't let on. And it's clear that Mom couldn't figure out what was holding back his love.

During the next three years, she taught off and on: eighth grade in Marshall, Michigan, to a rambunctious class of big-boned farm kids who liked to intimidate a novice teacher ("the spit-ball year," she called it); at a school for girls in Hyland Park; as a substitute in Cicero and at other grade schools; then six months of junior high English and grammar back in Ann Arbor.

In 1922, looking reluctantly back over her shoulder at Forman, Mom accepted Mel Dick's proposal. They had been engaged for two years, and it was a time for getting married. Leo and Verne had found wives, and each already had a child. For them, family life was a given. You went to college, got a job, married, had kids, and climbed the ladder of success—if you were lucky.

Mom, though, came to see her first marriage, like that of her parents, as a familiar pretense: "Knowing in your heart, deeply, your marriage is a culmination of your own burning desire to get away from home and live life, a possessive kind of caring for your husband, sexual attraction, a mixed, confused kind of knowing."

There had been "secret times of exploration high in the cold hills outside of town, on the front porch coming home from a dance, a sad, young, trial and error sort of sexual exploration." There had been feelings of pride, shame, and fear all tied in a bundle. The Puritan inheritance had sifted down from grandmother to mother— and now to daughter.

She recalled the white satin and lace wedding dress, the friends and relatives, the chicken sandwiches and spiked punch, coffee, and fruitcake, neatly wrapped in small waxed paper packages with white ribbon and a piece given to each person (a family custom).

They were young, romantic, and broke. Nine dollars between them. They went to Chicago, to a hotel room Mel had taken. They undressed, shy and hesitant. They made love. It was all a sham, she thought, as she lay wide-awake on the sheeted bed in the hot August night. This was no way to begin a honeymoon. This wasn't how it was supposed to be. Then Mel told her a story; a joke, really, about sex, one she could later never recall. It wasn't important. A small thing. But his crude attempt at humor hurt her and she pulled away. She climbed out of bed, slipped into her taffeta gown, and sat in the Morris chair by the window. When Mel asked her to come back, she didn't answer.

She thought about the "men are beasts" admonition handed down from her grandmother Clark. She could see her mother's drooping mouth. She hated the image. She had always hated it. And she knew that she was doing exactly what Rosa had done all her life.

Although Mom had taken a vow not to follow her mother's path, it would take long years of trial and error to break those patterns. But for the moment, the vow allowed her to laugh out loud, climb back into bed beside Mel and say, "It really was a very funny story."

Lettering show cards in Noble's store had paid off for Leo; by 1926, he was head of the creative department of Homer McKee advertising in Indianapolis. Verne was in Detroit, responsible for institutional ads for General Motors. Harry was at Yale, studying theater, and laying a solid groundwork for the unique showman he was to become.

Mom was living on Henry Street in New York, her marriage to Mel Dick having dissolved the previous October.

Though young, Mel was already set in his ways. Dinner would be ready when he came home. They would go to the movies on occasion, or sit at home and read, or talk quietly about their day. The companionable and poetic union Mom had imagined she'd find in marriage wasn't there. It was a relationship she didn't understand, a marriage whose ordinariness frightened her, and she didn't know how to change it.

Years later, in her diaries, there was regret but also recognition: "And so my dear first husband, while I was never able to express to you the pain of seeing and feeling your sorrow, your anger, your desperation at 'losing' me, I knew (my body knew) it would never work with us . . . I am everlastingly grateful that it was you, a fairly simple man, direct and honest, who aroused and let me know my own direct and honest heterosexual constitution."

Did she have doubts about her "heterosexual constitution?" Not likely. Perhaps the Puritan genetics were so ingrained, the contrast between physical attraction and the manner in which that was supposed to be satisfied so confusing to a young woman born in 1898, that she was simply unsure *what* she was feeling.

Her later diaries help fill in the blanks. October 25, 1972 rang a bell; the day of divorce, a feeling that she'd copped out, run away from a relationship she didn't know how to handle. "Somehow," she wrote, "beyond logic, beyond dreams, beyond ourselves, we begin to divorce, piece by little piece, of what we're made, without ever quite knowing how or by what means we learn."

There would be long, hard years before Mary Burnett sorted out the answers, before she became "Mom"; years filled with silly mistakes and brave experiments, happy times and terrible sadness. But for now, frightening as it was, she knew she had to make her own way. Eventually, she could sum it up:

Somewhere in early childhood the answers hide. But hide and seek are so long gone, and fear of what's behind the corner of the barn, the mulberry tree, the honeysuckle vine, or hidden with a bare foot, peeking out under the back porch. Fear of these, I think, could not shatter me again. Or could it?

So grateful am I dear people of the past that we've shared bits of time together, and I know, really I do know, no matter how much of our sharing seemed to come to nothing—I've never taken anything away from you nor you from me. We've just given each other ourselves back to ourselves.

After leaving home, my grandfather Noble lived alone for the next twelve years, mostly in furnished boardinghouse rooms. He never divorced Rosa, and she never forgave him for "deserting us." But he came back to Ann Arbor for weddings, birthdays, and other family events. He worked at a succession of jobs in Detroit, and as he promised, sent every penny he could to his wife.

Finally, in 1926, he became assistant manager of the Chase Mercantile Company in Pontiac, Michigan. He was there two years, until treatment for varicose veins, acquired partly from standing all his life, led to erysipelas, a general bloodstream infection. In those days, antibiotics didn't exist.

Within two weeks, Noble was dying. Leo and Verne came to the hospital along with their wives, Naomi and Laura. Harry, in New York preparing to go on the road with the show designed by Norman Bel Geddes, couldn't get away. Mom finished up her work sewing costumes for him, then took a train for Pontiac.

When she got to the hospital, Rosa and the rest of the family left the room so father and daughter could be alone. They talked quietly for a time, and he told her he had always loved her and that in spite of everything, he had always tried to do the best he could. Mom said she knew that. Then he looked up at her with a smile and said, "Sis, I wish you could learn to live within your means. You're really very extravagant, you know." Mom, who never had enough to be extravagant *with*, replied, "Yes, Dad, I'll try."

Then Leo and Verne and their wives were tiptoeing back into the room—without Rosa—and Noble pressed Mom's hand and said she should go get some dinner. She kissed him, got up from the bed and got her coat, then turned back at the door; her father was following her with his eyes. He lifted his hand and waved goodbye, like a little child waves, from the wrist.

"Goodbye, Sis," he said.

As she left, Verne followed her into the hall. "You shouldn't kiss him," he whispered, "It may be contagious."

"Verne," said Mom, "You'll have to lend me a dollar."

Grandpa's admonition to "try to live within your means" had great meaning for Mom, for it exemplified not the idea of miserly penny-pinching, but of taking personal responsibility, of using money for what one reasonably needs, and understanding that this is an important part of living an honorable life.

Mom cherished his memory, and sometimes found herself deep in conversation with him "when I'm muddled and can't find an answer." Her writing is filled with the same deep love of nature he had. And though she didn't understand his defense of her mother when she or her brothers complained of her prohibitions, she came to admire him for it.

In her later writings there even emerges a deep empathy for her mother and an understanding that she was also a woman created by her times.

Growing up, I always felt cheated by not having a grandfather. Dan Bessie died ten years before I was born; Noble Burnett, four. Couldn't one of them have waited a bit longer, taken better care of their health? Didn't they know they had secrets to pass on?

While Grandma Adeline Bessie was a gem, in my kid's mind, Grandma Rosa Burnett was no prize. I recall meeting her only once—in Connecticut at my Uncle Verne's, a year or two before she died in 1941. I was six or seven, and I remember Mom telling me that I had playfully lunged at her with a dime-store rubber knife.

"You're not my grandson," she's supposed to have replied. I can't vouch for the specifics but I do recall that whatever she said floored me. That evening, when I called to apologize, I began in a tiny disguised voice: "Hello, Grandma," I said, "this is Mickey Mouse." She hung up on me.

The wilderness inhabited by the Burnetts was not only one of noncommunication. There was also a craggy self-reliance bordering on often-unrealistic personal expectation. Unexplained prohibitions about sex fostered guilt and confusion. It took decades for some to find a clear stream leading out of those woods. Others never did; they just stumbled along, ducking low branches, and did their best to live within the narrow constraints of a complex heritage.

If the Burnetts have had a hard time in sharing deep feelings, they've also been there for one another during seasons when the rivers overflowed their banks. If Rosa's driving ambition pushed her children to success, none of them belittled another's lack of accomplishment. They hung together. Though his brothers may have looked askance, they never put Harry down for his sexual orientation. Nobody chided Mom because she never made much money or didn't "marry well." Noble's quiet compassion had a lot to do with fostering those attitudes.

It's been an erratic but powerful mixture those misty Scottish ancestors started to pass on a thousand years ago.

Somehow, it all filters down.

FIVE

battle of the century

From the doctor's point of view, contract bridge is the greatest outlet for excess nervous energy that one has at hand. There are thousands of people who are "bottled up," who are full of nervous explosive material which is in constant turmoil. Many such individuals can let off steam by reading an exciting detective story; others must get rid of this energy in some other way, and contract is the solution.

DR. HAROLD HAYES, IN *BRIDGE WORLD*

During the 1930s, Grandma Addie's cousin, Sidney Lenz, was one of America's great luminaries of contract bridge. And somehow, he gets mixed up in my head with Macy's Thanksgiving Day parade. It's all a blur: a gigantic Mickey Mouse and Pluto floating down Fifth Avenue, pie and sandwiches popping out of glass compartments at Horn and Hardardt when two or three nickels are fed into slots, and a brief but startling interlude with Sidney's sleight of hand. I seem to remember Grandma taking David and me to the parade, then to Sidney's huge apartment in the Waldorf-Astoria. One immense room held a billiard table and a ping-pong table. Glass cases lined the walls, with polished gold or silver trophies inside.

Then, Sidney. He had something of Uncle Harry's character—a ready smile and a compulsion to entertain—but without Harry's shy, boyish quality. Sidney loomed over us like some cosmopolitan Ichabod Crane. His eyes held me captive. To a six-year-old, he was incredibly tall. Gangly arms swept the air as jacks and aces flew up his sleeves then were plucked from David's ear. He slammed a ping-pong ball through his table and extracted it whole from underneath, disappeared colorful silks, then vanished a silver dollar and discovered it in the pocket of my shirt.

It may not all have happened on the same day. Perhaps it was Mom who took us to the Macy parade. A lot was going on during the late 1930s: we moved several times, Pop was in Spain with the Loyalists, battling General Franco, and our loquacious Grandma was filling us with so much gossip about friends and acquaintances, that it all blends like a bowl of melting Neapolitan ice cream.

I don't recall meeting Sidney again, but through Grandma's stories he became something of a myth.

At thirty-one, Sidney Lenz retired from business to devote the rest of his life to games. He died in 1960, twenty years before my infatuation with family began to emerge. Details about his early life are sketchy. Still, I've discovered a little.

The Lenzes were connected to Grandma Addie's Hungarian side of the family. They lived in Chicago, where Sidney was born in 1873, and moved from there to New York. At twenty-one, Sidney went to work, and within five years he had acquired a lumber mill and a paper box factory in Wisconsin. Did he take an active part in the enterprise, stripping bark, or pushing spruce and pine into the teeth of a whirling blade? Or was he an absentee timber baron? I wish I knew more. Clues suggest he may have had a hand in the notorious butter-boxes Grandpa Dan Bessie peddled up and down the East Coast, though final evidence is missing.

His *New York Times* obituary fills in a bit more, especially about his skill at games. Sidney excelled at whist and bridge, amassing "more than 1,000 trophies and other prizes in tournament play, a record approached by no other player." Table tennis, golf, tennis, bowling, cribbage (which he wrote a book on), any game or sport he tried, he quickly mastered. But then, he had the time, and apparently the skill and the patience, to master them.

He was also regarded as one of America's best amateur magicians.

Beginning in 1904, Sidney, by then financially independent, became interested in whist, which he'd dabbled in before, and in auction bridge (then a new game). Both quickly became a passion. He won his first tournament in 1910. By 1914, when auction bridge became an official tournament game, he became the first national champion. By the 1920s, he was writing books and articles on the subject (and supporting a widowed sister and a niece). He became bridge editor of *Judge,* a popular magazine of those years. *Lenz on Bridge* became a standard guide to the game and until his death was considered a classic. Until the 1930s, Sidney was a titan in his field.

For me, the thirties mainly conjure up my parents' five hard years in Vermont, living on welfare in Brooklyn, and Hitler's staticky speeches over the radio. But the decade was also afflicted with a virtual madness for bridge, a game I find incomprehensible.

The thirties probably needed bridge—at least the leisure class did—as a diversion from the gloomy images of everyday life. One idle matron explained that she was driven to it. Wives of the poor, she said, had much to occupy their time: washing, ironing, cooking, working in sweatshops:

> Alas, I can't perform these humble labors; they are all done for me. My husband leaves at nine and returns at six. What am I to do during that eternity of time? I am too fat for tennis; I'm afraid of riding in motors; cigarettes make me giddy; the current novels are all idiotic; my children are at boarding school, and so . . . I am literally forced to play bridge. Bridge is the rich woman's sweatshop. We are driven to it by a cruel, inexorable fate, just as the poor are driven to their sewing machines.
>
> from *The Mad World of Bridge,* by Jack Olse

Some were driven to more than just the game. When a Detroit woman made two misplays in a single hand, her partner shot and killed her. In a celebrated Kansas City case in 1929, a raging argument over a game reached its climax when John Bennett reached across the table and slapped his wife Myrtle several times, then got up and announced that he was spending the night in a hotel. Enraged, Myrtle left the room and returned brandishing a pistol. Bennett ran to the bathroom and slammed the door—just as two slugs ripped through the paneling. The door opened and the mortally wounded man staggered out, murmuring, "She got me."

Caught up in minutiae, America's breathless concern was not with the murder but with the bridge game! What hands were the players holding? What bidding system were they using? What effect did this have on events? The New York *Journal* solicited opinion from every leading authority, including Sidney. The consensus was that if Bennett had played a better hand, his wife wouldn't have called him a "bum bridge player"; the remark that set off the argument, and thus the murder, might never have been made. But no one remembered *what* hands the players held, and Sidney's speculation and that of other experts was just that—speculation.

Still, like the titillating details of cases from Lizzie Borden to O. J. Simpson, it sold newspapers.

Other cases were less brutal; one California woman merely asked for a divorce because her husband demanded that she change the bridge system she was using to the one he preferred.

Around 1925, a system differing from the then-popular "auction" variety of bridge had appeared on a cruise ship between California and Havana. Instead of having to simply win a given number of tricks, players had to "contract" for them before the bid. For more accurate bidding, they received extra points. Within months, contract was all the rage, though many older players refused to give up the more familiar auction variety.

Suffering aficionados soon had to wade through a steady stream of new books on bridge systems. There was the Bulldog System, the Picture Echo Calling, the Simple System, the Vanderbilt Club, the Power Control System, The Four Aces System, and literally dozens of others.

Into this *mélange* of confusion there arrived a clever, excitable player with a huge talent for self-promotion: Ely Culbertson. With his "Approach-forcing" system, Culbertson and his wife Josephine were soon the main subject of talk around bridge tables across the country. Ely plugged contract as a "social asset" and as the zenith of intellectual partnership games.

With the Culbertsons' increasing popularity, Sidney's books (as well as those of other experts) sold less and less. Innuendo and vilification had a field day, and Culbertson began carefully but deliberately baiting Sidney and the others. In the press and on radio, he accused them of trying to ruin his reputation, of calling him a gigolo and a "suspicious Russian." (He was born in Rumania.) As the leading member of the Old Guard, Sidney was singled out for special abuse. Finally backed into a corner, he and his cohorts bared their teeth.

A dozen of the traditionalists created an organization they called Bridge Headquarters. They would standardize the game, they said, with the "Official System." They issued a perfunctory invitation to Culbertson to join. He laughed in their faces. But he also loved a fight, so instead of joining he challenged Sidney, the best player in the bunch, to a match of 150 rubbers: five thousand dollars put up by Culbertson; one thousand dollars to be wagered by Sidney. Sidney could choose his own partner and would play the Official System against the Culbertsons, winnings to go to charity.

Sidney tried to ignore Culbertson, but Ely kept needling him. And as Culbertson's book sales soared and thousands of bridge teachers switched to the new system, Sidney, on behalf of the Old Guard, finally accepted the challenge.

A tedious legal contract was drawn outlining the rules of play. Sidney chose as his partner the brilliant young player, Oswald Jacoby. The starting date was fixed: December 7, 1931. The opening battleground, Manhattan's Chatham Hotel. Though it wouldn't have the devastating aftermath of the attack on Pearl Harbor exactly ten years later, bridge players, New York, and indeed, America, had no idea what was in store.

Telegraph rooms were set up, with wire services sending an average of eighty-five thousand words on the match around the world every day. Nor was a crew of shabby-suited hacks assigned to cover the event. Taking notes and calling in stories at one time or another were H. Allen Smith, Heywood Broun, Lucius Beebe, Damon Runyon, Westbrook Pegler, Grantland Rice, Henry McLemore, Ring Lardner, and Robert Benchley, the journalistic princes of the day.

Inch-wide cracks were cut into an expensive antique screen shielding the card table so reporters could look through; they rotated in fifteen-minute peeks. A large sign demanded "Complete Silence!" Tongue-in-cheekers implied that here was an event rivaling the sinking of the *Lusitania*. No sporting event then on record attracted greater public attention than the Bridge Battle of the Century.

The absurd importance given to it while America was in the throes of the Great Depression was staggering. Preliminaries began with an eight-course dinner costing ten thousand dollars. Speeches, interviews, predictions, claims, and counterclaims were splashed across the front pages. *Movietone News* spread the word on screens across the country. Cartoonists and vaudevillians satirized the match for weeks. Sportsmen that they were, Sidney and Ely declined offers to endorse everything from playing cards, cold cream, and cigarettes to bridge lamps.

On the appointed day, Lenz and Culbertson appeared in tuxedos. The referee, Lieutenant Alfred Gruenther (in later years, Army Chief of Staff) wore a uniform with gold epaulets.

They began politely enough, with Sidney's, "Where do you choose to sit, Ely?" Ely chose west. But almost immediately, Culbertson began a not-too-subtle game of psychological warfare. Night after night, he'd show up late. Sidney, usually unflappable, soon became furious. And Ely had other strategies; for example, regularly taking his meals during the match.

"My God, Ely," Sidney complained, "you're getting grease all over the cards! Why don't you eat at the proper time, like the rest of us?"

"My vast public won't let me, Sidney," was the retort.

And he got up every so often to rearrange the noise-silencing rug provided, or he'd sit contemplating a hand so long that Sidney finally began to doze off. Every night, Culbertson began play by asking Sidney and Oswald Jacoby, "Have you changed your system?" Even his wife Josephine, tiring of it, would remark, "That's getting a little monotonous, Ely."

According to the experts, the play of both teams was less than expert. Ego and psychological distraction dominated, with the nervous contestants playing like four old ladies in the weekly tournament at the Evangelical Lutheran Church of St. Joseph, Missouri.

Though play improved, mistakes still crept in. Like rival candidates sniping at a president whose popularity is on the wane, the eyes of a fickle public were on the mistakes instead of on the many brilliant hands played.

By the end of the 27th of a scheduled 150 rubbers, Sidney's team led by seven thousand points. Soon after, the Culbertsons took the lead. Onlookers could feel the momentum shift. Lenz and Jacoby seemed moody. On December 28th, a frustrated Sidney turned to his young partner and said, "Why do you make such rotten bids?"

Silence from Jacoby. "Shall we play another rubber?" asked Culbertson pleasantly. "Not with me, you don't," snapped Jacoby.

He rose and started to walk off. But when referee Gruenther advised him that the rules demanded another rubber, Jacoby sat down, stared at Sidney and told him that he'd made an "absolutely stupid defensive play" in the second rubber, and "you have the gall to criticize *me*. I'm resigning right now as your partner."

"Well, sir, all right, sir," Sidney stammered. But no apology followed. Jacoby left and was replaced by a friend of Sidney's, retired navy Commander Winfield Liggett Jr.

The drama proceeded, with the remaining excitement provided by Culbertson, when he got into a tiff with another bridge player in the pressroom. Names were called, challenges hurled, until Culbertson's wife arrived and removed Ely from the trenches.

The second half of the match was played at Sidney's apartment in the Waldorf, the same rooms where he entertained David and me a few years later. Victory for the Culbertsons had not been in doubt for some time, and they ultimately triumphed by 8,989 points.

Sidney rose and shook hands with Mrs. Culbertson. But he couldn't bring himself to do the same with Ely.

"I hated to beat you, Sidney," Culbertson said, and Sidney answered, "Oh, that's all right, Ely. You've got a wife and kids. What the hell." Then he turned his back and walked into the next room to meet the press, which was waiting expectantly for a sober analysis from the dethroned champion. Instead, Sidney started doing card tricks for them.

In spite of the mania, even conservative voices took a dim view of the affair. The *Christian Century* argued that "it is our overwhelming lust for the trivial that makes us like bridge and want to read about it," and went on to call The Battle of the Century "a Tom Thumb Congress of the American mind—a mind which prefers to dawdle over mythical difficulties and fence with hard situations which never exist, while men are asking for bread."

Following his loss to the Culbertsons, Sidney's bridge system

Grandma Addie's cousin Sidney Lenz at the time he made his fortune and retired to devote the rest of his life to games.

continued its eclipse. He played one more match in 1932, for the Eastern Contract Bridge Pair Championship. He won—and promptly retired. Like a good boxer who knows his glory days have faded, Sidney decided that taking a chance on another bloody nose just wasn't worth the trouble.

The gamesmanship, however, continued into his sixties and seventies. He kept up his whist and his bridge (as a pastime), along with table tennis, golf, and cribbage. And for years, he presented his amateur magic on cruise ships plying the Caribbean.

His longtime companion, Adele Hess, had begun a tradition of annual birthday parties for him, and these lasted until his death. Old friends, former bridge partners, and celebrities such as New York mayor Impelleteri, showed up. On his eightieth birthday, his old adversary Ely Culbertson put in an appearance. It had been more than forty years since the Battle of the Century. This time was different: Sidney shook his hand.

By all accounts, Sidney was a kindly fellow. "Never moody. Good, gracious, a perfect gentleman as well as a gentle person. Children loved him." These words from Adele Hess.

Apparently, that long-ago afternoon when Sidney astonished David and me with his illusions was no mere condescension to the grandchildren of a favored cousin, for in his obituary notice, the *New York Times* reported, "Mr. Lenz, in his eighties, retained remarkable skill both at games and at magic. He practiced sleight of hand for an hour each day, as he had every day since his boyhood, and he entertained children as an amateur magician until a year ago."

He also retained the "bridge player's memory," a memory incomprehensible to nonexperts. On one occasion, someone mentioned his partner in the Culbertson match, Commander Liggett, then dead some twenty years.

"I remember the last time I saw Lags [Liggett's nickname]," said Sidney. "There was a hand where he held five spades to the ace-queen, three hearts to the king, the ace and one diamond . . ."

Only Grandma Addie (and the Culbertsons) ever got the best of Sidney. Assisting him once in a magic show when she was in her teens, she helped him vanish a twenty-dollar gold piece. When he tried to produce it again, he couldn't. Red-faced, Sidney, like any good showman, cracked a joke and swung right into the next illusion. Always playful, Addie had slipped the coin into her bodice and never told him where it went.

I don't recall Pop ever mentioning Sidney. Maybe he regarded him as a wealthy idler. More likely, they had little in common. By 1924, Pop had graduated from Columbia, was losing a hands-on interest in *reptilia,* and would soon drift into an exciting new world; not a world with Sidney's kind of theatricality, but one with its own special magic: he was about to become an actor on the New York stage.

SIX

alvah: broadway to barcelona

*I had tried to get into some aspect of theater work even
before I was graduated from Columbia College in 1924.
First, I had wanted to be a drama critic. I saw John
Barrymore's* Hamlet *and reviewed it for my white-
haired professor, George B. D. Odell, author of the
monumental* Annals of the New York Stage. *In my
review I stated that "his ejaculation was superb." My
professor looked archly at me, wanted to know how I
knew, smirked and suggested I employ another noun.*

ALVAH BESSIE IN AN UNCOMPLETED AUTOBIOGRAPHY,
ONE MAN IN HIS TIME

⸙ When my father was young and preposterous and hoping to
bed every young actress on Broadway, his heart was broken by a
dazzling redhead who actually came from Keokuk, Iowa. Both were
bit players in Rogers and Hart's first musical, *The Garrick Gaieties of
1925.* Pop got nowhere with her, but she let him buy her dinners and
drinks, and she told him a story that nearly cost him his budding
theatrical career—not to mention his life.

She had had an affair with Philip Loeb, director of the *Gaieties*,
and then he had "dumped me on my ass" for another woman. The
redhead was still carrying a torch.

While in his teens, a fellow student had sold Pop a .32–caliber
revolver and a box of bullets. These he hid in a closet for almost ten
years. Now he retrieved the gun, loaded it, and carried it to the
theater three nights running, determined to avenge the rejection of
"so gorgeous, adorable, talented, intelligent and vulnerable a
creature as Keokuk Red." Philip Loeb never showed. The next night,
Pop didn't bring the gun. Loeb showed up. Pop thought to strangle

him, but even though Loeb was much shorter, he decided it might prove a formidable task. The next night, back came the revolver. Again, no Loeb. This went on for a week, "by which time I had cooled down to such a point that the very (unconscious) thought of what I *might* have done woke me in the middle of the night and I lay shaking in a cold sweat, sobbing quietly and invoking the name of the heartless beloved who did not even *know* of my mad passion."

Pop was not always victimized by such theatricality, but he was always theatrical. His dramatic persona was handed down from Grandma Addie; maybe even from Adolphe, the Old Gentleman himself. Or perhaps growing up with a father driven by an urgency to succeed in business simply fed a rebellious ego. Whatever jogged his insecurities plagued his youth, kept him on a committed course through his middle years, and helped create in his later years, a raconteur of heroic proportions.

My father had a nostalgia for his own life. Even total strangers were bombarded by kaleidoscopic anecdotes. These settled into mythology: his days as a libidinous young actor, his Paris of 1928, the Spanish Civil War. Much of it got into his books—especially Spain. And some, he only talked about. Endlessly.

He never completed his autobiography. When I asked why, he told me he'd become "bored with the central character." Not that it mattered; most of what he wrote was autobiographical. But long before I read his books, he wove vivid picture-stories. Though my own busy life gradually fogged the details, I was never bored with the central character. Often frustrated, but never bored.

After Pop died and I began sorting his literary effects, his early years came racing back. Some of his stories turn what was an often sad and troubling youth into lighthearted poking fun at his own immaturity. His Spanish Civil War diaries, with a drama and honesty that flows from the events themselves, reflect the deep changes he was going through. Everything he wrote is a part of the complex and caring father I never quite got to know.

Pop's interest in writing started in college, where he "walked around the Columbia campus wearing a Windsor tie and writing bad poetry." Even before his teens he'd been devouring books. He remembered bursting into tears one day in 1916 when his teacher pinned up a news item announcing the death of Jack London at forty. Pop had read most of his books by then, from *The Call of the Wild* to *The Sea Wolf.* And even *The Iron Heel,* "not one word of which I understood." But in 1924, he put literature on hold.

On his graduation from Columbia, Professor Ruth Benedict, the anthropologist, gave Pop a letter of introduction to Bertha Kalish, reigning tragedienne of the Yiddish stage, who was making her English-speaking debut in Tolstoi's *The Kreutzer Sonata.*

He bought a ticket and looked on, captivated, as in the final scene the actress became so overwrought when it was time to shoot her lover, that she fired straight up into the flies—and two men onstage dropped dead. Still weeping through her mascara, she greeted the eager hopeful backstage a few minutes later, with Ruth Benedict's letter in her trembling hand. "You vant to be an ektor?" said Kalish, "Very vell; you shall be an ektor. I vill make you leading man in my company." She told him he was very handsome, had an enormous talent (though she'd never seen him act), and gestured to the stage manager, waiting in the wings to close the house. "Spik to my manager," she said, "He vill arrange it." Then she vanished, sobbing, into her dressing room. Pop's adrenalin was pumping. "Did she promise you the lead?" sighed the manager. "Forget it kid. That's what she tells 'em all." Then he scrutinized the crestfallen young man and added, "You don't look like an actor to *me,*" and escorted him to the stage door.

At The Theater Guild, Theresa Helburn told him that if he'd only come that morning, he might have had a tiny part as a *conciérge* in Molnár's *The Guardsman:* "I would have carried a trunk onstage and deposited it at the feet of Alfred Lunt."

Then, luck. He bumped into a Columbia classmate who worked as a stage manager at the Provincetown Playhouse, by then relocated from Massachusetts to MacDougal Street in Greenwich Village. The company was short a Mexican seminarian, so Pop soaked his hair and slicked it back and spoke no lines—until the play died after six performances. The lead, Leo Carrillo, went on to become sidekick to *The Cisco Kid* in a string of TV potboilers. Director Stark Young went on to become the sort of distinguished critic Pop had first aspired to be, for *The New Republic.* Pop went back to the Theater Guild.

This time, Theresa Helburn had a job for him, understudying as an Italian-American in Sidney Howard's Pulitzer Prize-winning play of 1924, *They Knew What They Wanted.* When the actor playing Joe, a vineyard worker, couldn't perform at a benefit for the great Jacob Adler, "far gone in years and partially paralyzed," Pop was called on to do a scene with leading man Richard Bennett.

Bennett took Pop to his bachelor's apartment off Fifth Avenue to rehearse, disparaged the regular in the role, and told the novice he would show him how the part *should* be played. There, surrounded by walls covered with life-sized portraits of himself in various roles, Bennett set Pop's heart thumping with the promise that "When we take our calls, I will introduce you to the audience. I will say, 'I want you to keep an eye on this young man; he's the most brilliant young actor I've met in thirty years.' Your career will be *made.*" "Oh," said Pop, with astonishing modesty, "I hope you won't say that unless I deserve it." "You'll deserve it," said Bennett, "*I'm* directing you."

By curtain time, Pop knew the part cold. Relaxed and confident, he "sang like a bird" (the role called for a song) and was breezing through his lines when Richard Bennett entered, playing the role of Tony. Staggering drunk, shoes held aloft, Bennett commanded the stage, sweeping everything before him. Pop, frozen in place, did not even remember that he *had* more lines. Bennett immediately caught his protégé's stage fright and paraphrased them, delivering lines that had been written for two actors, but which worked just as well with Bennett delivering them alone. Pop sat dumbfounded, unable to utter a sound, until the curtain came down to vast applause. Pop was dizzy. They took four curtain calls, hand in hand, but "Mr. Bennett did not say one single, solitary word about me to that enormous audience and I finally realized what had happened."

Apparently, no word of this fiasco was leaked, for Pop's romance with theater lasted four years; ten dollars a week as an extra, twenty dollars for a bit part. He played a white-robed Klansman, a coal miner, and the Italian-American vineyard worker all on the same evening, in two separate theaters. (The Theater Guild shuttled the extras back and forth in cabs to save money.) He was a

Alvah (Pop), just before he went
on the New York stage.

Chinese courtier and a Nubian slave—the Guild hired no black actors until years later—in Eugene O'Neill's *Marco Millions.* He sang and danced in a male chorus in *The Garrick Gaieties.*

In spite of an excellent reading for Walter Hampden's *Cyrano de Bergarac,* he was only permitted to understudy, because, as Hampden told him, while he might play "clowns and other minor parts, you are not tall enough for the classical theater."

This infuriated Pop. So, resolving to end his theatrical career in a blaze of notoriety, he decided that some night when the actor playing the Vicomte de Valert (who is killed by Cyrano in a duel) got sick, he, as the understudy, would simply refuse to be killed. He would keep Cyrano (Hampden) dueling all over the stage endlessly, then coolly run him through with his own *epee.* (Pop had been a member of the Columbia fencing squad, and the stage dueling, in his eyes, was distinctly third-rate.) They would have to bring down the curtain. The unsung understudy would be front-page news in every paper in New York.

Alas, the actor playing M. le Vicomte never missed a performance during the entire run of the play.

Besides nursing a fevered imagination, theater offered tantalizing possibilities for a young man whose hormones were on fast forward. In a small part opposite June Walker, Pop took great pleasure in being kissed each night (and at two matinees); and when he discovered that the actress believed it was good luck to kiss an extra before taking the stage, he positioned himself strategically in the wings for extra smooches.

He was smitten with Lynn Fontanne, whose "voice, long before Garbo's, drove the male audience into sexual fantasies"; by his first lover, a British actress who cooled his ardor when he discovered her in bed with another woman; and by Gale Sondergaard, playing Queen of the Witches in *Faust*. ("After all, I was only one of the misshapen trolls and she never knew of my passion or frustration.")

He was briefly consoled by one of the other witches, who promptly gave him a case of gonorrhea that lasted six months.

Sometime in 1928, Pop met Mary Burnett, who four years later became my mother. An "older woman" (by six years), she was a painter, writer, and, with her brother Harry, a puppet-maker. This fascinated Pop. They were soon lovers, then breaking up, then lovers again.

Pop had also begun writing. He had a novel in manuscript and had translated the first of several works from the French, Pierre Louys' gently erotic *The Songs of Bilitis*. He was giving serious thought to writing as a career—or joining the army air corps.

Dreams of flying had filled his head since 1909, when his father took him to see Wilbur Wright circle Manhattan during the Hudson-Fulton Celebration. After failing an air corps physical because "Your left eye is different from your right," he went for a confirming opinion to a doctor friend of his brother Everett, who had been an examiner for the corps during World War I.

"Most people's eyes are different," explained the doctor.

"Then why?" asked Pop. "You are a Jew. The corps has yet to accept one as a student pilot."

So the acting continued. Pop was making twenty-five dollars a week when he reached his theatrical zenith, playing the bailiff in Ben Jonson's comic masterpiece, *Volpone* (The Fox). Alfred Lunt played *Mosca* (The Fly). Pop's role, whenever the proceedings fell apart, called for him to stride forth in a floor-length velvet gown, bang an eight-foot staff on the floor and demand, "Order in the *Court*! *Order in the COURT!*" And there was order, except on those occasions when actor McKay Morris, playing the Lion, looked Pop squarely in the face and crossed his eyes. Then "there was no longer order in the court but there was silence." And then laughter. From Pop. McKay Morris turned away. Morris Carnovsky, on the bench, betrayed a smirk. Lunt was staring at Pop; *scowling.*

After a repeat breakup the next evening, Pop was summoned to Lunt's dressing room. The Great Voice said, "Come in." Pop came in. "Close the door," said the voice. Pop closed the door. Then Lunt turned from the mirror, and in a low voice, told Pop that he had watched him in rehearsal, felt he had talent, and then "he lifted that great head and fixed me with those tragic eyes and said, 'You have done something—*for two performances now*—that is *impermissible* in my theater . . . in *any* theater! . . . You LAUGHED!'"

Pop explained that McKay Morris had looked cross-eyed at him, and that he couldn't help it. As he did so, he broke out laughing again—in Lunt's face:

> "You COULD help it!" cried Lunt, rising to his full six feet something and topping my laughter with his voice—"No ACTOR would PERMIT himself *to do such a thing—no matter WHAT was done in his presence! You are a DISGRACE to the theater and if you are here tomorrow night . . . I . . . WILL NOT . . . GO ON!*"
>
> "I'm sorry, Mr. Lunt," I said, "I didn't—"
>
> "You may leave," he said, dropping his voice an octave and turning back to his image in the dressing-room mirror, with the sigh of a broken heart.

Pop was crushed. If he showed up the next night, Lunt would not appear. Worse, he'd be blacklisted from the theater. Timidly, though, he did show up the next night and actually set foot on stage. And so did Alfred Lunt. But Lunt did not deign to look at him "and neither, oddly enough, did McKay Morris."

But something had finally come home. As the bored stage manager of Madame Bertha Kalish had said before escorting him to the stage door, "You don't look like an actor to *me.*"

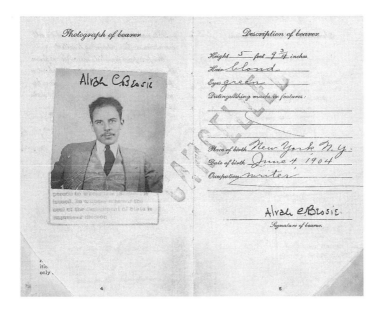

The aspiring writer on his way to Paris, 1928.

I knew I wasn't. I had spent four years getting exactly nowhere on the New York stage; unless you consider a six-month case of gonorrhea somewhere. I had somehow acquired 1,000 books (mainly by theft, I'm sure) during my four years in high school, four in college, and another four on the stage, and I decided that there was only *one* thing for me to do; I would sell the books for one dollar apiece and go to Paris—to write. And that is what I did.

Make it 1,001 books he swiped (at least), because I have the tattered Bible in which Pop began recording family births and deaths in 1929. On the flyleaf he's inscribed, "Stolen from the *S. S. McKeesport*." The *McKeesport* was the rusting freighter he took to France in October of 1928. Grandma Addie saw him off at the Hoboken dock, with a tearful plea to the smirking third mate to "take care of my baby."

Mary (Mom) was living on Bank Street then, struggling to paint, and helping Harry with his puppets. Her father had died that year, and she was trying to get a handle on her own life.

The *McKeesport* actually bent amidships during heavy swells, and Pop was sick as a dog for the first two days. During the next eleven, he recorded his impressions of the voyage and the crew and drafted his first short story, "Redbird," on an Underwood he'd brought along. (All his life, Pop typed with two fingers. I timed him once; he could peck out eighty-five words a minute. Accurately.)

Literary Paris was in full swing when he arrived. Harry and Caresse Crosby's Black Sun Press was publishing Oscar Wilde and D. H. Lawrence. Nancy Cunard had begun Hours Press. Expatriate journals were ubiquitous. Hemingway, though, was in Key West. Scott and Zelda had gone home. Pop never sat in on Gertrude Stein's salons, never met Ezra Pound or James Joyce—though he browsed at Shakespeare and Company and bought *Ulysses* (along with *Lady Chatterley's Lover*) from Sylvia Beach herself. And he "actually saw Matisse with one of his models at *Les Deux Magots.*"

With Parisian women, he struck out. Not for lack of trying; the virtuous were simply *too* virtuous. And the bout with gonorrhea had so terrified him that when an ancient streetwalker "straight out of Toulouse-Lautrec" approached him on the Boulevard Raspail, he quickly said, *"Non, merci."* As for a bewildered girl at the American Express, she'd barely opened her mouth to ask an innocent question when Pop said, "No, thanks," and hurried away.

Still, he found plenty to fill his days. One of his letters of introduction opened a door to Marlon Brown, a "relatively bad actor" he'd seen in a Chekhov play in New York. Brown was what was then called a Remittance Man. Scion of a wealthy Philadelphia family, he frankly admitted that he was paid to stay away from home. (He drank.) Waking at noon, he'd sit for an hour or more in his grubby room in the crumbling Grand Hotel des Principautés Unies, singing opera. He knew every painting and sculpture in The Louvre, dragged Pop through endless galleries of that vast museum, and "between bar-prowling from noon to dinner time to midnight and to dawn, was a gratis tour guide."

He also told Pop where he might find a job. Dropping the name of renowned correspondent Vincent Sheean, and lying about having worked on *The Boston Globe, The Baltimore Sun,* and *The Philadelphia Inquirer,* Pop landed an assignment on the *Paris-Times,* an English-language newspaper that came out in the afternoon and merely rewrote the French morning papers.

The publisher, G.M. Archambault, demanded "good stories, no matter how you tell them." But within two weeks, Pop objected to having his stories cut to where they were indistinguishable from the routine newspaper writing Archambault had said he hated.

"Are *you* telling *me* how to run my paper!?" he shouted. "Go to the *caisse* and get your pay. I'm sorry to lose you; you're a good newspaperman." (Archambault would be imprisoned years later as a Nazi collaborator. "He was a fascist even in 1929," said Pop.)

Between assignments, Pop did his share of café-sitting, often with writers Whit Burnett and his wife Martha Foley, then reporters on the Paris *Herald.* In his *The Literary Life And The Hell With It,* Burnett recalls that Pop came to Paris "when many Americans who have since become quite proper and Communistic were then cluttering up the Dome and the Select and contemplating their art and their navels and the pearly drink called Pernod."

A week after Archambault sacked him, Pop wandered into the Café Balzar to meet Burnett, Martha Foley, and Rex Stout (now best known for his *Nero Wolfe* mysteries). If getting plastered in Paris is *de riguer* for writers, so is literary embellishment:

[Bessie] was in a gay mood and no slight snifter would suffice. He could, he said, drink beer in quantities hitherto unconsidered by the average man.

When it became evident that Mr. Bessie wanted beer, we commanded beer. Martha took a small quantity, *un bock . . .* Rex lingered, but finally ordered a *seidel.* Someone else ordered a *distingué.* And we suggested that Mr. Bessie take a *formidable.*

"What," asked Mr. Bessie, is a Four-Me-Dawble?"

"It," someone added, "is a beer."

"If it is a very large beer," said Mr. Bessie, "let them bring it on."

When it arrived, it was lugged laboriously in between three heaving huskies, purpled with their labors and exertions. A table by itself was set aside and the *formidable* was hoisted up and onto it. A *formidable* contains God only knows how many gallons of beer. Only half a dozen Paris restaurants consider they can afford to own the monumental glass container.

Burnett has Pop attacking the *formidable* for twelve hours, by which time, "he had not drunk a single foot around the vast circumference of that magnificent glass washtub of beaded amber fluid." Suffice it to say, he drank enough to pass out. When he woke next morning in his room on the Rue Servandoni, he called the Burnetts. They told him that Rex had taken him home in a cab.

Before that memorable binge, Rex Stout had cultivated him, taken him to La Tour d'Argent and other chic restaurants, listened into the small hours while Pop read his short stories aloud, and said he would not—as one of the owners of The Vanguard Press—publish *Itinerary*, the novel Pop had brought with him to France. He simply didn't like it and felt that the stories the young author had read that evening proved he could do much better.

Whit Burnett had a better opinion of *Itinerary*. "*That* was a novel," he said, "full of humor and young love." Pop ultimately agreed with Stout. Sometime over the years he lost the manuscript, "like so much of my young life." I could kick him.

Weeks earlier he'd written to Mary in New York, asking her to come to Paris; they could easily live on twenty dollars a week. Now she answered, saying she couldn't. Unemployed, broke, but having had "the presence of mind to put $80 away to assure my passage home," he decided there was no way he could remain in *La Ville Lumiére*. In February of 1929 he returned home. "Redbird," the story he'd written on the way over, appeared that same month in *transition*, the most well known expatriate review published between the wars.

⤵

Pop returned to an America in which millions would soon be unemployed. More fortunate than most, he drifted through a series of jobs: office manager at a publishing house whose owner he'd met through Rex Stout, editor in another house that went broke, proofreader and fact checker on *The New Yorker* (Pop once told me he never planned a career move in his life. It all just "happened.")

And he was still seeing Mary. By the middle of 1930, she had tired of their off-again, on-again relationship. She called from Oyster Bay, where she was working in a bookstore. "I'm sick of this affair," she said, "Come out tomorrow and marry me or to hell with you." They were married on the second of July.

By mid-1931, the Depression was grinding the nation down. Mom had lost her job. Pop's poorly paid translations from the French kept them going. Some days, a fifteen-cent bowl of minestrone was all they could afford to eat. But they kept checking the want ads. One day, a notice placed by an architect with a summer home in Vermont caught their attention. He was looking for a bright young couple, the wife to cook, and the husband to do chores, empty the garbage, drive the station wagon, and play chess with the drunken guests when they came up over the weekend.

The job paid twenty dollars a month for both, plus room and board. They took it. When the architect closed up in September, Mom and Pop decided they liked Vermont. They found an old house for seven dollars a month, scraped together furniture at an auction, and moved in.

Landgrove, where I was born in 1932, was (and still is) an idyllic village nestled in a rustic valley. The seven houses, built in the early 1800s, were falling apart. People in the surrounding hills, often illiterate, got along by hunting or hiring out. Some brewed moonshine ("panther piss").

My parents' stories brought the locals to life for me. Lucy Chadwick, who lived in a ramshackle cabin and never bathed, helped bring me into the world. When she died, Pop helped the local undertaker ready her for burial. Along with neighbor Orville Holcomb, Pop was coming along a road one night when a bootlegger's truck hit a ditch, sending all the kegs into the air and bumping into the under-brush. Delighted to assist the driver recover his cargo, they also spirited a keg—for later consumption—into the woods before finishing the job.

These stories and more were incorporated into Pop's writing (though not without dramatic license).

He sent off letters to New York magazines, asking for books to review. Some dribbled in. And he sold a few short stories. He bought an ancient Plymouth for ten dollars and went to Manhattan to call on contacts. On one of these trips he met a man whose influence would alter the course of his life: Kyle Crichton, then editor of *Scribner's Magazine*. Pop asked for books to review. "I don't have any," Kyle replied. Then, noting Pop's basset-like expression, Kyle asked, "Do you need the money badly?" Pop said he did. "In that case," said Kyle, "we have books to review."

Crichton not only sent four or five books a month, he also sent occasional small checks and boxes of food. He visited during the summer, talked politics, and in between, sent Marxist pamphlets. Still, Pop told me that he and Mom spent their first three years in Vermont "gracefully starving to death." Confronted for the first time with real poverty, living and working among others in the same boat, Pop began relating theory to practice.

Between writing, raising chickens, and growing peas, lettuce, and cabbage, he hired out to a potato farmer, taking his labor out in trade. That fall, when the A&P truck came around, the produce man offered to buy a thousand bushels at fifty cents a bushel.

The farmer was outraged:

> "Damned if I'll sell my potatoes for that price. It cost me more than that to grow the damned things. I bought a potato digger. I bought chemical fertilizer. What the hell kind of a price is that?"
>
> "Well, that's what we're offering," said A&P.
>
> "Before I'll sell potatoes at fifty cents a bushel, I'll let 'em rot in the cellar!"
>
> And that is precisely what he did. He also gave them away to anybody who wanted them.
>
> The next summer, he decided that he would plant just enough potatoes to feed his family, and when the A&P truck drove up that fall, the buyer offered him $1.10 cents a bushel—and he had none to sell.

It made no sense to Pop that the price of potatoes being bought from the farmer should be $.50 one year and $1.10 the next. There was even more demand from one year to the next. And there were just as many potatoes being produced, "except by my farmer friend. Why should the price suddenly go up and down?" He decided the prices were being manipulated by the people who bought the potatoes from the farmers. This jibed with the pamphlets Kyle Crichton had been sending. He began studying: history, political economy, Marxist economics and philosophy. Pop's radicalization had begun.

⌒

My first images date from Vermont. Vague, happy memories: feeding an ice-cream cone to someone's pet raccoon, picking wild

(Right) Dan Bessie, age 2, in Landgrove
Vermont, 1934. (Below) Alvah Bessie
writing a story, Vermont, 1935.

blueberries, trudging through drifts with Pop to meet a snowplow,
a large protective German shepherd named Jobie.

By 1935, when my brother David was born, we had moved to
another rented house near East Dorset. On his third try, Pop was
awarded a two thousand dollar Guggenheim Fellowship in creative
writing, making possible the completion of *Dwell in the Wilderness*,
which was quickly accepted by a publisher. Most reviews were
thoughtfully favorable, but the book sold hardly at all.

He bought a new Ford roadster with the money, which irritated Mom, for they had a mountain of bills and personal loans.

The marriage had been shaky from the start. Pop says he was an "adolescent cynic" when they got together and describes Mom and himself as "ivory tower artists." He'd been flattered by her encouraging opinion of his work, and he didn't want to lose that or the intellectual stimulation. Still, by the end of the first summer in Vermont, Pop was having an affair with young Mary Sullivan, who he'd met on his first trip back to New York looking for work. And the Guggenheim money quickly ran out.

Soon after David was born, we moved briefly to Connecticut. Pop, feeling trapped in the marriage, had lost most of his desire to write.

Whenever times got hard, Mom told him, as she often told David and me during our lean years with her, "something will turn up." (One of her favorite characters was Wilkins Micawber in *David Copperfield,* whose motto this was.) Remarkably, something almost always did. In this case, a friend of Pop's "practically made a job for me," offering him the position of assistant editor on two Sunday magazine sections of *The Brooklyn Daily Eagle.* So, toward the end of 1935, we moved to Brooklyn.

Pop always worked best with a deadline. He began writing again: book reviews, motion picture and play reviews, editorials. His fifty-dollar-a-week salary supported us decently in 1935.

In 1936, Pop joined the Communist Party. (Mom never did.) He would stay for twenty years. Like the million Americans estimated to have been members at one time or another, he saw socialism as a more just and humane way of organizing society.

Also in 1936, a violent seamen's strike hit the East Coast. It was all too common for a sailor assigned to picket duty on some far-flung pier to be found dead in an alley, his head split open by a baseball bat. Pop wrote publicity for the National Maritime Union, while Mom organized a citizen's committee to support the strikers. It met in our living room on Joralemon Street near the docks. Rough-looking seamen, thick cigarette smoke, and a buzz of activity filled the living room as David and I crouched on the stairs, listening, until we were spotted and hustled off to bed.

Later, Mom told my father that she'd had a brief affair with one of the seamen. Hastened also by Pop's preoccupation with work, their marriage was heading for the rocks.

And Pop was soon involved in another strike, this one on his own paper, *The Brooklyn Eagle.* The owner had bought a rival paper and decided he'd fire the staff and have the *Eagle* employees put out both. The newly formed Newspaper Guild threatened to strike. A meeting was called with the owner, who "actually burst into tears," called his employees "one big happy family," and told them if he had to support two staffs he'd have to close both papers and "none of us will have a job." It sounded persuasive. Nevertheless, the Guild voted unanimously for a strike. The publisher capitulated, hired the staff of the *Brooklyn Times-Union,* and made more money than ever.

Partly to escape from the marriage, Pop was spending much of his free time fulfilling his lifelong ambition to learn to fly. (He also helped organize a flying club of Communist Party members who were pilots.) One day, he brought home from Floyd Bennett Field, Lee Gehlbach, a famous test pilot he'd met, whose celebrity was starting to fade. Lee, charming, and an alcoholic, was broke and had no place to say.

Mom and Lee quickly became close. Gehlbach, though, didn't love her. To Pop, that didn't matter. Mom's declaration of love for the flyer was all the excuse he needed. In spite of her desire to work on saving the marriage, Pop told her he was moving out—which he did, early in 1937.

There followed almost immediately, one of the two critical events shaping Pop's life: Spain. A year earlier, a Popular Front government of liberals, Socialists, and Communists had been elected in this laregly peasant country. In July of 1936, an army revolt led by General Francisco Franco broke out in Morocco. It spread quickly to Spain, and many divisions of the army joined with right-wing groups eager to overthrow the legal government. In August, a nonintervention pact sponsored by Britain and France was signed by twenty-seven nations, including the United States. Germany and Italy, which had also signed, ignored the agreement and supplied Franco with guns, planes, tanks, the air arm of Germany's Condor Legion, and one hundred thousand Italian regular army troops. Only Mexico and the Soviet Union supported the legal government with military aid. Convinced that Spain was Hitler's dress rehearsal for world war, a trickle, then a flood of volunteers from many nations began finding their way into Spain to fight beside the Loyalist army.

These events quickly absorbed my father, so much so that he would soon exchange his typewriter for a rifle.

$$\approx$$

Pop's interest in Spain had first been piqued when the *Eagle* sent him to interview André Malraux in 1937. A dashing figure in his Spanish Republican Air Force uniform, Malraux had come on a speaking tour to raise money for medical aid for Spain. Pop met the tall, pale author of *Man's Fate* in a Manhattan hotel. Fascinating not only because of what he represented, Malraux also impressed Pop because "he was the only human being I had ever met who could speak and exhale [cigarette smoke] simultaneously through both nostrils."

The interview so outraged the Catholic Church in Brooklyn (which supported Franco) that it demanded equal space—and received three times as much. In disgust, Pop quit the *Eagle* to work for the Spanish Information Bureau, churning out press releases and pamphlets on events in Spain. In 1937, millions of Americans were supporting the Loyalist cause. Marches and rallies were constant, and I recall Pop taking us aboard a ship with a huge red cross on the side, where a crowded fund-raising party for Spanish relief was going on. (My most vivid memory is of a cartoonist drawing big pictures of Mickey Mouse for a group of us kids.)

And thousands were volunteering for Spain. The Communist Party fostered recruiting, but few needed encouragement. Thirty-three hundred Americans volunteered (between 25 percent and 40 percent, Party members). Sixteen hundred of those who joined the Abraham Lincoln Brigade lie buried in Spain.

Some were looking for adventure. Others went on impulse. But most gave up jobs, left friends and families, to fight in a war that was, as some said, "none of their business." By aiding Spanish democracy, they were also acting to stop fascism.

Friends my parents knew from the waterfront strike were going to Spain. The night before he sailed, Mom sewed the buttons on seaman Richard Tynan's coat. In January of 1938, Pop decided to volunteer. At thirty-three, he was a bit older that most.

His reasons for going were both political and personal. Spain coincided with a long-felt compulsion "to complete the destruction of the training I had received all through my youth." By submerging himself in a large body of men (something he had never done), and "seeking neither distinction nor preferment"—goals he *had* been pursuing—he hoped, through "self-discipline, patience and unselfishness," to destroy forever the middle-class demons his father had worshipped.

Perhaps Spain would make him more of a man, but he was still a writer. As he moved toward the Spanish border, he was already filling the first of four pocket diaries with the staccato rhythms that would later help him recapture the immediacy of all he went through that year and lend flavor to a book he had in mind.

> Beziers-Wednesday, February 2, 1938. By car into the country (18 men—American, German, Rumanian, Italian, Czech, Serbian) at 12:45 P.M. In barn from 1:15 to 8 P.M. More men—Danes, Germans, etc. 8 P.M.—autobus through Narbonne, etc., to close to frontier—10:45 P.M. March over Pyrenees—rain, wind, pitch black. Over 40 men. Walked all night—at dawn reached summit of second range of peaks and border. Dawn in Spain—magnificent rugged country. Cork trees with trunks stripped, gray green of olives ripening, lemons ripe.

> February 3rd—rivers winding silver in distance. Masonry houses, composite stone, brick, fieldstone and blocks. Tile roofs. First Spanish—three women—salud. Cold, hungry, exhausted.

> Guide Portuguese ex-smuggler—little fat man with raincoat and umbrella. Took long way around to avoid French border patrol, possible injury or death to men. One fell, cut face. In all, march of about 30 miles, 11 hours, to foot of Pyrenees on Spanish side and trucks.

The footsoldier in the Abraham Lincoln Brigade
in Darnos, Catalona, Spain, in 1938

With the Non-Intervention Committee (led by British Tories and joined by France, Russia, Italy, Germany, and Portugal) imposing a land and sea blockade, ostensibly to keep the conflict from escalating, volunteers had to sneak into Spain.

Four hundred men filled the camp at Figueras, "a babble of tongues." They drilled and marched and listened to a Polish volunteer play the violin and a little Irishman sing bawdy songs. Then, packed into a slow, dilapidated train, they chugged toward the training base at Tarrazona. The Americans passed the time remembering the words to "Rosy O'Grady," "A Bicycle Built for Two," and "I Didn't Raise My Boy to Be a Soldier."

This was a new kind of army. Democratic. On duty, men saluted their officers. Otherwise, they were "Sam," "Milt," "Steve," or "Comrade." They elected a political "commissar," held meetings where any problem of food, mail, clothing, shelter, military orders or discipline, tobacco (the absence thereof), tactics, and personal behavior could be worked out. Majority opinion ruled.

While he was learning to be a soldier, Pop kept taking notes, observing. His letters home were filled with sketches (in colored pencil), describing what he saw. Feeling his drawings might, in enemy hands, help identify where the brigade was located, the censors objected: "Comrade, I've written you before about this, but once more and then I will take action. Don't draw pictures (even for your children) of panoramic vistas or views 'from where you are.' Explanation for this is superfluous, you should realize. Censor responsible."

In mid-February, he came down with the flu after a long stint on guard duty and was left behind when new recruits were sent to join the brigade. He recuperated, went on guard duty again, and kept taking notes: "Late afternoon—barrel-organ in the street playing 'Music Goes Round and Round,' 'Popeye the Sailorman.' Children of all ages listen and dance. Little kids (3–4) wearing short smock, no pants. Beautiful kids, large intelligent eyes. Hang around barracks all day. Some, toughened, orphans, beg and smoke cigarettes, have learned all military drills from watching."

The international situation was tense. In March, Hitler seized Austria. British prime minister Chamberlain, playing Hitler's game, supported Germany's territorial claims.

In Spain, a spring offensive was being planned against Franco, and there were rumors the fascists would use gas. Pop wrote in his diary, "I wonder about Mary and the kids . . . whether they are eating regularly enough, have a roof over their heads."

Though Mom and Pop had separated before Pop left for Spain, they kept up a regular correspondence:

Dear Alvah,

Dan takes a keen interest in Spain and gets me the *Times* and the *Worker* each morning so we can find out how things seem to be moving. I haven't told him what you are doing, but he seems to know it, as well as many other things, without being told.

When you think of me and the kids, you must think of us as
we are . . . cheerful, comfortable, nourished and busy.

Mom tried to keep up his spirits. But we were on welfare, and she
didn't look for work that entire year. With Pop away, she felt her
place was with us. Grandma Addie helped. So did Uncle Verne, Kyle
Crichton, and Pop's cousin, Mike Bessie. I sold used comic books on
the corner (two for a nickel) and gave the money to Mom.

Pop completed his training and with other fresh troops was
moved by truck toward the front. They slept on the frozen ground of
an olive grove, then were marched to join the Lincolns, a part of the
Fifteenth Brigade, dug in high in the rugged hills of the Aragón
range: "The men are worn and discouraged, individualistic. It
appears the brigade took a terrific licking at Belchite and elsewhere
(they came out of action yesterday), lost lots of men and equipment.
Can't say how long we will be here. Learned of death of Tynan
(sailor we knew back home), also Howard Earl, who was on the
Lafayette coming over and wangled his way into the last draft by
lying about his experience—he had none."

The Americans were decimated. There were no rifles. Food was
at a premium. Pop's priorities changed: "This day swapped high-
class Spanish dictionary for fine brass spoon."

A soldier quickly learns that half of any war is waiting. Pop
waited while the brigade was reorganized, waited through driving
rains, waited in hope that the French would permit supplies through
the border, waited on guard duty with orders to shoot any non-
civilians who didn't reply to a challenge. Often, he simply observed
the cycle of life: "Edifying sight: dung beetles rolling away pieces of
your recent crap, in which to lay their eggs. Thus, in one of many
ways, we contribute (even on a hilltop in Spain) to the balance and
economy of nature. They make balls about $3/4$ of an inch in diameter
and roll them away. A beetle without a ball will try to take one away
from the other."

Then everything changed. They were marched off twenty-six
kilometers past Gandesa to a camp in the hills; then, four days later,
when rifles were brought in, to front line positions in the mountains:

March 31—Hot firing from one ridge to another. Our first action.
Several wounded, including Sgt. Ben Finkel, leader of our

platoon. Am now *cabo* [corporal] of scout squad. Impression—
lack of fear while under fire; fear returns during lulls in fighting.
Several close calls—snapping of near bullets, singing of far.

Battle from 9 A.M. to dark. Sent on patrol alone, 3 P.M., to make
contact with unknown forces. On return at 5, sent with machine
gun squad to place gun further on right flank. Placed it under
hot fire from snipers and machine guns. Out till midnight—
nothing up. No food all day or night; no sleep except in snatches.
At midnight they opened up hot, thinking us attacking. Half
hour of fire. More wounded. On guard, 12 to 2 A.M., slept 2 to
4:30 A.M.

The men didn't know it, but they were surrounded. A decision
was made to move around the fascist lines after dark and take up
new positions. Scouting ahead, Pop and his machine gun unit lost
contact with their company and walked directly into the fascist
camp. As they started to run, they could hear the enemy behind
them, shouting: "Halto! Los Rojos! Halto los Rojos!

They ran all night, "shedding equipment and ammo. Hiding in
woods, moving east all day—given water and nuts by evacuating
peasants." Finally, after twenty-five hours of continuous flight, they
reached the town of Mora del Ebro. Almost immediately, the fascists
arrived. The Americans blew the bridge and retreated to the
opposite shore. There, they found hundreds of men from all the
International Brigades, demoralized men wandering around
without command, looking for their units.

Seventy-five percent of the Lincoln Brigade had been killed,
captured, or were missing on the opposite side of the Ebro. Franco
had almost cut Spain in half, and the chance of meaningful support
from outside was fading fast.

Slowly, they began to regroup. Herbert Matthews of *The New
York Times* came by, along with Ernest Hemingway, who gave Pop a
pack of Lucky Strikes. Now there was time to relax a bit, time to
remember that far from wounded and dying men were children
who waited and wondered when their father would come home:

Sunday, May 15, 1938

Dear Poppy [my mother wrote for me],
    We went to see the May Day parade and it was big. Mommy

took us and we saw the Spanish Loyalist veterans. I gave Mommy a little card for Mother's Day. I got a bow and arrow for Easter and it broke.

Dear Alvah,

Needless to tell you of the concern we have here, and how anxiously we await word of your whereabouts. Nothing has reached us from you since April 6th, which was when Matthews' piece appeared in the *Times,* mentioning you among six who escaped miraculously.

All of you should be heartened by the relentless efforts being made here on Spain's behalf. Even brother Leo, awakening to something or other, sends me a check, stating, "to help along a good cause"—which made me happy.

Salud, Mary

Over the next five months, while the Loyalists prepared for a major offensive, Pop and his comrades were marched from location to location, dug trenches, stood guard, battled lice, trained Spanish recruits (sixteen to eighteen years old), ducked artillery shells, nourished rumors of going home, heard talk of fascist advances, and tried to keep up their spirits.

They were fighting the good fight, but everyday life was the same as in any war:

April 15: Face badly swollen. Spanish dentist lanced gums; says tooth must be extracted or abscess will recur. Catching up on sleep.

April 23: Going out every other night to fortify trenches on bank of Ebro from 7 P.M. to 4 A.M.

May 3: Appointed last night Sergeant-adjutant to Aaron Lopoff, Company Commandante of Company 2 . . . Job will be arduous, especially under fire.

May 10: Much rain the past few days; making it miserable for all. No rifles for the majority yet. Many [Spanish recruits] are so young they cry when reprimanded.

May 19: Today cold, wind, damp. Morning spent in school

building. The kids are more like children than men or soldiers. It is doubtful if they have any conception of what they are going into. These aspects of the moment make an older man sad for them and the losses they will inevitably suffer in the next action. It is shit that such babies should have to know this sort of thing—it is shit that anyone should have to know it.

May 20: Tonight the food reached a new low—garbanzos, a few shreds of greens and canned beef. It is apparent that the country is sacrificing a great deal and suffering a great deal to supply us with arms.

May 27: Yesterday at 4, started 15-kilometer march to a position about 20 kilometers from Lerida. Aviation active all day— artillery in distance—artillery all night.

Four months in Spain, and Pop had seen only three days of actual fighting:

June 3: If this percentage obtains there is a fair chance of surviving! Three envelopes from Brooklyn this morning—letter dated May 15, enclosing fine drawings by Dan; 2 envelopes with 30 cigarettes—a fine birthday present for tomorrow.

June 4-5-6: Morale, per se, is none too high among the Internationals, most of whom have been here a long time and want badly to go home and talk of nothing else.

June 14: No mail today. Weather continues cold and windy, with occasional cold rain—two nights ago it rained all night, drenching all. A more wretched body of men could not be found in a month of Sundays.

Ten days later, the government was finally ready to attack:

July 24: (midnight)—July 15: moved out and down to the Ebro. Crossed under combined fire of artillery, air-bombs and strafing, early in morning of the 25th. As we were crossing in boats, a cat-walk bridge of barrels and planks was thrown across. First experiences of air-bombs and strafing; awful feeling; alleviated considerably if you fire at the plane instead of just lying on your face.

He was in and out of heavy combat for the next month: dodging sniper bullets as a scout and a runner, hugging the ground during pounding barrages and praying a shell wouldn't blow him to bits, following on the heels of his commander, Aaron Lopoff, as they led their terrified young Spaniards in an assault on a fascist machine gun position. In a night attack on a strategic hill, Lopoff, by then a dear friend, took a burst of machine gun fire to the head and was carried away on a stretcher.

The Ebro offensive was major news in the States:

Dear Alvah,

Even Dan knows that you are again in action. The night of the 27th I looked down into the street and saw the headlines. The next morning Dan got an earful when he went outside (since the neighbors all know his Pop's in Spain). So what does he do? He comes in with a stick of wood about six feet long and makes me saw out a trigger notch so he can be a Loyalist in action.

When I awoke the following morning he had already dressed and gone out. I saw him down there all by himself skittling around with his six foot rifle.

We think about you all these days, about all fathers every-where, most of whom are fighting in one fashion or another.

Love, Mary

In early August, Pop heard about a possible job as frontline correspondent for the brigade paper, *The Volunteer for Liberty:* "Ed Rolfe told me just before the action started that it would be my last. Frankly, I hope so. Not only because I fear for my life—and I do—but because I truly feel that I have learned as much from front-line experience as I will. That, as a soldier, I am a negligible quantity, showing no possibilities of leadership. I might, now, and quite possibly, be of some use as a writer."

After three weeks of rumor and tension, the job came through, and he started work on August 28—my sixth birthday. For a month, he shuttled back and forth between companies, gathering infor-mation under fire and feeding copy to Barcelona.

On September 8, Pop learned that Aaron Lopoff had died of his wounds. He remembered that when the Company was ordered to take a hill "at all costs," Aaron had given him an address, "just in case," and had in turn ordered him to stay back to provide cover and care for the wounded. And he remembered that as they waited by the Ebro that July morning for their turn to cross, Aaron had called to him: "His face was bright like the face of a happy child, and we went around the cane and stood looking at the water. Broad and placid in the sun, it was filled with little boats, little rowboats full of men, moving sedately back and forth across the river, drifting somewhat with the swift current. 'It's Prospect Park in the summer time!' he said. 'It's wonderful!'"

On the thirteenth, Pop was trying to convince headquarters to release Jim Lardner, son of humorist Ring Lardner (and the last American to volunteer) to be his assistant. Second in command George Watt refused, stating that "Jim Lardner was learning things that would mature him, make him a good writer."

A rumor that the volunteers would be leaving in a matter of days was squelched by word that they were going into combat again. Finally, on the twenty-second, the International Brigades were ordered withdrawn—but it came too late to prevent the Lincolns from moving into the lines.

Jim Lardner, who volunteered for a scouting patrol, was the last American to be killed. He was twenty-two.

Pop was assigned to Barcelona, writing for *The Volunteer for Liberty.* He would be almost two more months in the small part of Spain that the government was fighting tenaciously to hold, months when the volunteers were entertained at fiestas and paraded down Barcelona's broad Diagonal, while the government struggled to overcome endless internal and international bureaucracy in preparation for their departure.

In late October, they were trucked to Ripoll, near the French border. Hemingway and Herb Matthews showed up again and bolstered them with news of the government's ability to hold Franco on the opposite side of the Ebro—temporarily. The inevitable death of the Republic came four months later.

On December second, Pop and his companions finally left, in a sealed train directly to Paris, and from there to Le Havre, where Vincent Sheean, like Hemingway in Spain, appeared suddenly with whiskey, cigarettes, chocolate, and sandwiches. Later, Brigade commander Milt Wolff, Pop, and a group of others went "over the fence" into Le Havre, where they released their pent-up energy and frustration and disappointment about Spain in a night-long binge, culminating with a dinner of *pate de fois gras, chateaubriand,* fried potatoes, mushrooms and garlic, ice cream, coffee, *calvados,* and "champagne in floods," all on Sheean's tab.

French seamen were on strike in Le Havre, so instead of sailing on the *Normandie,* they were shuttled to Cherbourg, for departure on the *Paris.*

In New York, Pop was met at the dock by a *World Telegram* contact, who said his managing editor wanted to see him about a series of articles on Spain. Excited, he dashed off a sample piece describing the all-night hike across the Pyrenees, avoiding French patrols.

"Good copy," said the *Telegram* editor, "but not exactly what we're looking for."

"What exactly are you looking for?"

"You know. The romance. The adventure. Beautiful dark-eyed señoritas in lace mantillas. Color stuff."

Instead, Pop peddled his articles around town. There were no takers. At Random House, Bennett Cerf gave him a cast-off overcoat ("The one the French workers had provided on our way home was rather odd-looking for New York"), but no book deal.

An agent sent him to Maxwell Perkins at Scribner's. Perkins said he'd think about it. Another dead end, thought Pop. But the "hand of God" intervened in the person of Ernest Hemingway. Pop's agent called and told him to call Perkins to discuss a contract.

He called. Hemingway, said Perkins, had visited him the day after their interview, and when Perkins told him about the book Pop wanted to write, Hemingway had said, "Grab it. It'll be the best book written by any of the guys."

Despite a full-page review by Vincent Sheean in the *Herald Tribune,* a good review in *Time,* and a flock of other publications, *Men in Battle* sold little outside the Left, "for it appeared the week that Hitler invaded Poland, and people had other things to read—the newspapers." The world war that the forty thousand international volunteers for Spain hoped they might prevent had begun.

One melancholy task remained. Pop went to visit Lopoff's

parents. They wanted him to stay. They took him into Aaron's room. "This is his desk," they said. "You could use it. He made this model airplane. These are his things . . . you are the same size."

Pop choked back his tears and left as quickly as he could.

～

Spain would always be a big part of my father's life. After *Men in Battle,* he lectured and wrote an endless number of articles and stories about his experiences and about the war. He was immensely proud of his participation, and as long as he lived, he had a deep love for the Spanish people and their heroic fight. The struggles all people went through to overcome their troubles and get ahead would always move him, and this concern animated his writing from then on. Spain had changed him profoundly and had solidified his politics and his basic humanitarian outlook.

113

And he passed much of it on to me; from my late teens and into my twenties and thirties, while friends were buying the 78s of Sinatra, Crosby, or Nat [King] Cole, I was singing the songs of the Abraham Lincoln Brigade.

Into the fall of 1939, Pop was busy writing about the year fighting for the cause he believed so passionately in, but it wouldn't be long before he'd be crafting another tale—the story of a sad, simple man who came into Mom's life, David's and mine, soon after Pop came back from the Spanish Civil War.

Some would compare it to Dreiser's *An American Tragedy.*

SEVEN

harold

If you prefer illusion to realities, it is only because all
decent realities have eluded you and left you in the
lurch.

GEORGE SANTAYANA

⤙ Harold told us stories. The loft in the dilapidated barn David
and I played in all through the summer of 1940 was a kid's fantasy.
We had hay fights, created secret tunnels among the bales, or
jumped from one to the next as we listened to Harold spin a yarn.
He'd stop talking half way through, then wander off to his chores; so
we'd tag after, impatiently demanding, "What happened next?"

"Why then the polliwog that didn' have no tail looked at the
other polliwogs an' says, 'You guys don' need t' think y'r so smart
'caus you got tails an' I ain't got a tail.'"

"Didn't he really have a tail?" asked David.

"He really didn' have no tail at all," said Harold, "an' that made
him feel bad 'cause nobody likes not t' have what everybody else has
got, even if it's on'y a tail."

"So what did he do?"

"Nothin' to it. He hid hisself un'er a lily pad an' when a certain
polliwog come along that he didn' like, he come out an' he snapped
his tail right off. Then he waited till all the other polliwogs come

swimmin' by, an' one by one he snapped off all their tails, so that none of 'em had a tail, an' then they was all alike."

"Why didn't the polliwog buy a tail?" David asked.

"He didn' have no money."

"That's a silly story," I said.

"I s'pose," said Harold, and he began tickling David and me and chased after us, knowing we wanted him to keep it up, but finally letting us escape through our secret passage in the hay.

That year and a half in Bucks County was a disjointed reality. Images crowd my memory: Mom heating endless pots of water so David and I could take our Saturday bath in a big galvanized iron washtub, the hurricane that rolled up our tin roof and threw the outhouse a hundred yards into a muddy field, the Rhode Island Red hen whose broken leg Mom bound in a splint, the Schwinn bike Pop bought for my eighth birthday.

Mostly, though, I remember Harold.

We rented from the Diarmans, a farm couple straight out of *American Gothic*. Harold Frisbie, their hired man, did odd jobs for them and worked the fields adjoining our house—soybeans, mainly, and the long summer grass that became fodder for the animals.

In a sense, we had two fathers. Pop drove out from New York fairly often, less frequently after he began courting Helen Clare Nelson, the McGraw-Hill editor and "blond bombshell" (his words) who became his second wife. They'd met at a party for veterans of the Lincoln Brigade. Pop followed her home and then pursued her relentlessly for a year before she married him.

Harold was around almost every day. Short and wiry, his arms were like oak, and he could jerk bales of hay back and forth like a longshoreman. His big rough hands were as gentle with David and me as they were forgiving of the cheap strings on his old guitar. His laughing eyes made it easy to ignore his crooked, tobacco-stained teeth as we rode next to him on the harrow or the hay baler, or as he sat in the kitchen drinking Mom's coffee.

Always, there were his remarkable stories.

"I was in Alaska once. Went with a group of pursuit planes inna Army. I was in Europe, too."

"When was that?" Mom asked.

"Oh, a few years back. It was a secret air mission. Saw Hitler an' Mussolini."

I asked him what they looked like.

"Oh, jes' like you seen 'em inna movies. Talkin' an' stickin' out their jaw. Little guys, both of 'em, look scared."

Then he'd change the subject or start splashing bath water over David, who splashed back from the tub.

His ragged backcountry speech never bothered us, nor did the dirt under his fingernails. If the stories sounded far-fetched, that didn't matter. Harold was simply Harold. We'd known people like him before.

Mom had a talent for spotting kind-hearted "strays," as she called them. In Brooklyn, she discovered Charlie Peterson—Petrix, we called him—living on a park bench, shabby, cold, and near starvation. Mom bought him a secondhand overcoat, took him home, fed him, and let him sleep on the kitchen table. (He preferred the table.) Mom trusted Petrix completely. He took David and me to the Prospect Park Zoo, taught us to box, and, like Harold, kept us spellbound with his eye-popping adventures.

Uncle Harry had moved us to Pennsylvania in the spring of 1939. A photo I've inherited shows boxes with our belongings lining the porch of the hundred-year-old stone farmhouse near Doylestown; I'm trying out the pump handle (for the place lacked indoor plumbing). Harry's caption reads, "I took my sister and family to the country to start life anoo."

In another snapshot, the blue convertible David and I rode in during our California visit in 1944 is parked near the house. Pop must have been visiting, for one of his letters to the "blond bombshell," dated "Tuesday in Pennsylvania," says "Mary's fairy brother stopped in at 7:30 this A.M., resplendent in black suit and brand new Packard Super-8 roadster, on his way to Hollywood."

Nineteen thirty-eight had been a hard year. Mom and Pop had separated, and by the time Pop came home from Spain, the divorce was final. But they remained friends, and over the next few months, Mom offered moral support while Pop wrote *Men in Battle*, his classic memoir of the American volunteers in Spain. Even before his

(Above) The one hundred-year-
old farmhouse we rented in
Bucks County. (Right) Mom
with Dan and David in Pennsylvania, 1939.

return, Mom wanted to get away from the city. Brooklyn held too
many memories: a failed marriage, months on public assistance,
thoughts of suicide. As always, she pulled herself through.

Mom always felt she had a calling. If she was unaware this
would someday involve helping children get a decent start in life, by
the time we moved to Bucks County, she may nevertheless have had
clues, for the old farmhouse was an ideal place to board city kids.
Before Harold showed up, two or three children came out from New

York for the summer. The following year brought four or five. Mom cooked their meals, read us all stories at bedtime, and gave everyone the run of the farm.

I pledged a seven-year-old's undying love (simultaneously) to Pam, an ample nine-year-old with glasses, and to Sylvia, a small, softer girl in pigtails. We cuddled under blankets, explored forbidden zones, and made elaborate wedding plans. A precocious *ménage à trois.*

We had chickens. The Diarmans had cows, along with two immense plow horses, Prince and Valiant, which Harold cared for and on whose sturdy backs the summer kids were occasionally permitted to sit. Diarman loved to catch me off guard while he milked the cows, aiming a sudden stream of warm milk, and emitting a raucous cackle when I didn't jump out of the way in time.

With summer over, I began attending a one-room country school. Until my birthday bicycle, I walked the mile, trudging through foot-and-a-half-deep snow in winter. Of thirty students, five were in my second-grade class. Third grade had a single pupil. Each grade would be called to the front of the room to read or to recite sums. The teacher is a blank, and aside from these spare details, all I remember is an insistent cast-iron bell she rang when lunchtime or recess ended, and a huge maple tree just outside the school—strictly off limits. We climbed it anyway.

The following spring, Harold began showing up more often, usually for dinner. David and I were sent to bed while he and Mom sat in the kitchen, smoking and talking. After school one day, Mom called me to her room and told me that she and Harold were thinking about getting married.

"Would that be all right with you?" she asked.

"Would Harold be our father?"

"No, you and David have a father. But Harold would be my husband."

The rosy images of marriage to Pam and Sylvia filled my head, and I guess I must have said "OK," because in no time at all we were knocking on the door of a Lutheran minister in Doylestown; then David and I were looking on as Mom and Harold exchanged vows; then Harold was secretly handing us each a dime as he whispered, "Now you boys be sure'n call your mom Miz *Frisbie,* hear? Miz

Harold and Mom in 1940.

Frisbie." He bounced around as excited as a puppy, and I recalled Pam's wide-eyed account of what would then transpire: "As soon as the man and wife get married, they go in a little booth and do something, and pretty soon a baby comes!" I peeked around doorways but finally concluded that the parsonage didn't own such a booth.

As we left, Mom was radiant. We piled into the old jalopy Harold had borrowed and went for a long ride in the country. He stopped at a store, where David and I bought Pepsi-Cola with our dimes. Then we drove home—the world's shortest honeymoon.

Memory is a fickle companion, and I probably felt less easy about the marriage than the years allow. In another letter to Helen Clare a week after the wedding, Pop says Mom has told him that I'm going around with my suitcase packed, intent on coming to New York. "He wants to get settled in his mind that I'm still in the picture." Promising to show David and me a good time, he then adds that "he who has children has given hostages to fortune."

Harold's fortunes, too, had begun to change. His job at the Diarmans must have ended, for he hung around the house a lot that summer. He built furniture from scrap wood, helped nurse David and me through chicken pox, spent hours puttering in the barn, and began to lose the buoyant enthusiasm which had so delighted us.

Sometimes he'd disappear for days. "Looking for work," Mom said. Once he came home beaming. He'd earned a few dollars and wanted to take David and me to a show. We hitched a ride into town on the back of an old pickup to see *The Gold Rush*. I watched, fascinated, as Charlie Chaplin ate his own shoe, then grumped when Harold told me it was made out of licorice candy.

In the early fall, he spent days in the kitchen, carving and fitting out half a dozen full-rigged scale models of the Pilgrims' *Mayflower*. These were displayed in a local gas station, where he eventually sold one for five dollars. Then he disappeared again.

October 1940. Pop had been sending occasional money orders to help us out. In a letter dated the seventeenth, Mom thanked him for the latest and mentioned that Harold had gone off to smoke out an old friend who he hoped would take a mortgage on a house he'd told Mom he owned in New Jersey "to keep the creditors from descending with weapons." She wheedled kerosene from a local garage to keep the stove working and fed us potato soup until his return. He didn't show up as promised on Sunday, nor all day Monday. Mom had two potatoes left in the house when he finally "drove up in a 1941 Buick at 1 P.M. [on Tuesday]. I just sat down and let her rip. We'll hold off the dogs yet, and make a go of everything."

Harold was limping badly as he climbed out of the Buick. "I jes' stepped on a rusty nail, that's all," was the excuse. Mom insisted he get an antitetanus shot. Another bill.

David and I were excited. We had a *car*! We could *go* places! New York, maybe. No such luck. We settled for an afternoon drive to Allentown, where, said Harold, a man lived who owed him money. The man wasn't there. We turned for home, arriving after dark. As the Buick pulled in, I saw two men wearing overcoats standing on the porch. Harold got out to speak with them. Mom hustled David and me inside and upstairs and told us to get ready for bed; then she started downstairs, saying she'd be right back.

We were in pajamas when Mom came back. Obviously upset,

David and Dan in front of the car that Pop often borrowed from actor Morris Carnovsky, Bucks County, Pennsylvania, 1940.

she said the men were soldiers, and that Harold had to go with them. He was being taken into the army. He'd be back soon.

Hours later, Mom woke us; Pop was standing next to her. I was happy to see him but confused when Mom said we were all going to his place in New York.

"Tomorrow?"

"No, honey, right now."

David and I were bundled into the back seat of the Chevy Pop often borrowed from his actor friend Morris Carnovsky, and we set out for the city. I woke up once during the trip and looked out. The car had stopped. A sign outside the window said, "Blue Ball Gasoline." A nearby clock read two A.M. I wondered why we were going to New York in the middle of night, and as I drifted back to sleep a fuzzy image materialized: Harold, smiling broadly, as he marched up and down in a smart military uniform.

Pop and Helen Clare, married by now, were living in a small apartment on East Tenth Street, so we stayed with them only two weeks. Mom located a flat in the Village for three months before moving us to Danbury, Connecticut, in the spring of 1941.

With a loan from my Uncle Verne, who lived nearby, she opened a small day-care center in our house.

All through that year Mom was often away for a day or more, visiting Harold "in the army." Toward the end of November, she was gone several days. When she returned, she had his guitar with her. She asked David and me to come upstairs. We followed. In her room, she sat on the bed, David next to her, while I stood in the doorway, as she said, "I have something I need to tell you boys."

"I know what it is," I said.

"What?"

"Harold is dead, isn't he?"

Mom burst into tears. Between sobs she managed to ask, "How did you know?" At the same moment, David said, "No, he isn't, he isn't!" Mom told David it was true and that she was terribly sad.

I didn't know how I knew; I simply knew. I asked if he'd been killed in the army. Mom said yes, "in the army." David and I never asked for details. We simply accepted it. We held one another tightly, and cried for a long time.

Summer 1943. We had moved to Poughkeepsie. Mom pursued a Master's degree in early childhood education at Vassar College, and at the same time, ran a preschool for the city. We talked about Harold from time to time. For me, his guitar became a tangible connection to the man who was no longer there, and I liked to sit and strum it occasionally.

With the end of the war, Poughkeepsie decided that day care for children of working mothers was no longer essential and reclaimed its building. Mom waged a long battle to keep the school open but finally had to concede. During the fight, she received a good deal of support from a kindly janitor at the school. In gratitude, she gave him Harold's guitar before we moved west. In a way, it was a symbolic letting go of the past.

California began another life. Mom worked two nursery school jobs at the same time. I became preoccupied with new friends, weekends on the beach, drawing cartoons, and at fifteen, trying to fathom the mystery of girls.

Pop had written three books by this time, and I had read none of them. *Dwell in the Wilderness, Men in Battle,* and his third, the novel *Bread and a Stone,* sat gathering dust.

One summer evening in 1948, Mom and I were sitting around talking. Somehow our life in Pennsylvania came up.

"What about the time you were married to Harold?" I asked. "I guess I never understood all that."

Mom looked at me for a moment then said, "Just a minute." She got up and pulled the copy of *Bread and a Stone* from the bookcase. "You might want to read this," she said, "then we'll talk." I went to my room and opened the book. Two hours later, and half way through the novel, I came downstairs. Mom was reading a newspaper. "This book," I said, "it's about you and Harold, isn't it?" Mom nodded. Fascinated, yet a bit annoyed, I asked why she hadn't told me before. She answered simply and directly: we'd been too young. We wouldn't have been able to understand. She knew that in our own good time David and I would ask. I had asked, so now we could talk about it.

Pop had written it all down. With only slight modification, *Bread and a Stone* told the story of everything that had happened in Bucks County. He'd created a remarkable fiction, but a fiction that was true to the actual events. After Harold died, I had only an eight-year-old's impressions to remember him by. When I finished Pop's book, the disjointed images began to merge. Everything made sense. Though I'd accepted Mom's explanation, I'd always felt an unresolved "something" around Harold's death "in the army." Now I knew why.

During the Spanish Civil War, Ernest Hemingway had taken a pair of 7.65 Estrella automatic pistols off a dead officer in Franco's army. These he sent to Pop's friend, Ed Rolfe, who gave one to Pop. It was with some reluctance that Pop loaned Harold the gun in September of 1940. Harold said he wanted it to clean out skunks around the property.

Pop thought Harold a "queer duck" and never trusted him. He'd been worried about the relationship since Mom and Harold first met. The marriage upset him. I'm not sure he understood Mom's loneliness, nor her feeling that Harold's gentle nature and his patience with David and me was enough to overcome the cultural and intellectual gulf between them.

By the time Harold asked to borrow the Hemingway gun, things were desperate. After losing his job at the Diarmans, he'd looked everywhere for work. He'd spent weeks hitching the back roads, stopping at farms, gas stations, anywhere his skills might be useful. He never had more than half a dollar in his pocket, so Mom made sandwiches for him to take on the trips. Though he found occasional day work on a road crew at twenty-five cents an hour, that didn't go far. His scale models of the *Mayflower* didn't sell.

Mom owed more than three hundred dollars in bills—to the grocer, the phone company, back rent to the Diarmans. Harold was especially concerned (we discovered later) that the milkman would stop delivering milk for David and me if he wasn't paid.

In early October, he saw a letter to Mom from a Doylestown department store. Though he read poorly, he could tell that the letter threatened legal action if the bill wasn't paid. He was convinced Mom would be put in jail. But he didn't know how to talk with her about such things. As the man of the family, he had to do something. He told Mom he was going to Trenton, New Jersey, to see if he could borrow money on the house he allegedly owned.

Bread and a Stone dramatizes the scene as Harold leaves—putting on the too small overcoat Pop had sent, and Mom asking, "Do you really think you can raise some money on a mortgage?" then digging into her purse for two dollars for his bus fare. He doesn't let her kiss him goodbye. He can't take a chance. If she put her arms around him, "she'd o' felt the gun in my pocket . . ."

Harold's statement to the sheriff in Laporte, Pennsylvania, traces his movements: "Before I left home I had made up my mind to come up to Eldredsville [three hundred miles from where we lived] and stick up a fellow by the name of Lyman Snyder, who is a storekeeper. I used to knew Lyman for a good many years and knew he did a good business. I knew he could have enough money on hand for me to pay off my debts."

He hitched rides to a friend's, where he stayed overnight. The next day he continued toward Lyman Snyder's store. A white vehicle approached far down a road, and since state troopers' cars where white, Harold threw the gun into the bushes. The vehicle turned out to be a truck. He retrieved the gun and moved on.

A Ford stopped and the driver offered a lift. He decided to hijack the car in order to facilitate the holdup. He made several attempts to take out the gun but lost his nerve. He got out of the car and headed on foot toward Towanda. He caught another ride, then, on foot again, decided to detour through Forksville, where he'd worked as a boy. The Forksville sheriff, Raleigh Beinlich, had treated him kindly in years past.

About 1 P.M., Edward Lee, sixty, a popular, well-to-do lumberman, drove toward Forksville, where he planned to pay taxes on a house he owned on a nearby lake. Lee's new, maroon, five-passenger Buick coupe pulled up next to Harold, who climbed in.

In *Bread and a Stone*, Pop duplicates a conversation between Lee and Harold, the essence of which Harold later told Mom:

"Howdy," says Lee, "I allus pick up folks on the road; make a point of it."

"That's right kind of you," says Harold.

Lee then questions Harold about where he lives and what kind of work he does. When Harold tells him "there ain't no work," Lee becomes testy and asserts that "there's work for any mother's son that wants it bad enough!" Then he rails against Franklin Roosevelt's New Deal and "all these women he's got in office" who are "runnin' the country to the dogs." He chastises Harold for not voting in the recent election and tells him that if he'd voted for Willkie (the Republican candidate), he'd have a job by now.

Harold decided to take the car. Looking for a match to light a cigarette, he put his hand in his jacket pocket. Instead, his hand found the automatic. He gripped it, pulled it out, and told Lee to stop the car and get out. "He stopped the car," says Harold. "He didn't move and I repeated, 'Get out.'"

In the novel, Harold suddenly panics, decides not to go through with it. With his gun hand he lunges for the door handle. But Lee grabs his opposite wrist and starts twisting. Harold turns back to face Lee, brings the gun up—and it discharges. Lee swings his door open and stumbles out, pulling Harold with him, twisting his wrist with both hands as hard as he can, and crying, "God damn you, you son of a bitching bastard!"

Harold can feel the gun firing, leaping and jerking in his hand as Lee, still pulling on him, drags him toward the rear of the car. In seconds, it is over. Lee slumps to the ground. Harold looks at the gun. The chamber is empty. He looks around. There is a house, but nobody is near it. "He listened; the echoes were dying away and then it was silent. His ears were ringing."

No cars were coming. No one had heard the shots. Edward Lee was barely alive as Harold hefted him into the car, piling him onto a stack of Willkie posters in the back seat. His intention: to "take this guy to Forksville to a doctor and put him out along the road in front of the house." Harold got back into the Buick and drove off.

During the shooting, a bullet had crashed through Harold's left foot, shattering two toes. (This was the reason he came home limping.) He stopped by a creek to bathe the wound, and there discovered that Lee had died. He dragged the body from the car—along with the Willkie posters—and left it on a bank of the stream, hidden beneath a small bridge.

Harold left clues a seven-year-old could figure out. Two women had seen him riding with Lee. A group of highway workers saw him driving Lee's car back and forth along the highway before entering the forest road where he disposed of the body. On the way back to Bucks County, he bought gas, boots, and heavy wool socks. A clerk recalled him. He'd stopped to have his foot treated and had given the doctor his correct name.

The troopers didn't have far to look. Lee's body was quickly discovered. Everywhere, it seemed, people knew Harold Frisbie. Police traced him to a Salvation Army hotel in Philadelphia where he'd often stayed. From there they tracked him to the Doylestown minister who presided at the wedding—and from whom he had borrowed four dollars a week earlier. The minister supplied our address.

Sensationalizing the arrest, lumpish copy in *Startling Detective* magazine has two cops, guns drawn, bursting into our farmhouse, where Harold sits on a chair bathing his wounded foot. When Harold says that he stepped on a rusty nail, one detective tells the other to "Go out and look at that Buick. I'll stay here with our friend, 'Three-toes.'"

Bread and a Stone describes it differently. Mom is in the kitchen as the troopers arrive. She opens the door; they enter and ask for Harold, who is upstairs bathing his foot. She calls him; he comes down, is handcuffed and led away.

And my vivid memory is the one described earlier, with two men in overcoats waiting on the porch as we drive in from the long trip to Allentown.

Though he had no advance plan, Harold did make an effort to hide the murder. In New Jersey he bought an old car for twenty dollars and switched plates on the Buick so that his story of going to Trenton would fit. He told Mom he'd borrowed the Buick from a brother being sent overseas. After cleaning the Hemingway gun, he returned it to its shoe box in a dresser drawer.

Bullied by the Doylestown police, Harold first created a fictitious aviator, "Harvey Betz," who had done the killing in an argument with Lee. Yes, he'd been there, but Betz pulled the trigger, took Lee's money, and gave fifty dollars to Harold.

Nothing held up. Lee's Pennsylvania license plates were discovered in the barn; Harold's left shoe, with a bullet hole through it, in Mom's bedroom closet. When Sheriff Beinlich (the sheriff he'd known as a boy) arrived from Forksville, Harold burst into tears and confessed everything.

When he was killed, Lee had over three hundred dollars in his wallet, enough to cover Mom's debts. Harold gave it to her, telling her he'd mortgaged the Trenton house. When all the bills were paid, four dollars remained. The day before his arrest, Harold drove to Doylestown and returned it to the minister he'd borrowed it from.

Lee's murder was headline news in eastern Pennsylvania. Harold was branded a vicious criminal. Sheriff Beinlich called him a "bad egg," with "a record as long as your arm."

Mom's immediate reaction was to get David and me away from wagging tongues. She didn't want me to learn about it at school the next day. That's when she called Pop to come for us.

Unaware that the Hemingway gun had been used in a killing,

Pop took it back to New York that night, where he left it with his brother Everett. The next day, Pop and Mom returned to Doyles-town for questioning. Nervous and frightened, Pop first denied knowing about a gun, then quickly told the police where to find it.

A few days later, Mom took a bus to Laporte, Pennsylvania, to see Harold in the Sullivan County jail. It depressed her to discover him in a four-by-eight-foot cage. She'd put on her best clothes and wore a new hat, borrowed from Helen Clare. And she'd applied nail polish, something she never did. She wanted to cheer Harold up. But it had the opposite effect.

"You sure spruced up," he said. "You walkin' out?"

Mom assured him that divorce was the farthest thing from her mind. She was there to see him through the ordeal. This touched Harold, and everything he'd always wanted to say but never could came tumbling out: the deceptions, the outright lies. He admitted not owning a house, not having a brother in the military, never having been a test pilot. He'd wanted to tell the truth, but felt that if she'd known he was a nobody, she wouldn't have liked him. "I ain' so bright," he told her. "I don' even know enough to work an' keep you an' the kids good after we got married."

The *Towanda Daily Review* interviewed Mom, and played up her story in a box on the front page:

Can Anyone Still
LOVE
A Mate Found to Be A
MURDERER?

Read One Woman's Reaction on Page 6 Today.

The story exploited the angle of a cultured university graduate married to an illiterate ex-convict. She had not known of Harold's long prison record or his lack of schooling. She had not known he couldn't read or write until after they were married. She had not known so many things. But Mom had her priorities straight, declaring, "there is much more to life than just an education; it is the human qualities that count." Nothing that she learned turned her against Harold. "I am standing by him," she told the reporter,

Daily Review

TOWANDA, PA., THURSDAY MORNING, JANUARY 16, 1941.

FRISBIE FRANKLY TELETLS OF MURDER

Court Adjourns To Febuary 15; Arguments Then

"I Just Started Firing. I Don't Know Why", Killer Tells Sullivan County Court; Kindness Brought Confession.

Laporte, Pa., Jan. 15. — Taking of testimony was concluded this afternoon in the case of Harold B. Frisbie, hitch-hike slayer of Edward Lee, prominent Forksville lumberman, and the Court set February 15 for the submission of briefs and arguments by opposing counsel. Whether the final decision will be made on that day or later was not indicated by President Judge E. B. Farr, who with his associate judges, George Bown and Don Hughes, have been taking evidence for the past two days without a jury.

Since Frisbie pleaded guilty on a general charge of murder Tuesday morning, the responsibility for deciding his fate rests entirely with the Court. The judges must decide the degree of guilt and if it should be the first, must determine whether the penalty should be life imprisonment or death.

Frisbie was on the stand most of the day, telling an almost unprecedented "hard luck" story in which he described details of his life from the time of the death of his father when he was only three days old to the present time.

He was so willing to talk and answered questions even

Sullivan County Slayer

'*I Love Him*', Says
Mrs. Frisbie; Tells of
Home Life of Killer

Strange Background to Murder Case
in Sullivan County Court; University Graduate
Wife of Illiterate Ex-Convict.

"because I love him. After all, you cannot tear your heart out and throw it in the garbage can."

He had deceived her, she felt, because he was living in a kind of dream world. Rejoicing in the marriage and in the home they both shared, he was also terrified that if she found out about his past, her resentment would bring everything crashing down. He'd wake to find that it *was* only a dream. "If he only had told me," she said, "I would have been able to help him, but I believe he was so happy it just didn't seem to him that it was true."

On January 14, 1941, Harold pleaded guilty, so no trial took place, simply a hearing to determine his sentence. Mom felt that knowing Harold's background might sway the three-judge panel.

It had been a sad history: a family torn apart when his father died three days after Harold's birth; a stepfather, Fred Beckhorn, who beat him with a rubber hose or steel rod, "very stiff an' thick around as your finger," for infractions such as talking back or coming home five minutes late from school. When his mother tried to interfere, she was beaten as well. Harold ran away three times.

One year, Beckhorn forbade him to go to a Christmas party. Angry, Harold sneaked out with a friend. On a lark, the friend decided to burn down the local schoolhouse, while Harold, who refused to join in, kept watch. Harold was seen and arrested. The other boy got away, and Harold took the blame. Why not? The sheriff treated him better than his stepfather did. (This was the same sheriff whose jail Harold would be sent to following his arrest for murder.)

From the Sullivan County jail, Harold was sent to reform school, where his treatment changed 180 degrees. Violation of the rules brought more beatings, with birch rods soaked in vinegar, leaving blood running down his legs.

Two years later he was paroled into Beckhorn's custody. The violence resumed. Finally, one day after he'd been beaten over the head with a pitchfork, Harold left home for good. There were short-term jobs as an airport mechanic, in a West Virginia coal mine, and day work as an itinerant carpenter. His mother died around this time.

His "long prison record," in addition to the reform school, turned out to be a second term, for stealing a jug of cider from a half-brother, and two terms in the New Jersey State Prison for auto theft. In both incidents he'd gotten drunk and taken cars on joyrides. One belonged to a brother-in-law, who, after receiving a wire from Harold that he'd bring the car back the next day, turned him in anyhow.

Harold's court-appointed attorney put a doctor on the stand who testified to Harold's abused childhood and that he had the mental capacity of a child of ten or twelve. "At heart," said the doctor, "he is honest, but the good qualities have not been developed." The doctor, M.E. Hydock, was the same one who had treated Harold's foot the day after the killing of Edward Lee.

The *Towanda Daily Review* was genuinely sympathetic toward Mom. The newspaper reports her squeezing Harold's hand to bolster him when he began to cry and giving him a "come on, brace up," look, when, on the stand, he seemed on the verge of breaking down: "The spirit of the woman in standing by a man who . . . faces possible electrocution, gripped the imagination of the huge crowd that jammed into the hot, stuffy court room. Even Special Prosecutor W. G. Schrier shook hands with her . . . and expressed his sympathy for her in suffering through such an experience. 'It is a terrible mess,' he said. And Mrs. Frisbie agreed."

None of it mattered. Not the long recitation of Harold's tragic life, not his terrible fear that Mom's creditors might send her to jail, not his explanation that he hadn't intended to shoot anyone, not his deep sense of remorse. The law was unequivocal. When a man goes out with a loaded gun, it takes for granted that if he's forced to use it, he will use it. Even Doctor Hydock had to admit that Harold knew right from wrong.

On February seventeenth, Harold was sentenced to death.

While the long appeal proceeded, Mom began a "correspondence course" with Harold, teaching him to write. During visits she talked about the case, about his life, and reassured him of her love. And she sent money for cigarettes, soap, and other necessities. Instead of spending it on himself, Harold saved it, and at Christmas a package arrived from the Sullivan County jail. Inside, we found a box of handkerchiefs for Mom and toy trucks for David and me.

The Pennsylvania Supreme Court heard the appeal. Though one justice voted for life in prison, the others upheld the verdict. The Board of Pardons heard two appeals. Denied. Though, for the first time, a plea for mercy based on diminished capacity was allowed in Pennsylvania, and it set a precedent. Desperate, Mom went to see the Governor. His "hands were tied."

On November 24, 1941, a one-paragraph article in the *New York Journal American* announced that "two more condemned murderers died in Pennsylvania's electric chair at Bellefonte early today." One was "Willie Jones, 26, Allegheny county Negro," convicted of killing a man during an attempted street holdup.

The other was Harold B. Frisbie, 33.

~

Bread and a Stone sold few copies. Within a month of publication, America had other things on its mind: Japan had attacked Pearl Harbor. This was Pop's third book in a row to die quickly, even though critics from the *New York Times* and the *Saturday Review of Literature,* to the Book-of-the-Month Club, were enthusiastic.

While under contract at Warner Brothers three years later, Pop gave Bette Davis the novel to read. Pop, who indulged a brief fantasy that he would someday marry her, hoped to interest the then-reigning queen of Hollywood in portraying Mom in a film version of the novel. Twenty years later, he vividly remembered their conversation over lunch in Warner's Green Room:

> DAVIS (emphatically): I want to play that woman.
> ALVAH: I want you to.
> DAVIS: There's only one thing wrong. You've got to find some way to save the man's life. He simply can *not* be executed.
> ALVAH: But it's the logic of his life and—
> DAVIS: I *know* that. But it makes for a downbeat ending. It will send people out of the theater feeling sad.
> ALVAH: It's a sad story.
> DAVIS: You think about it, Alvah. You find a way to save his life, and I'll get Jack Warner to buy it.

Jack Warner didn't buy the novel. Pop could never find an honest way to write a happy ending. For another twenty years he tried to find someone to film Mom and Harold's story.

In 1985, my then-partner Helen Garvy and I raised $425,000 to produce a movie based on *Bread and a Stone.* We called the film *Hard Traveling* and shot it in the fall of that year in and around Santa Cruz, California. During the next year and a half, Helen and I appeared with *Hard Traveling* at festivals and premiers as near as San Francisco, and as far away as San Sebastian (Spain), Florence, and Moscow.

Audiences were invariably moved by the story. In Moscow, a large group, many of them middle-aged women (some of whom had perhaps lost their men during World War II) crowded around Helen and me, anxiously wanting to know what happened to Mom after Harold's execution. In Seattle, a women I'd known when she was a girl in Pennsylvania in 1940 heard me on a radio interview, came to see the film, and spent an evening telling us how faithful we were to events as she recalled them. In Utah, a woman whose husband was in prison for killing a man during an argument came up, weeping, to tell me "it was the best film I ever saw."

A few people, often younger professional men, felt the film urged special pleading for a man whose hard luck story read like that of many others who had overcome misfortune and clawed their way to the top. Harold, they felt, probably got what he deserved.

I saw it differently. I remembered a gentle and loving man, and that colored my thinking. A victim of terrible abuse, Harold did not become an abuser. Told he was lazy and worthless, he tried in every way he knew to support us. Growing up with sarcasm and hostility, he became a lively and inventive storyteller. Watching his mother beaten, he was a model of consideration toward Mom. That he wasn't able to overcome all the negatives before tragedy took over had more to do, I believe, with not meeting more people like Mary Burnett much earlier.

Mom never knew about *Hard Traveling*. I believe she would have recognized herself and smiled and shaken her head—and cried a little. And afterward we would have talked for hours. There were so many questions I wanted to ask, so much I'd like to have known. But that seemed OK. A chapter of my life had closed. And I knew what Mom must have felt when she left Harold's guitar behind in Poughkeepsie. Devoting the rest of her life to working with young children, seeing they got the chance Harold never had, that was what she needed to do.

For me, it was also time to move on. Remembering Mom's gentle strength and firm kindness was enough. She passed on to me an enduring ability to pull myself through hard times and fight for what I believe in. She left me with memories enough for a lifetime. She gave me Harold.

And Harold told me stories: "You're good," he said, grinning. "I'll show you a trick."

I got off the bike, the Schwinn Pop had given me for my eighth birthday, and Harold got on. The bike gathered speed as he raced around the barnyard. Suddenly, he jerked hard on the handlebars, pulling the front wheel off the ground and peddling around on just the rear one.

I was impressed. "Where'd you learn to do that?"

"Inna circus."

"Really?"

He nodded. "I was a trick clown in t' Ringlin' Brothers once."

"I don't believe you," I said.

He got off and rested the bike against the gate.

"I c'd tell you more, but you wouldn' believe that neither."

"Harold," I said, "I'm going down by the pond to catch a spring peeper. Do you want to come?"

"Can't, I got chores."

He smiled his crooked, country smile, and I started off. Then I turned back.

"How come," I asked, "they peep when you're far away, but when you come up close, they stop?"

"You'd shut up y'rself," Harold said, "if somebody was after you."

EIGHT

mary: the rarest bird

They are looking; they're thinking what a big nose you have, what big feet, what a frumpy figure, what a tacky dress. Then immediately, as though by some enchantment, her lips would be dry, her throat would ache, she could feel her enormous hands dangling at her sides for all the world like a pair of hot-water bottles tied to her sleeves and her legs would be heavy.

FROM *DWELL IN THE WILDERNESS*

Against the June sky she was like a cameo done in some strange and disturbing medium. The curved throat, the strong chin, the full expressive lips, the Roman nose, the low forehead, the sleek lacquer of black hair pulled smoothly over her head to a knot low in the neck—she was like the portrait of a Messina coin, or a bas relief from a Roman theater.

FROM *BETTER ANGEL*

March 2, 1978. A hard rain had been falling most of the day in Los Angeles. The answering machine held an urgent message, asking that I call the residential care home where my twenty-two-year-old brain-injured daughter Lisa was living. It turned me inside out, for even before I picked up the phone, I was certain that she had died. Lisa's death was accidental. She had been alone in her room, lying in bed after breakfast, and had choked after throwing up. Bronchial aspiration is the clinical term.

I called Mom. I didn't tell her what had happened, but I think she also knew. We shared an empathy. She could sense I was holding a terrible secret, and I had to force back tears in order to navigate the

Mom in Vermont, 1931.

wet streets to her small apartment in Santa Monica. Then I collapsed. Even at almost eighty, Mom's big heart and gentle strength were all for me. Her pain was as great as my own, but she sat quietly, just listening, as I poured out my grief. She knew she could cry later.

A familiar reality shaped my mother, one governing the lives of most women coming of age before 1920. Trained to be wives and mothers, many were alive with possibilities they never realized, or discovered too late.

Mary Burnett had long ceased to be the insecure figure Pop drew from her journals and memories for his portrait of Martha in *Dwell in the Wilderness.* The lacquered black hair that Chloe pulls into a low knot in Forman Brown's *Better Angel* was gray now and cropped short; the regal face, soft and sagging. But her eyes, keen and inquisitive, belonged to a woman who didn't need to hurl back insults when a young girl on a bike yelled, "Get out of the way, you old hag," as Mom made her way along a narrow sidewalk toward the corner store. "Had its humor, its sorrow, its particular thing," she noted in her journal.

Mom was an observer, a watcher. The diaries she kept from grade school on were a private garden where she could plant thoughts, feelings, and conversations that grew into ideas. She looked back to understand what lay ahead. It was all of a piece: a self-dialogue, a grounding that helped her make sense of a trying past in order to keep the future on an even keel.

137

Recreated in fiction by Pop and by Forman, Mom ultimately defined herself.

Life in New York from 1926 to 1930 contrasted sharply with her marriage to her first husband, Melvin Dick. In Chicago, Mary had mainly stayed home while Mel, with meager success, sold Hoover vacuums door-to-door. Alone in New York (having arrived with four dollars), she got a piecework job decorating gift boxes. With her marriage and her dreams of a romance with Forman both dead, she started smoking, drank too much, and wandered in and out of relationships. She roamed Manhattan, stayed up until dawn painting and sculpting, and escaped into her journals.

Working with brother Harry creating puppet costumes in a Greenwich Village basement, she felt "torn between wanting to do them right, and a ghastly feeling of failure." With Harry and his partner Roddy, she toured New England while Forman was in Europe. Harry introduced her to Bill Stahl, the Columbia classmate who had led my father into theater; and through Bill, she met Pop. Here was the world of arts and letters Mel was never a part of, here was a man who could play the role Forman found impossible to fill.

They began living together off and on, spent long evenings critiquing one another's work, and argued over Mom's attraction to the teachings of religious mystic Emanuel Swedenborg. (Mom looked at all ideas with an open mind, selected from each what worked for her, and shucked the rest. In later years, Khrishnamurti, with his concept of "freedom from the known," was a favorite.)

Several budding young talents became their friends, including James T. Farrell (before his Studs Lonigan trilogy) and Alexander Calder (just beginning to experiment with mobiles). When they could scrape together a few dollars, they went to see *Blackbirds of 1928* or *Mourning Becomes Electra,* but this was rare. They were existing on next to nothing, and Mom's later diaries recall little happiness during those years. (Most journals before 1931, she destroyed).

While Pop was off being the American expatriate in Paris, she took a bookstore job at Oyster Bay. She recalled the tall, lonely man who owned the place, his awkward attempt to romance her, the gulls accompanying her silent walks along the Long Island shore, their high-pitched shrieks echoing her isolated frustration.

Marriage to Pop, she saw, as she did with Mel, as a way to break out of the rut. But it was more than a year after his return from France before she told him, "Marry me or the affair is over." And so, they were married. They rented two rooms on Sydney Place in Brooklyn Heights and struggled to survive. A year later, after Pop's clipping and filing assignment at the *New Yorker* ended, they moved to Vermont.

From Mom's Landgrove journal:

Saturday & Sunday, September 19, 20, 1931

His telegram says, "See you tomorrow afternoon. Your loving husband, Alvah."

Oh boy! Today then.

Debts:		Possible income for the month:	
local	$11.91	Kirstun–advance on possible stories	25.00
groceries	$17.00	Scribner's–review	6.00
		Article (1st of four–Brooklyn Eagle)	10.00
		Saturday Review–3 possible reviews	15.00
total	$28.91		$56.00

Hope, hope, hope. Your ineffectual efforts. If you had the slightest idea how ridiculously happy I am. Oddly too, I seem to recognize our present as the one thing I'd always looked forward to, and it's so much like I'd hoped it would be. How could I be anything but happy under the circumstances. Oh, comes the old finger-wagging. Watch your step, Mary, watch your step, try to keep prepared, there will come times, take it easy, take it easy . . .

Mom and Pop in Vermont.

Pop had hitched to New York to look for work. Even with slim pickings such as these, the possibility of a month in which income exceeded outgo was reason enough to break out a bottle of Heindrich someone had given them. It seemed so incongruous, Mom thought, sitting in a cozy living room in a ten-dollar-a-month ramshackle house, looking out on glorious mist-shrouded mountains, and drinking an almost record-best champagne from jelly glasses.

While Pop was writing stories and reviews and slowly crafting *Dwell in the Wilderness*, Mom made friends with the locals and played the writer's wife when editor Kyle Crichton or other New York friends drove up for the weekend.

Her mood swings, timed as much to the seasons as to Pop's struggle to make a living, found expression in her writing:

Monday afternoon, November 16, 1931

Each day moves drearily toward the next, and there is sun

and wind, and then the snow, and after that the dripping from the eaves and slush under foot. Sometimes we cannot bear the strain of waiting, waiting, everlastingly, while the slow days pile up into a month, and still no money comes nor any word.

Then, when the moments come too full for holding longer, we explode in our respective ways. Perhaps he will sing loudly, madly, for a while, then lapse into a somber brooding—or perhaps he will go to the shed and saw and chop the great birch chunks with a strength I never knew he possessed. And I, most surely I am apt to throw the pots and pans on the stove with a bang, or take my wrath out on the harmless kitten, booting him none too gently out the back door. Then the tears will come, and in shame, and I'll blubber, "If you had to wait, and wait and wait—" There is no knowing, there is only to go on waiting, through the centuries of this life.

In 1978 she looked back on these passages and penciled in beside them, "What an idiot I was, what a coward, what a baby."

With my impending birth, Mom's gray winter passed. She noted the budding spring, uncurling maple leaves, a distant fox barking, as she and Pop stood on their broken-down porch in the moonlight.

On August 28, 1932, twin sons arrived; one, stillborn.

Pop cried as he dug a grave in the little cemetery down the road and buried the shoe box that held his tiny son. Mingled with my mother's joy was a soft sadness that would last a lifetime. Her journals are filled with dream scraps of "the little be-be," and she sometimes talked to it as to a spirit guide (as she also did to her much loved father).

Still, motherhood was mainly a happy time, and in later years she often flashed back, relating a moment when she'd open the door and look out "not on the recently tarred street of Santa Monica" and the porch covered with scraps of paper and dots of paint left by her grandchildren and the neighbors kids, but on "the hills of Vermont on a bright October morning of 1933." She remembered her year-old son pulling himself to his feet on a kitchen chair, then, a month later, walking erect "into his father's 'office,' the writing room where he was not allowed to touch anything and where his father went to write and couldn't write. So I looked out this October morning over the Vermont hills, knowing as I looked, there were 30 years between

Uncle Everett (Pop's brother) with
Dan in Vermont, 1933.

then and today, and that I could hold it there in memory for as long
as I will live."

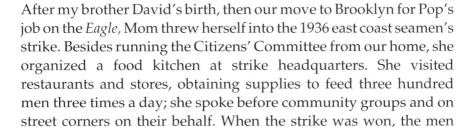

After my brother David's birth, then our move to Brooklyn for Pop's
job on the *Eagle,* Mom threw herself into the 1936 east coast seamen's
strike. Besides running the Citizens' Committee from our home, she
organized a food kitchen at strike headquarters. She visited
restaurants and stores, obtaining supplies to feed three hundred
men three times a day; she spoke before community groups and on
street corners on their behalf. When the strike was won, the men
voted her an honorary card in the National Maritime Union.

Perhaps the strike helped to take her mind off the threadbare
fabric of the relationship. I sometimes wonder if when Pop brought
home test pilot Lee Gehlbach—"the saddest man I ever met," he
called him—he had a hunch this would kindle Mom's attraction to

lost souls. Pop was, after all, looking for an excuse to break the marriage. (The affair with Mary Sullivan he'd begun while living in Vermont continued.) Years later, Mom described him charging into their bedroom and stuffing clothes into a suitcase.

"Gotta go," he said, "Gotta get out of here."

"Take it easy, pal," Mom replied. "I'll make some coffee. Sit down and we'll talk it over. We can work things out."

Pop would have none of it. He stomped out and took a room in a nearby hotel. Whatever distress David and I went through was cushioned by his almost daily appearance. And Mom, even with her own hurt, had more sympathy for Pop and for Lee (who remained friends) than she did pity for herself.

Would psychological hindsight see her as a doormat? Did she push back feelings, masking anger? That's a hard call. As a kid, I couldn't make such judgments. She could certainly unload on David or me when we tried her patience, but even as an adult I rarely felt any tightness or suppression in her. Mom simply had a compassionate door that was always wide open to anyone, the same door she opened for me on the day that Lisa died.

Mom's own hurt had developed in her a profound understanding of children. She knew they needed to grow at their own pace. While Pop was in Spain, she wrote him about the fistfights I had with the Italian kid next door, the stitches I needed after falling off a chair and cracking my head open after surviving an afternoon of Push-O races. (But she didn't tell him about the beefy teen who chased me for blocks, slashing the air behind my neck with a pair of enormous butcher knives.) Though the Brooklyn waterfront was a minefield through life, Mom refused to tie us to her apron strings:

> Take Daniel . . . For a barely six-year-old he's been through some tough paces in this tough but lovely block. The only blond in the block, a newcomer to the street, a kind kid to boot, he's had his troubles, but you should see him now. He's one of the gang. When I see him coming 40 miles an hour down the street on his bike, missing cars with a seventh sense my heart ain't where it ought to be, but I let him go because he needs it.
>
> David can run him a pretty close second (especially today) when he climbs up the ladder off the fire escape right on to the roof.

Grandma Addie (Pop's mother) didn't approve, she said, though she "hasn't fainted yet," and she added that I wanted him to come home, "war or no war."

Pop was risking his life, so Mom felt her job was to provide for David and me, hold herself together, and let him know that everything was fine. On the rare occasions when despondency crept into her letters, she'd admit to being a hermit, and that "to one as loves people as much as I do it's a pretty sad mess. Don't want to try figurin' out anything anymore . . . except how to make a living and be of some use, without too much dissipation of energy."

She was in and out of a dark depression for most of the year, but when Pop returned, she began working with him as she always had, offering advice and encouragement as he wrote *Men in Battle*. For Pop, it was "emotional torment, reliving the experience so soon after living it." They tried briefly to rekindle the romance. It didn't take. Time to move on.

Mom had been corresponding with Burt and Marion Lutton, old friends from Vermont now living in Pennsylvania. She thought about moving there but had only a vague idea about how to survive. When Pop finished *Men in Battle,* she made the decision to move. It was closure on a long chapter in her life and the opening of another one—shorter, but written with far more drama.

The farm we rented was half a mile from the Luttons. When Burt Lutton learned that Mom was about to marry Harold Frisbie, he called Pop to tell him about it, predicting "tragic consequences." Pop rushed out from New York. His notes from the period say he found Mom "belligerent in the extreme" and "near hysteria" over his attitude toward her marrying Harold. She accused him of "always trying to spoil my plans" and "probing into my affairs and wanting to know things."

It's probably true. Pop could be a snoop and a busybody; it complemented his theatricality. But he also cared about her, and though Mom's compassion for the underdog may have colored her judgment, she took people at face value. If a person was honest and caring, and Harold was both in his treatment of her and of us, that was what counted. On the day after Pop's visit, they married.

Mom with Helen Clare, Pop's second wife, 1941.

Three months later (October 1940), Pop and Helen Clare were also married. Mom's big heart went out to them, writing that she "felt good all over to know that two swell guys are taking a pot shot at happiness. Here's to you both, and Harold sends the same."

And she quickly dispelled Pop's concern over what David and I would think about a new woman in his life, telling him and Helen Clare to come visit "at any time of day or night. Psychology be damned. Kids can understand anything when it's given to them reasonably."

Through the months that followed, the mounting bills, the killing, then Harold's arrest and trial, Mom defended her marriage with Harold to Pop. In a union compounded of loneliness, empathy, and delight over the ease with which David and I took to him, she saw Harold beginning to change. He was like a thistle with a slowly opening but delicate blossom, and this helped her downplay his quirky tall tales and the cultural canyon separating them. Most of her doubts and fears (though some were expressed to Helen Clare) were given free reign only in her head.

Following Harold's arrest, everyone expected Mom's collapse.

But it wasn't to be. Not yet. First came the trial, then a year of appeals. Mom had made a pact. No stranger to suffering, she would never let a fellow human being go through a crisis alone.

When she visited Harold in jail, she told him he had to tell the truth, even if that was hard, even if he'd only felt safe inside a cocoon of lies. During the trial she reinforced that; told by a reporter that she had the sympathy of many because of the bitter experience, she replied, "I do not need sympathy. He does not need it. He needs to have backbone."

Through most of that year we were living in Danbury. In addition to frequent trips to visit Harold, consult with his attorney, or appear before the Pennsylvania Board of Pardons, Mom was simultaneously running a preschool for the children of working mothers out of our home.

When Harold was executed, friends were astonished at her acceptance of his death. She plunged into building the school with the same energy as in the seamen's strike. She spoke before the Rotary and other groups to raise money and tried to win support from the Board of Education. I remember her determination—and her exhaustion, the nights David or I sat on the edge of her bed, rubbing her weary feet. Twice, she closed the school (there was no question of making a living; Uncle Verne shouldered the deficits), only to reopen it after the mothers' desperate pleas. She didn't like depending on Verne or on the small help Pop could offer, and she thought of taking work in a defense plant. But this would leave David and me alone, and that she wouldn't do.

A noble effort. But the years of caring for others, while trying to find herself at the same time, had finally caught up.

Her notes looking back on the winter of 1943 describe day after mechanical day: breakfast, packing lunch boxes, laundry, cleaning (I remember rearranging the furniture a lot), shopping, dinner. Underneath, she felt a "gnawing sorrow," with less and less caring. She saw herself as a "poor mother," dragging along under a cloud of terrible guilt. On an evening in March, she plodded up the stairs, lay on the floor of her room, and decided that nothing held any meaning. The only thing she could do was to take her life.

All that night, she fought the decision. She sat on a window seat, hand on the phone, ready to lift it when the "tenuous thread that held me to the living" finally gave. "Send someone to get me quickly," she would say, not sure if, in the interval of lifting the receiver and hearing "Operator," lightning would strike and she would end it all. But the slender dawn of a cold and gloomy morning found the thread still holding.

She walked into our room, looked at David and me sleeping, and wondered what would become of us. She tried to think she could go on automatically doing everyday things, and by so doing, bring life back into focus. But as quickly as it flared, the spark died. The old depression had come back and taken root. "Mind and body," she wrote, "were going down together."

Then, suddenly convinced her body was riddled with cancer, she called a doctor and made an appointment.

That day, she went to the basement furnace and burned decades of accumulated papers and correspondence; there would be no hint she had led anything but a circumspect life. After that, she headed downtown. What she wore or how she traveled, she didn't recall. She only remembered being in a bank, looking at her check stubs to see if there was enough left to cover two or three small bills "which loomed like mountainous amounts too long owed." At least her brothers would be able to say that she left her affairs in good shape. And she thought of her father's final admonition before he died: "Take care of yourself, sis. And remember, try to live within your means."

There was no cancer. The doctor told her she was in excellent health. Mom paid him and started for home. She had walked only a block or two when, once again, suicide clouded her thoughts:

> Being seen by people was insufferable. They knew me; a despicable, loathsome "thing." I must get away quickly, out of sight, up the side streets, through the alleys—but where? To the lake? Suppose I didn't drown? What then? My kids; what of them? No! I couldn't. But where, how, what else? Then the impulses began to quiet and I plodded up the long hill to the only place there was, the house that could no longer hide my shame.
>
> When I reached home it was dark and the boys ran out to meet me, crying and frightened.
>
> "Where have you been? Why didn't you come home?"

Where had I been? Just the long, shadowy secret way home. But I couldn't tell them. I could only keep on dissembling.

She tried to cheer us, tucked us into bed and told us to "Sleep tight, don't let the bedbugs bite."

She dreamed of her parents that night: of her mother, somber and disapproving, of her own funeral. In the morning, she thought of hanging herself from a water pipe in the basement. It was all part of a "secret world," fractured and tormented.

A few days later, as she was cooking oatmeal, I asked her, "Mom, don't you undress when you go to bed?" She looked down at herself. "Your clothes look like you slept in them," I said. "Are you sick, Mom?" After David and I left for school, she sat at the kitchen table, her morning coffee cold and untouched. "A dirty mother," her secret world said, "I am a dirty mother." Guilt and shame sent her upstairs to grab her winter coat and into a frantic search for an old felt hat "I had once worn casually and smartly, to now pull down over my ears." Although the moment passed, "this time," she wrote, "I knew where I was going."

What chain of events led Mom to call brother Verne and have him arrange for professional help is unclear. Her thoughts that morning were on a nearby river bridge. First, though, she sat in a small café and drafted suicide notes on napkins. She searched for the right words then became stumped over where to leave the note. Again, the moment passed.

A few days later she admitted herself to the Payne-Whitney psychiatric clinic of the New York Hospital.

One of Mom's great gifts was an ability to use others as a mirror in order to see herself more clearly. Emotionally isolated and lacking perspective in the year following Harold's execution, she had no such mirror. When she entered Payne-Whitney, that began to change. Instantly.

Lunch on the first day was a catalyst: "From long experience I was accustomed to being polite and making conversation when thrown in with strangers. My three companions slumped in their chairs, staring at the tablecloth. I felt sorry that they should look so miserable and picked up the basket of rolls, passing to each one in turn. 'Won't you have a roll?' I asked." The other women neither glanced at the basket nor gave any indication they'd heard her. Several attempts at conversation were fruitless. She began to feel she was back home in Michigan, forced to endure a meal with a hurt and petulant mother. One young woman sat through lunch with her hands in her lap, eyes fixed on her plate. Another, about Mom's age (she was forty-four), picked at her food then pushed her plate aside and began to sob.

Slowly, Mom became aware of sunlight slanting through the windows, the chatter of the nurses. The dining room felt unreal, "like a chamber unearthed from some ancient, long-buried city." An inner, life-giving force began to stir. She looked up and smiled and said "thank you" to an attendant when the food was served.

Then she looked around at the remote and sullen faces of the other women at her table. Something was familiar: "That's me," she thought. She felt like running away and hiding from the shame of this realization. "I'd had the feeling before. I saw myself in the shuttered personalities of these three women, and I didn't like the reflection. I ate the meal with difficulty."

Each piece of the impersonal routine on that first day strengthened Mom's resolve to get out of the place as quickly as possible: the removal of a sharp-ended comb from her dresser, a nurse's attempt to help her bathe, a game of cards with no conversation, preparations for a walk in the garden.

Events surrounding that walk were a huge emotional kick in the pants. After dressing for outdoors and huddling in a corridor for twenty minutes, doors were unlocked and locked, and the women were herded "like so many cattle" from one floor to the next, and finally to a small formal garden bordered by a high wire fence, facing the East River. Bitterly cold, they walked around and around under a light snowfall. Patients from other floors who were there seemed much more sprightly, talking and laughing. Half an hour of this and they were "herded once again from one elevator to another back to the seventh floor and into our rooms."

While the experience was still too new for Mom to be objective, and while it had only been twenty-four hours since she'd entered the hospital, she was already beginning to emerge from the fog. There would be more hard days, but these became less and less frequent. Within two weeks, Mom had permission to leave the grounds for short excursions with sister-in-law Laura or with other friends. Within six weeks, she was visiting David and me at The Curtis School, a dark, Dickensian institution for boys in Connecticut, where Uncle Verne had enrolled us for the balance of the spring term.

David, called "Little Bit," became the mascot of the older boys, talked them out of bouncing me on a rail (which they threatened), and won a special award for all-around achievement when the school closed for the summer.

By May, Mom was out of Payne-Whitney and staying with Verne and Laura at Tumble Brook Farm, their *House and Garden* paradise just outside Danbury. In June, David and I joined her. We spent two weeks at nearby Lake Waubeeka, swimming, catching bass and sunfish, and soaking up sage advice about girls from sixteen-year-old Bob Dennis, who managed the lake and its seven rustic cabins.

While David and I were packed off to Camp Nawaakwa for the summer, then to Greer School for the fall term, Mom, who had come out of Payne-Whitney with new insights about herself, was piecing her life back together. By September, she had a job: the city of Poughkeepsie hired her to run a city-owned day-care center, which, like her school in Danbury, took in children of working mothers.

Though summer camp was a blast, and Greer School was at least bearable (I had to wear knickers for the first time), we missed Mom something fierce. Typically, she answered our sad letters wanting to come home with cheery ones of her own, decorated with little stick figures:

November 23, 1943

To think of it. Only 4 weeks from now you will have a Christmas vacation.

Won't it be jolly, though. Dan, I'm afraid we won't be able to have two boys in on Christmas day, because of room here. It won't be very simple. But perhaps they can come in for a day. You decide what's best.

This is tin can week here in Poughkeepsie. We have opened and flattened about 100 cans in the nursery. If you were here I would have you jump on them to flatten them.

We will buy the Cub Scout suit, Dan. You'll be glad to know your Mom is getting a raise in salary.

Christmas, 1943. We were in two tiny second-floor rooms in Poughkeepsie. Grandma Addie came up from New York. Pop was in Hollywood, writing movies (we saw his *Northern Pursuit*, starring Errol Flynn, during the holiday), and he could afford to indulge David and me with wooden rifles and machine guns, toy planes, and games—everything a World War II era kid was nuts about.

Mom spent a good part of the vacation nursing David through strep throat, which left him with a hearing loss he only learned about years later. At the time, his illness seemed a small price to pay. Mom was our old Mom again, and we were together.

The next two and a half years raced by. A buddy and I skimmed dozens of now priceless old movie posters (who knew?) off the balcony of the condemned Rialto Theater. The Santa Fe *Chief* took David and me west to visit Pop in July of 1944. With Mom, we spent another month at Lake Waubeeka. At school, you chose sides: Crosby or Sinatra. I had a crush on curly-haired Anna Kearin, got beat up by Henry Stevenson, had a paper route, and lost myself in movies. (*King of the Zombies* flickered off one April day in 1945, as the manager came on stage to announce that FDR had died.) David and

I stayed up past midnight with other revelers on VJ Day. And I started drawing cartoons.

Mom gave us plenty of latitude. If we acted responsibly, we could do pretty much as we pleased. Prohibitions were minimal. When we had a problem, she was there to talk it over. When we were confused, she suggested instead of lectured. When I discovered the delights of "self-abuse" (Pop's joking term) and my conscience got the better of me, she said it was normal—though underneath, I caught a shadow of the midwestern morality she'd grown up with. By the third time I "confessed," she shouted, "Ok, enough! You're getting to be a pain in the neck." She could swear too, and sing an occasional bawdy song: "Oh the buccaneers had hairy ears, they pissed through leather britches; they beat their cocks against the rocks and swore like sons of bitches."

While running the day-care center, Mom was also attending Vassar College part time, working toward her master's degree in early childhood education. Exhausting years, but a foot rub from David or me brought a big smile and renewed energy.

With the end of the war, Federal funding for the day-care center, covering a third of the cost, ran out. In March of 1946, the city argued that Poughkeepsie had only committed its third as a wartime measure. (Parents paid the rest.) Only five children were described as "war connected," and another seven were hardship cases. The city refused to continue its share unless parents would cover the other two-thirds. Since this would have been impossible for many, the city was asked to supply an extra $533 a month.

Mom swung into action. Nights, as I lay in bed listening to *The Shadow* or *I Love a Mystery,* I'd hear her pecking at the typewriter or making calls. She debated on the radio and mobilized a Parents Emergency Committee, which in turn rallied the community. Social welfare groups sent resolutions calling on the city to come up with extra money. Every few days the campaign made the front page of the *Poughkeepsie New Yorker.*

Mayor Doran discovered that five of the kids lived "out of town." (A few blocks beyond city limits.) It would be "illegal for the municipality to contribute to their accommodation," he said. Mom's letter urging city support was "non-informative."

So she wrote another, outlining the financial facts and arguing that the center was needed by working mothers, helped returning servicemen adjust to civilian life, and fostered healthier, happier children. It "goes beyond mere custodial care," she wrote, "and brings to this community a service for which it should be proud to assume responsibility."

More charges were hurled: the center's supporters had a plan to expand it to accommodate four hundred children, costs to the city would be astronomical, not every parent was a working parent, the center had outlived its usefulness. Over the next two months, Mom countered these charges, point by point, and built more support. Doctors, ministers, psychologists, the PTA, YWCA, and the highly regarded director of Vassar's child study program joined in.

Still, it became apparent that the old boy network running Poughkeepsie had no interest in continuing the center, even when the State of New York agreed to fund 49 percent of costs, with parents and friends putting up the rest. On Sunday, March 31, Mayor Doran ordered the center closed.

When Mom went in that afternoon to retrieve personal items, a hurried scuffling greeted her as she unlocked the door. Looking cautiously around, she discovered the mayor and other civic leaders hiding in the girls' bathroom. They'd been checking out the building, planning for its development as business offices.

The town fathers had been stringing the parents along, implying that the conflict was all a matter of $533 the city couldn't afford. Eventually, they agreed to accommodate the seven hardship cases at another day nursery. The local Jewish Community Center opened its doors to the rest of the children.

Weeks earlier, Mom had gone to Albany to try to meet with Governor Thomas E. Dewey to appeal for state funding. Though he wouldn't see her, on April 1 he signed a bill providing $1 million in aid for local childcare projects. "The continuance of the program for child care centers," said the Republican governor, "is justified by the conditions which arose out of the war and which have not completely subsided." Mom had lost, but she had also won.

Before our move to California, she asked David and me if there was anything special we'd like to do. We'd always wanted to take a trip on the Hudson River Day Line. So on a balmy Saturday in May, we all boated down river to New York, where my brother and I spent the afternoon at Coney Island stuffing on hot dogs, bashing one another in bumper cars, and scaring ourselves silly on the parachute jump.

In June, David and I left for Los Angeles, once again on the *Chief*, while Mom stayed behind to tie up loose ends.

Soon after Mom arrived in California, Pop arranged with director Lee Strasberg, an acquaintance since Theater Guild days, for her to rent his home near the beach in Santa Monica while Strasberg was in New York. At fourteen, I set up a "studio" on a glassed-in porch and between painting and cartooning, pored over his collection of gory volumes on the French revolution.

Making ends meet required Mom to work two jobs: directing a parent's cooperative nursery school in the morning, and a day-care program for the city of Santa Monica, afternoons. Vassar's widely respected curriculum, plus her master's degree (and three years in Poughkeepsie) had won her a modest reputation. In Santa Monica, she would fully realize her ambition to help children develop within a secure, structured environment, which at the same time encouraged an easygoing creativity.

Children's innate curiosity demands they have buckles to unbuckle, locks to unlock, laces to tie and untie, bolts, latches and eye-screws to open and close. Long before they appeared in toy stores, Mom put together her own boards with these challenges. Play-Dough appeared a full twenty years after Mom began mixing colored dyes into big bowls of flour and water. If budgets didn't allow for supplies her kids needed, she'd often buy them herself.

For The National Association for Nursery Education she wrote a mass distribution pamphlet, pointing out that children, left to their own devices, would gravitate to a favorite wet spot; behind a bush, near a leaky faucet, or in a puddle after a rain. If these natural urges were inhibited by admonitions to "Get out of the mud," or "Do you want to catch your death of cold?" she suggested this could lead to kids sneaking off to play in the mud anyway, or learning obsessive cleanliness, or that dirt was one of the "bad" things of the world.

Mom's schools always had a hose or two, plenty of dirt in the yard, and clay, sandboxes, messy paints, gloppy dough, blocks, cardboard and wooden boxes of assorted sizes to climb on or under or pile into towers. And bigger objects (not only a jungle gym): a rusting Chevy she'd get the fathers to remove the sharp edges from, then paint; an old fishing boat she discovered and had hauled into the yard on a trailer.

Many kids of three and four, Mom found, were already burdened with ingrained habits that made cooperation difficult. She worked hard with parents to try to help them unlearn the training that triggered these patterns in their children. She went to meetings and conferences, wrote evaluations for the city, organized parent committees to fix or paint or schedule the week, and came home bushed (by taxi if she was too tired to wait for the bus; Mom didn't drive), only to get up at six-thirty the next morning and start all over again. At the end of 1948, she resigned the city job to devote her time and energy exclusively to the co-op.

On weekends, she took anxious calls wanting to know what to do about Bennie playing with himself, or Suzie, who was trying to choke her little brother.

At the same time that Mom was steering hundreds of kids toward a head start in life, she was also raising David and me—in her own inimitable way: David recalls a day shortly after we moved to California when he called an older boy a "fag." The boy warned him not to say that again. When the boy next appeared, my brother, by then big enough to lick me, and feeling his oats, called out, "Hey, you queer!" The older boy proceeded (in David's words) to "beat the shit out of me." As David, bruised and battered, tried to defend himself, Mom came rushing out of the house to demand, "What's going on here?"

"Ma'am, your son called me a queer."

"Did you call him that?"

When David answered that he had, she turned on her heel, and without a word, walked back into the house, as the boy continued pummeling my brother.

Perhaps empathy for her own brother, Harry, got to her and she decided that David needed a lesson. Usually, she talked things out with us; like the time when David, then eight, was asked to take part in a minstrel show. When he asked Mom what it was, she told him and added that she thought it made fun of black people. Personally, she wouldn't be in a minstrel show, but "you have to do what you think is right." David mulled it over and decided to drop out, even though his best friend was involved.

In 1949, Mom sold a story based on an incident between us to *Parent's Magazine*. I'd come home late from school and told her I was going to a basketball game. My Whizzer motorbike was laid up for repairs, so I called friends for a ride. No answer. I decided to borrow David's bike. Mom objected; it was raining and dangerous and the game was ten miles away. She thought I shouldn't go. I blew up and stormed out, telling her to mind her own business, nobody was telling *me* what to do, and that if I couldn't take the bike, I'd hitch a ride. When David asked Mom what she'd do when I got back, and she replied, "Nothing, he'll cool off," my brother suggested she ought to knock me silly.

Ten-thirty. I called to say I was on my way home. Mom was in bed. Instead of relief and a "Thanks for calling," something else was triggered. "Peeved" that she had to worry at all, she felt herself building "one of those undignified, slightly mopey, hurt-feeling moods that more properly belong to the adolescent."

I came in buoyant, excited about the game (we'd lost, but it was close), and faced a pouting mother who proceeded to lay on a thin layer of guilt. "Aw, I'm sorry," I said. "Forget it," said Mom. When I went up to bed without telling her any of the details of the evening (as I usually did), Mom initially felt she'd "won." Then, as always, she began to sort it out:

> And my thinking went something like this: When they're little and defenseless we lose our tempers, yell and scream at them on occasion, are immediately sorry and ask their forgiveness, hug them and make up. Because of their strong need for our love and their complete dependency on us and that love, they have to take it. Then they grow up, blow off steam under inner pressures, just as we used to do, and we can't take it. Nice how-de-do. As though we hadn't given them enough feelings of guilt without loading on more.

She recognized that I had called the minute I got back to town, that I was sorry, that ultimately, *she* was the one that could have handled it better, and that "no self-respecting parent can say to a boy

Pop, Rose Kuras, Dan Bessie, and Mom on Dan and Rose's wedding day,
January 23, 1953.

Dan, Mom, and David (about to leave for
Korea), 1955.

Mom with Lisa, 1956.

going on 17, 'I forbid you to hitch a ride.' About the best that can be done is what you've already done during the preceding years—and trust that it made some sense."

Here then, was the essence of our mother. As David and I went on through school, married, and began making our way in the world, with me following in Pop's artistic and political footsteps, and David becoming involved in sports, then training as a physical therapist, Mom was always there, cheering from the sidelines. Never directive, she applauded our successes and never condemned our blunders; that was simply how people learned. Problems, confusions, uncertainties, though, she'd try to help us sort out. She was a careful listener, who could distill complex ideas into a few words. David puts it best: "She didn't need to say much; her example was more significant than any particular commentary."

Gifted with the ability to sense quickly where people were emotionally, Mom also knew how to enjoy them at their own level. When my kids stayed with her overnight (which was often), she could as easily get down on the floor with Tim for a game of pick-up-sticks, stay up until two watching *Wild Strawberries* on television with Joe, or, when he began studying philosophy, keep up with him by reading Gregory Bateson:

> December 18, 1975–5 A.M.
>
> Dear Grandson Joe,
>
> Have been caught up . . . in his book by a phrase, "Blake sees, not with his eyes, but through his eyes." This has taken me to Emerson who was one of my loves from high school, and to this big book, "The Roots of Consciousness." Have thought you could be interested in some of it.
>
> While I believe most other members of my family are more concerned over the conventional "senility" pattern they sense and fear emerging in their mother, their aunt or whatever, than with who I am, do want you to know, somewhere along the way, just what kind of a being your grandmother is, caught between two worlds but still alive and kicking in this one.

My daughter Lisa, I believe, challenged Mom more than anyone she'd ever known. Locked into an inner world of pain and fantasy, Lisa, since age eleven, had been in a succession of state hospitals and private and public board-and-care homes. My wife Rose and I, fearing she might do harm to her brother Tim, had reluctantly agreed with professional advice that "this is best."

At "Grandma's," where Lisa could draw, color, pound clay, or walk around muttering to herself until Mom said, "Enough!" (which stopped her for maybe ten seconds), Lisa found unconditional love. There was an immense caring and honest compassion, but also a frustrating uncertainty over how best to guide her. Mom equated Lisa's bizarre yet somehow magnetic behavior with the secret world she herself had known twenty-five years earlier, and with the people and experiences she'd gone through at Payne-Whitney.

On Christmas, 1967, after the floor had become a sea of holiday wrapping, the turkey picked to the bone, and my little family packed into the car, Mom waved good-bye. Then, after a refreshing hour of sleep, she woke to reflect on Lisa, and wrote that "even I, only the grandmother, can never hope or expect to make or have a life long separate from this ravaged young girl. Each of us must contribute in

Mom with big brother Leo, mid-1960s.

the best way possible to help find a home for this lost little soul within the bursting-out-of-clothes girl. How, God only knows, but somehow. 'Possessed' is the only word I can find. Must try to sort it out."

At sixty-seven, Mom retired—but only from the workaday nursery school routine. For the next fifteen years she was a neighborhood grandma to dozens of children, a confidante to their parents and to a legion of friends. If she wasn't flying to Chicago when nephew Joe Burnett needed her to care for his four kids while their mother went through a personal crisis, she was taking two-hour bus rides to Hollywood to spend days snipping and sewing costumes for Harry's puppets. When I decided to give up a truck-driving job to apprentice on Tom and Jerry cartoons at MGM (thirty-six dollars a week to start), Mom somehow came up with extra money to help my growing family survive.

She read endless books, took painting classes, and writing courses by correspondence. She took a couple of nostalgic trips east, one to old haunts in Greenwich Village, Danbury, then on to Woodstock, New York. For a time, she thought of settling in that colony of music and art:

August 29, 1968

I sit now and look around, wondering if I will walk into this little house again come October, November, December, and be, in a strange way, glad to be "home."

Now even, I think of the horror of Pennsylvania and the night, with the boys tucked in their father's car in their pajamas; again I know "I will never be back here to this house."

I think of Vermont (the September dawn when I paused at the top of the hill as I walked down to Chertaneux for milk, the morning we were to leave with grandma, Danny and Dave, and said to myself, "I will never be back here!"

And now, my little house, I look around and I don't know. You are full of swinging days and nights with grandchildren, visits with Ida, Bill, Vicki, of puppets, of notebooks, of Christmas and Thanksgiving, of visits with Dave, Merle [David's second wife], of many dreams, of all that has taken place since I returned last October.

Perhaps—probably, I will be back, for it holds, this little house, only good, and Hoshi [a neighbor's Siamese], who always waits for the lamb.

It holds the water bugs who have come and gone, it holds the blood-splattered kitchen of a year ago when I tore open my leg, it holds a million. It has been a good little place, and as I write it seems I am leaving it for someone else. There is food on the kitchen shelves, and coffee, tea, canned milk and sugar. There is toilet paper, paper towel, bath towels, blankets, soap, a leaky faucet, writing paper, envelopes, vacuum and dustpan, garbage can, dishes, pots and pans. The pilots are on, the telephone is only "temporarily disconnected, vacation rate." The gas is paid, the electricity is paid and they will continue. The *LA Times* is paid through the 31st, will stop until my return.

Oh dear God, I cannot know. Each day flows into the next.

Her mind was a bubbling stream, drawn from a broad river of memory and experience. She noted people, nature, feelings; everything from "the blue top button of her blue sweater sparkling in the light from the tall wicker lamp" to "the pigeon cuddling, shiv-ering in the corner of a shelf outside the door of Harry's workshop," to the small creatures who shared a Woodstock path with her as she went for an autumn walk, to "the yellow caterpillar on all its tiny sturdy

Mom and Uncle Harry, 1960s. *Inset*, Mom with Forman, 1921.

legs, below, ahead of me in the gravelled road on the way to the lake
this morning. Silently knowing where (and how I ask does it know,
its problems as complex perhaps but different from yours and mine)
to go, then still moving as fast as it can go, for I seem to feel a
caterpillar cannot hurry like a cockroach or a mouse when you snap

a light button in the kitchen and lift a foot to take the first step onto the old linoleum."

Her broad connection with life ranged from studying Paul Klee, to nights of cutthroat pinochle at Harry's; from seeing *Cabaret* with Forman and watching Michigan football on TV, to hours spent trying to draw "a poetic onion." Growing old, she took with large grains of philosophical salt, relating the process not so much to Mary Burnett as to humankind in general.

Even at seventy, she entertained thoughts about finding a new companion—perhaps Bill Stahl, the New York friend who had introduced her to Pop so long before. (They met again on one of her journeys east.) If the notion was romantic, this was because Mom *was* a romantic. But she'd also made peace with herself. She'd burned her bridges and reconstructed her life and she was content with what she had created. If a man came along, that would be delightful, but if not, that would be all right too. She had a strong sense of her deepest needs: "And now it's time to pack the memories, the madnesses, the wounds of childhood and youth, time to put them all away I think, and search, rather, for the sights and sounds from birth that form into a beauty, a riot of color, at times; at others, the calm and soothing blue of certain sky."

Not long after Lisa's sudden death, Mom began slipping into a gentle forgetfulness. I could sense that she felt her work had come to an end. She could pack her bags. It was as if she decided she'd had enough of reality. There had been so much taking care of others: her mother, Mel, Harry, Pop, Harold, Lisa; thousands of children and anxious parents; and David and me—especially David and me. I like to believe that her gradual shutting down was Mom's quiet way of asking for the one thing she had never asked for: to be taken care of at last.

When she could no longer live on her own, even with the help of friends who dropped in daily, my brother and I moved her north to his home in Marin County. David insisted. Nor was it a payback for all she had given him. Mom had simply been, besides his wife Carolee, his dearest friend. For him, it was completely natural.

Mom died on a rainy Wednesday in March. Like Lisa, she was

alone in her room at the time. Although they had been divorced for almost forty-five years, Pop, deeply affected, wrote a brief, poignant notice for a local paper.

My own hurt was also deep, but it didn't linger. We didn't need a formal good-bye. We'd made our peace as we moved through the years. Letting me fight my battles on Brooklyn sidewalks, reading David and me to sleep with *The Wind in the Willows*, crying with us over Harold's death—these were all a part of getting us ready to live our own lives. They were her gifts. And without precisely saying so, she directed that we pass them on.

My mother never became famous. She wrote no books. But in a way, she was the rarest of birds, for the compassion she offered to everyone who crossed her path during her eighty-four years was drawn from a deep well of self-discovery. It was genuine. And she could always detect those occasional times when there was a smidgen too much of the martyr in her unselfishness, or when self-pity poked its head in at her door. She could spot those demons and tell them to "crawl back in your hole."

Then she'd chuckle inside and pull out her journal and jot down her thoughts—never forgetting to add, "Don't ever take yourself too seriously, for if you do the world and all its people and all its beauties will escape you."

163

a long way from otsego

*The thing you need to guard against most, Brown, is
your facility.*

ROBERT FROST

Forman Brown discovered that *Better Angel,* the classic gay
novel he wrote in 1933, and more than fifty years out of print, had
been reissued in paperback only when a friend told him he'd seen
copies in Hollywood's A Different Light bookstore.

He set out to investigate:

INT. A DIFFERENT LIGHT BOOKSTORE. HOLLYWOOD,
1987—DAY

An ELDERLY WHITE-HAIRED GENTLEMAN enters. Tall,
spindly, and wearing a puckish smile, he waits, clucking his
tongue over a lurid title, while a CLERK completes a transaction.
Then he steps to the counter.

OLD GENTLEMAN: Uh . . . Pardon me, do you happen to have a
    novel called *Better Angel,* by one Richard Meeker?
THE CLERK: Yes, indeed. It's very well written and quite popular.
    I think you'll like it.
OLD GENTLEMAN: I'm sure I shall. You see, I wrote it.

CUT TO PUBLISHER'S OFFICE. BOSTON, MASS.—DAY

A SECRETARY pokes her head into an office and addresses her boss, a tall, harried YOUNG MAN.

SECRETARY: There's some old guy on the phone, says he'd like to speak with you.

YOUNG MAN: (picking up the phone) Hello . . .

OLD GENTLEMAN'S VOICE: You're the publisher of *Better Angel*?

YOUNG MAN: That's right.

OLD GENTLEMAN'S VOICE: The book you discovered by accident, and decided that since the copyright had expired, you were free to publish it?

YOUNG MAN: Yes . . .

OLD GENTLEMAN'S VOICE: The book your introduction calls, "possibly the first novel published in America to show male homosexuality in a positive light?

(as the publisher sighs)

And in which you also say, "Alas . . . over a half century after the novel's original publication, we are unlikely to discover what happened to the author, Richard Meeker?"

YOUNG MAN: Yes, but look here, I simply can't—

OLD GENTLEMAN'S VOICE: Well, I hope you're sitting down, because this is Richard Meeker.

As Forman Brown, my cousin thrice removed had been a partner with Harry and Roddy in Turnabout Theater. As Richard Meeker, he was the author of a pioneering gay novel, written when he was still deep in the closet. The moment he claimed credit in his own name, at the age of eighty-six, he stepped out.

Everyone needs a relative like Forman Brown. At ninety, he walked two miles every day to plunk out nostalgic tunes for Harry and the other retirees in a Hollywood nursing home. At ninety-two, hospitalized for a week after his ancient green VW was broadsided while exiting a parking lot, he decided it might be a good idea to give up driving. But when I called to urge a speedy recovery, his big complaint was that he still didn't have enough to occupy his time. (Forman worked best with an assignment, and contracts weren't exactly rolling in.)

As his ninety-fourth birthday approached, he was getting ready for another in a string of personal appearances for *Turnabout*, a video documentary I produced that celebrates the theater and its three partners as well as Forman's life as a gay author. And he was eagerly awaiting the third printing of *Better Angel*—this time, with his own name on the cover. He had waited sixty-two years for that event.

As with Uncle Harry, I didn't really get to know Forman well until he was in his eighties. There was much that Mom hadn't told me about the puppeteers or that she had mentioned only in passing. Reading *Better Angel*, then discovering Mom's diaries, prompted me to badger Forman about his younger years, and this helped me fit together what until then had been scattered scraps of memory.

He and Roddy had been together almost sixty years, but even after they became lovers in 1926, Forman was still uncertain about how to deal with his sexual orientation.

My mother and Forman seemed like an ideal match. They were both curious, aesthetic, and captivated by literature. Mom was already at college when Forman arrived in Ann Arbor to room with the Burnetts. She was quickly smitten. Forman fell easily into the role of swain and admitted to having encouraged her, discoursing on classical authors and reciting to her on Sunday canoe trips or outings at a nearby lake. How many sensitive young women of the 1920s could remain unmoved by a handsome young poet's alliterative description of her, "half seen, half lost in forest lake, in lake and fern, in fern and brake, a tendril's turn revealed your hand, and then your face, in fairyland of frozen lace?"

Mom was inspired to express her own feelings:

> The blossoms have gone from the tall pear tree,
> The hyacinth is dead,
> But you have come home to comfort me
> And summer is here instead.
>
> The quivering leaves on the tree will die,
> And you'll be going too,
> And I will wish in my heart that I
> Am summer or part of you.

At the time, Forman had "hoped it would work out." But it didn't work out, so Mom, baffled, drifted into the unfulfilling marriage to Melvin Dick.

My friendship with Forman was new when he told me he had hoped it would work out, but this comment was shorthand for the emotionally searing process he and Mom went through. While briefly attempting a romance with her (he had met Roddy by then), he was also testing a long-held feeling that he was by nature homosexual.

When Mom left Mel Dick and moved to New York, she and Forman took walks by the East River and went to concerts or to a movie, where they could "sit restfully in the dark, the flicker and shift of reflected light playing over them and their quiet neighbors while the organ trembled melting sentimentalities."

The characters in *Better Angel* representing them act out an awkward passion, attempting a romance that is never to be. As they walk through Central Park, Forman is finally able to talk about his homosexuality. Shocked at first, Mom cries briefly, then dries her tears and says, "This may be the thing that's ours exclusively, yours and mine." All the others, she says (indicating strolling couples) will "go on in the old way [but] we'll go on in the new way, and build, oh who knows what?"

While the words are from a novel, Mom's quick recovery and her acceptance is typical of everything I know about her. Bill Buck, a Turnabout regular in its last years and a friend to both Mom and Forman, had his own take on their nipped-in-the-bud union. That it was never consummated struck him (from the vantage of the 1990s) as romantic soap opera. "One wishes that friends will find happiness," he wrote me, but in the long run it had the most satisfactory conclusion. It "is the stuff for later reflection and possible heartache . . . for the same scrapbook with a dried, pressed prom rose . . . Bittersweet but not high tragedy."

Mom and Forman remained friends for life.

By the time the closet door was jerked open six decades later, Forman had no regrets. Unlike Harry, to whom coming out was a bit unnerving, Forman stepped into the welcoming sunshine of the 1980s gay pride movement. Acknowledging his gayness was a matter of enormous satisfaction.

The process by which my gentle and talented relative developed from a somewhat troubled young man to an unusually well integrated old man, began in Otsego, Michigan, in 1901.

Before her marriage, Forman's mother and her twin, who died young, had played the cornet in a "ladies band." Later, she sang in the church choir, and as "Mrs. George R. Brown," composed songs. (She detested her given first name, "Pet.") Forman ascribed "such musical talent as I have" to her. His father and both uncles owned newspapers. George's was *The Otsego Union*. His sister, Forman's Aunt Belle, who lived with the family, was the reporter, typesetter, and bookkeeper.

Forman was a spoiled child, fussed over by his mother and aunt. They dressed him in middy-blouses, which he hated; paradoxically, they let him braid and comb their hair, and when nobody was home he found himself drawn, "willing and yet reluctant," up the stairs to his mother's room, where, naked, he tried on her clothing and jewelry. In school plays, "if I could be the queen, the heroine, that was what I loved most."

Homosexuality was unknown to Forman's mother, who "would have been shocked to discover that such a thing existed." Still, she must have dished up some rare emotional supplies, for she nurtured his creativity, told him to stand up to the boys at school who called him "sissy," and somehow encouraged a "pride in difference." (These words from Forman's book, fifty years before the gay liberation movement hit full stride.)

Even his father, though disappointed that Forman didn't like baseball or other "boy" activities, supported his literary talent.

Sexuality was another matter. When I think of my own "sex education" in the late 1940s (a film on reproduction among farmyard swine, with appropriately vague explanations, was shown to separate classes of giggling boys and girls), Forman's introduction seems catastrophic.

"Self-abuse" (while a gratifying discovery) held unspeakable terrors. By chance, he discovered an ad in a cheap magazine, suggesting that "losing your Manly Vigor . . . through bad habits formed in youth" would be addressed in a pamphlet "sent in a plain wrapper." The pamphlet confirmed his worst fears, his guilt over the "unpardonable sin" toward his own body. The "secret vice," he learned, was responsible for insanity, feeblemindedness, loss of memory, and all sorts of ghastly diseases he had never even heard of.

Religion further fed his demons. Like my encounter with the orgasmic pigs, Forman suffered through a Sunday afternoon "fathers and sons" meeting, part of a series of church revivals, in which the pastor, after lecturing on the evils of swearing, gambling, and drink, and after warning the older men about the sins of adultery and fornication, let loose on the "horrible things that had happened to boys who had let "this insidious vice [masturbation] get hold of them."

It all made him quite sick, and even though his father reminded him to "pay attention to what he says, playing with yourself is bad business," when the meeting is finally adjourned, Forman's character in *Better Angel* feels as if can breathe again. Dodging the moral brickbats, Forman gave himself over to schoolwork and the arts. "I was always the best student in my classes," he wrote, "and of course, valedictorian of the class of 1918—Otsego High School. Rah! Rah! Rah!"

By the time he enrolled at the University of Michigan, he was sure he would be a writer. An early poem, "The Ruse," from *Walls*, a thin volume published privately by his father, testifies not only to Forman's developing talent but also to the sexual ambivalence that later found expression in the attempted romance with my mother:

> What struggle has a tree to be a tree?
> What dare expends a flower to be a flower?
> Yet I through every whirling perilous hour
> Must battle all my fellows to be me.
> There is no answer to this mystery,
> That men must point and laugh, or frown and glower
> While I fight back, or failing, couch and cower;
> No answer but to battle, or to flee.
>
> There is no answer, but there is a ruse—
> Whose fruit is silence and much suffering:
> The wall invisible, which fains a truce;
> Yet it confines me in so close a ring
> I tremble lest it burst, and set me loose,
> A stark, terrific soul, some silver Spring.

Forman Brown in Ann Arbor, Michigan, 1922.

The years 1922 and 1923 were "Elysian ones for budding campus poets," wrote Forman, in a humorous memoir for the "Michigan Alumnus" bulletin. Robert Frost was poet in residence. Students put out a small magazine called *Whimsies,* and though some "cringed at the title, we were silent, since we hoped one day to see in its pages a poem bearing our name." Frost regularly invited a dozen or so aspiring writers to his home, where they might spend an "electric evening with Vachel Lindsay," or sit at rapt attention while Carl Sandburg strummed his guitar and sang cowboy laments.

Most memorable of all was poet and literary critic Amy Lowell. Costume from another era, Amy's satin dress with a lace choker was "so engineered with stays that it must have been hideously uncomfortable, for, let's face it, Miss Lowell was more than pleasingly plump—she was monumental." She wore pince-nez glasses attached to a gold chain that, when not in use, "zipped back on a reel pinned to her expansive and shining bosom. This was sufficiently intimidating . . . but when she lighted up a very long and black cigar, she presented a spectacle such as Ann Arbor had never seen."

Forman recalled Miss Lowell entering a crowded auditorium, a tall reading lamp in one hand and a pile of books in the other. With no light plug in sight she called out, "*Boy!*" whereupon the janitor, an ancient bearded gentleman, shuffled on stage, surveyed the situation and "'lowed as how she needed an extension cord."

Needless to say, the cord produced was miles long, and while the janitor, Robert Frost, and Professor Strauss of the English department began attacking the "octopus-like problem, Miss Lowell stood . . . arms akimbo, commenting volubly on the ineptitude of men in general." After further convulsions, Miss Lowell quieted the by then hysterical audience, and "her reading of those passionate and often fragile verses, seeming so incongruous from that corseted and massive female, was a triumph of the spirit over the flesh." Heady days for a youthful poet.

"If Harry hadn't led me astray into the world of puppets," Forman told me, "I'd probably have wound up a frustrated lecturer in . . . the North Carolina College for Women. It was here that he served as an assistant professor of English in 1925 and 1926, and where, on being hired, the Dean advised him "to always keep your office door open when you're interviewing one of our young ladies." Little did the Dean realize how uninterested he was in their young ladies.

When the fall term of 1926 ended, Forman started for Europe, stopping off in New Haven to visit Harry (then studying at Yale). There, he met Roddy Brandon for the first time. The attraction was immediate, and they spent several nights together in a "dark and dustily exotic studio." This was his first real romance—love, he was certain. Though less for Roddy, Forman left a few days later with "many kisses and many promises of what my return would be."

In Paris, he roamed the Left Bank. He spotted Isadora Duncan in a square at Cannes, heard an aging Yvette Guilbert (the chanteuse immortalized by Lautrec), met a slew of young American artists, and discovered Frank Harris, author of the then-scandalous *My Life and Loves,* living above Nice. So he biked up, wangled a dinner invitation, and was presented with an autographed copy of Harris's biography of Oscar Wilde.

All the while, he kept up a chatty correspondence with his parents, which his father ran as a column in the *Otsego Union:*

Cagnes, France—December 24, 1926

Yesterday, Bill and I spent the day, or most of it, in Monte Carlo. We went in to Nice in the morning, had lunch there . . . I left him in the roulette halls and went to a symphony concert in the theater. A young violinist, Nathan Milstein, played, and he was quite the finest I've heard since the first time I heard Heifetz.

"Bill" was a popular young New York actor and amusing raconteur, Alexander Kirkland. The center of attention wherever he went, Kirkland swept Forman up in a whirlwind of activity. They explored England together, auditioned as entertainers at Cannes' swank Negresco Hotel, and shared a studio in Cagnes-sur-Mer.

In St. Paul de Vence, they took rooms in an old house on a hill, with a red-tiled roof and a blue door opening onto a garden. Forman could sit by the open window, "with the sun streaming in, the orange tree just beneath humming with a busy warbler, a shepherd across the valley leading a flock of sheep along the slender white road beneath the fringe of grey-green olive trees, and having at my side your letter full of tales of ice and snow—the paradox is almost too much."

What the *Otsego Union's* "continental correspondent" *didn't* report was that he'd met Kirkland crossing to Europe on the *Leviathan,* had been "seduced" by him, and learned, for the first time, that he and Harry and Roddy were not sexual freaks. When, in a somber tone, Forman told Kirkland he was beginning to suspect there were "more than a few others who feel as we do," Kirkland fell on the floor in a laughing fit.

"Why," replied his friend (when he could control himself), "there are *millions* of us all over the world."

Odd as this now seems, Forman's only experience had been with Harry and Roddy; and though a few others in their circle were gay, and though his reading suggested, "There was Plato, beyond a doubt. There was Cellini, and Michelangelo, and Shakespeare. There was, I felt almost certain, Shelley," he had been living, until Europe, within the same snug cocoon of innocence as had Mom, and his sexual ambivalence had not abated.

Then too, literature on homosexuality was rare. Gay bookstores, a gay press, gay movies; these didn't exist. "The whole question was pretty much taboo." So Kirkland's hysterics over his naïveté came as a revelation.

Better Angel dramatizes the moment when Forman accepts his gayness. After describing his own first love affair, the Kirkland character probes his intended conquest's still repressed feelings then says he's diagnosed his case and offers to prescribe.

"Prescribe," says the neophyte.

"Come here," says the tutor, "You're going to take the cure." He takes the young man's hand and pulls him, "bemused and uncertain," toward the bedroom.

Although they would never meet again after Europe, Kirkland's prescription validated Forman's growing awareness of his sexuality. The experience with Harry, then with Roddy, and with Kirkland, inspired the novel. In the few gay novels published before his came out, the hero had committed suicide. Forman wanted a hopeful ending. The title came from Shakespeare:

> Two loves have I of comfort and despair;
> Which like two spirits do suggest me still;
> My better angel is a man right fair—

The final line (which Forman omits on his title page), "The worser spirit a woman coloured ill," refers to the Sonnets' Dark Lady, who was vexing Shakespeare. Whether or not "loves" was used in its generic sense, it was a comfort, in 1933, for a young author cloaking his sexual inclination to position himself in such distinguished company.

Hooking up with Harry and Roddy not only created family, it also provided a space in which Forman's poetry could freely bubble. It had to, in order to fuel their work during the next sixty years. Robert Frost's admonition to him in college to "guard against your facility," was intended as a friendly warning, for Forman was nothing if not facile. Consider "Mrs. Pettibone's Chandelier:"

This is the story of Mrs. Henry Pettibone,
she was afflicted with taste.
Her friends were all contented to accept things as presented,
but Mable thought her duty was to fill the world with beauty,
so something always had to be replaced, replaced,
so something always had to be replaced.

Mable persuaded Mr. Henry Pettibone
to buy her a crystal chandelier.
But no sooner had she bought it, and hung it,
than she thought it made her furniture look shabby,
so she up and called a cabby,
and hurried to tell Henry her idea, idea,
and hurried to tell Henry her idea.

Well Mable persuaded Mr. Henry Pettibone
to let her refurnish their abode;
so Mable soon ran rife with Hepplewhite and Duncan Phyfe,
till she found to her dismay that the house was too passé
to provide a proper setting for her Spode, her Spode,
to provide a proper setting for her Spode.

Well Mable persuaded Mr. Henry Pettibone
their domicile was awfully out of date;
so he let her build another, so much grander than the other,
that she found to her chagrin that Henry never would fit in—
she would have to get a more distinguished mate, oh yes,
she would have to get a more distinguished mate.

Well Mable persuaded Mr. Henry Pettibone
to give her a fine divorce.
So she hurried out to Reno where one night at the casino,
she met Mount Moretzi Nevel, who was stylish as the devil.
She attacked and took him home by force, of course,
she attacked and took him home by force.

Well Mable discovered Mount Moretzi Nevel
was so stylish he glittered like a jewel.
In fact he was so charmin' he made her look quite common.
She was sorry she had got him, so one afternoon she shot him,

for Mable couldn't stand to look a fool, a fool,
for Mable couldn't stand to look a fool.

Before they electrocuted Mrs. Mable Nevel,
she said these words for all to hear:
"Never let your taste outstrip you,
if you do it's bound to trip you;
and although you may adore it if you lack the setting for it,
never never buy a crystal chandelier, my dear,
never never buy a crystal chandelier.

175

Between composing all the music and writing all the lyrics for both the puppet and variety stages at Turnabout, Forman hired out as a "lyric doctor" for the Los Angeles Civic Light Opera.

Along the way were songs for Sophie Tucker's one-woman shows, special material for Shirley Booth and Imogene Coca, lyrics to fit the score for Nelson Eddy's film, *Knickerbocker Holiday*—and a frantic call one evening from the by-then ancient Rudolph Friml, who pleaded, "Brown, can you come up here and help me out? Mrs. Kennedy wants a special number for one of those musical evenings she puts on at the White House. They need it by tomorrow." (It was Jackie's birthday.) Forman raced up to Friml's home in the Hollywood hills and labored over the piano into the small hours. Months later he received a thank-you note from Jackie's office, along with a recording of the piece. The Marine Corps band was featured, backing a lusty baritone.

Critics loved Forman's work. *Billboard* once placed him "in the envied niche beside such great masters . . . as Moss Hart, George S. Kaufman, and Morrie Ryskind."

The rhyming continued long after Turnabout Theater had been converted to an antique store, long after freelance assignments stopped trickling in. While Harry sat knitting his little woolen hats for children, "to keep my hands busy," Forman sat composing their annual holiday card:

Two crusty old codgers, one day each November,
remember a date coming up in December
requiring a greeting they yearly contrive
to prove to their friends they're really alive.

So they cudgel such brains as they still may possess
to concoct a greeting they hope may express
the old Christmas wishes for health and good cheer
sufficient, they trust for at least one more year.

So here, from these two obsolescent old chaps,
(one making verses, and one making caps)
to add to the clutter that's so customary,
their fondest good wishes!
Signed, Forman and Harry

Immediately after Forman stepped out as Richard Meeker, he began to be lionized, mainly in the gay community, where *Better Angel* is recognized as a classic. Robert Kiely, Loker Professor of English at Harvard, placed the book on the reading list for his course on twentieth-century literature, in company with *Ulysses, Lord Jim, Homage to Catalonia,* and *Lady Chatterley's Lover.* A *Los Angeles Times* reviewer confessed to initial skepticism, feeling this "was the sort of thing every college teacher does slyly—adds one or two unknown writers to his required list to show his independence and demonstrate the breadth of his knowledgeability."

On reading the book, the reviewer decided he was wrong. "Long before gay liberation," he wrote, "*Better Angel* resounds movingly with the anarchic note of pride in difference," He then described it, "thoroughly modern in its voice . . . Brown's book is not only a very good novel about coming out, as it has been called; it is a very good novel, without qualifier, a book that contains excellent writing, sophisticated humor, universal insights. 'The whole problem of life is to get enough moments crowded into it so the places between won't be so deadly.' That is a sentence any writer would be proud of."

Forman, of course, ate up the notoriety, especially at events such as an AIDS Quilt fund-raising banquet to which Bette Midler invited him. (Forman had sent her a recording of his songs, along with a copy of the book.) There, she surprised him by belting out one of the raucous numbers he'd written for Elsa Lanchester.

As important to him as this later applause were letters he received from gay men around the country when the book first appeared in 1933, for *Better Angel* let them know that they were not alone. One letter writer was "positive that every one of the 'boys' will offer up a silent prayer for a work so well done"; another, a respected citizen of his community (having married for self-protection), said he had "known the nameless longing," and felt he had "thwarted something in myself that would have made my life much happier"; still others, lonely and isolated, wanted to meet Forman. And some simply needed to acknowledge his courage.

As did Roddy: "The thing I hate most is that a book so beautiful and so worthy must be treated with such secrecy, and yet you are helping the day when we need no longer fear or flinch from those who do not want to understand, who have never felt the loneliness and longing I did until I met you, MY BETTER ANGEL."

Modern reviewers were surprised to discover that when the book first appeared, there was little negative reaction, thus exploding a myth that early gay books were always buried. "In fact," says Forman, "there were excellent reviews." The *New York Times* called it "a well-written novel on a sensitive theme." A modest commercial success, it went into a second printing. And before its rediscovery in 1987, one publisher, capitalizing on its theme (the story includes almost no sex), issued a pirated copy in the 1950s with a lurid cover, and the provocative title, *Torment.*

For me, Forman became something of a role model for "growing old gracefully." A cliché? Perhaps. But in his case it was true. A simple and direct man, he didn't make life more complicated than it needed to be. He didn't analyze or agonize over the past. And when he did look back, it was with clarity, with a lack of recrimination, and without an attachment to the emotional wounds others often bottle up inside.

I think about that as the years slip away. Perhaps, aside from digging for family roots, this is what led me back to the Turnabouter's door in my late forties.

"Coming out" in his eighties, Forman was once more at center stage. He stepped into this new spotlight with the same steady ease and lack of concern for stuffy opinion that characterized his long, satisfying, and very accomplished life. He had come a distance since the day his parents drove him halfway across Michigan to the Burnetts' big rambling house on Munroe Street. A far greater journey than the one from Otsego to Ann Arbor.

With Roddy, Forman found the great love that his protagonist in

Forman Brown behind his piano at the Turnabout Theatre, 1941.

Forman Brown on his eighty-eighth birthday.

Better Angel had longed for. Even with muddy detours along the way, these were few and far between. And they were "so long ago, and so long forgiven," that he could end his novel, after the characters representing himself and Mom had spent a frustrating night, and after he and the Roddy character reunite after a long absence, with the certainty that their love "was as absolute and as right and as restful as this pale and now fading light of the March afternoon."

After Roddy died, Forman discovered a greeting his partner had saved, written (by Forman) on Roddy's seventy-second birthday, which was also the fiftieth anniversary of their first meeting in 1926:

> My love: I'd love to write a verse
> that would warm your heart, and fill your purse,
> and make you know that in all this earth
> there's not one thing of any worth
> that hasn't *you* as part of it,
> as bones and flesh and heart of it.
> And should you ever have a doubt
> just take this scrap of paper out
> and know that what I write is true—
> you are my world—my world is you.
>
> Love, F.

If I believed in a life after death, I could imagine the two reuniting again the moment Forman died, the day following his ninety-fifth birthday. I'd probably spot them wandering past some pink cloud, Forman penning a witty verse to be sung by the heavenly choir, Roddy fretting over how they'll seat everyone, and Uncle Harry meandering along behind, hoping there'll be time to squeeze in a few minutes with his marionettes.

TEN

an ink-stained wretch

Leo's appearance was singular in contrast to the popular
notion of a great advertising chieftain. He was short and
slope-shouldered, with a paunch. His waistcoat and
lapels were sprinkled with ash from the Marlboros he
smoked. A large double chin gave him a faintly froggy
aspect at times, and when he spoke, his voice was a gruff
burble. In his sixties, he had the vitality of a Cape
Buffalo, and no one could stay with him for more than a
few laps.

FROM *THE LEO BURNETT BOOK OF ADVERTISING*

When you reach for the stars you may not quite get one,
but you won't come up with a handful of mud either.

LEO BURNETT

When my uncle Leo died in 1971, the Burnett Agency was
fifth largest in the world, with three thousand employees, offices
from Chicago to Kuala Lumpur, and annual billings of $389 million.
Glowing tributes appeared in everything from the *New York Times*
and *Time,* to *The Daily Journal* in Caracas, Venezuela. Eulogies
poured in from every corner of the globe. He was "Leo the Lion," "a
giant of advertising," "a famed copywriter," a "pioneer in his field,"
and "one of America's finest gentlemen." They recalled his career
and recited his honors, from a Gold Medal from *Printer's Ink,* to
Marketing Man of the Year. He had been a trustee of the American
Heritage Foundation, chairman of the Advertising Council, and
director of the Hospital Planning Council for Metropolitan Chicago.
Contemporaries, from Putney Westerfield at *Fortune* to Robert
Sarnoff at RCA, extolled his virtues and said he would be sorely

missed. The Boy Scouts and the Crippled Children's Society testified to his loss.

To the man himself, he was "an ink-stained wretch."

Leo got his hands dirty. His fat black pencil obliterated mediocre copy and scribbled in his own powerfully simple words. He was known to snatch an ad presentation back from a client who had already OK'd it, because he thought it wasn't good enough. When his intimidating lower lip began to tremble, the Creative Review Committee knew that Leo was about to exercise what he called "instant democracy"—the idea was lousy and his "boys and girls" had to start over. The characters and campaigns created under Leo's critical eye have become a part of media folklore: the Jolly Green Giant; the Marlboro Man; the Maytag Repairman; the Good Hands of Allstate; Tony the Tiger; Morris the Cat; the Friendly Skies of United; Charlie the Tuna; Snap, Crackle, and Pop; and the Pillsbury Doughboy.

Leo rose at five, worked until seven-thirty, ate breakfast, and was in the office by nine. Most of his life he worked 364 days a year, taking Christmas morning off—and occasional Saturdays at Arlington, for he loved the ponies. (It's been said he always won because he bet on every horse in every race.) Until the day he died, he kept two secretaries working full speed, full time. He "was the only man I knew who worked harder than I do," said David Ogilvy, another advertising giant. "The thought of Leo ringing me in New York at 2 A.M. and asking me to meet him in Chicago for breakfast with some fresh campaign ideas was more than I could bear." Others caught glimpses of him in airports, "chugging around the country like a perpetual motion machine," lugging a huge portfolio of presentations to show to clients.

One of Leo's associates recalls him always wearing expensive, custom-tailored suits, "even when we were darn near starving in the early days of the agency. Why, I will never know, because within an hour they would look as if he had slept in them, and within twenty-four hours his suit could include a gravy stain or two and the ashes of three or four packages of cigarettes."

Marlboros may have helped do him in. Formal photos often show him fingering one, the smoke curling delicately above his head. And heart attack was no stranger to my uncle, though his first, years before, had been only a mild warning. A workaholic to the end, Leo was at home in his study writing notes for a meeting when my aunt Naomi, who minutes before had come in to ask, "And what would you like for dinner, you old sweetie?" returned to find him slumped over his desk.

Advertising was his lifeblood. More than fame, money, or becoming the biggest, his great passion was stringing words and images together in such a way that consumers would think, "That's a hell of a product," instead of, "That's a hell of an ad." His client loyalty was legend. At an annual marketing meeting of the Kellogg Company, Leo's voice suddenly grew weak and he collapsed into his chair, faint from the low blood sugar from which he suffered. "Candy bar," he whispered. One of the group leaped to his feet and began hurdling chairs toward a vending machine when Leo lifted his head and cried hoarsely, "Make sure it's a Nestlé."

It began with apples. Monday, August 5, 1935. The GOP was meeting at Chicago's Edgewater Hotel, mapping plans to defeat FDR. In Cook County, 285,000 families were on relief. New Oldsmobiles were selling for $675, sirloin steak for twenty-nine cents a pound, and the Thompson chain of restaurants offered a breakfast special of a fried egg, bacon, and buttered toast for fifteen cents. America was stuck in the Great Depression, and Leo, who was opening his own agency, in a suite at the Palmer House, had been warned that he would soon be out on the street selling apples along with thousands of others.

Back at the Burnett home in St. Johns, whenever someone was invited into the parlor (usually kept closed), you knew it was a friend. If the fruit bowl "with those great tasty apples" was offered, said Leo, you knew it was a *special* friend. He never forgot the symbolism. To this day, desks on all twenty-seven agency floors at 35 West Wacker Drive's fifty-story Leo Burnett Building have a big bowl of Washington State Red Delicious apples. More than half a million are given away each year in Burnett offices in nearly sixty countries.

His other symbol was a hand reaching for the stars.

We were still living in Vermont when my uncle opened shop. My brother David was four months old, and while times were hard in 1935, Pop's Guggenheim for *Dwell in the Wilderness,* his book about the Burnetts, helped keep us afloat.

Having left the Homer McKee agency in Indianapolis in 1930, where he'd spent ten years churning out ads for the now dimly remembered Stutz, Peerless, and Marmon automobiles, Leo had moved on to Chicago, as creative head of Erwin Wasey and Company. Naomi had stayed behind to have her third child, my cousin Phoebe. With the same gutsy independence that drove his grandfather George Burnett west along the Erie Canal, Leo started the company on his own hook. The fifty thousand dollar line of credit a friend helped him obtain was never used. Instead, he borrowed on his insurance.

And he did something else unusual. The Leo Burnett Company began with three clients: Hoover vacuum cleaners, Minnesota Valley Canning Company (later, Green Giant), which he took with him from Erwin Wasey, and Realsilk Hosiery Mills. After a long battle, Leo bought out an investor from Realsilk who had come aboard, owned 40 percent of the Burnett stock, and wanted more say than Leo and his seven associates were willing to relinquish. From then on, my uncle was adamant that Leo Burnett would remain a privately held company, owned by its employees. And it remained so until 1999, when the agency merged with British and Japanese interests.

Over the years, Burnett became famous for what came to be called "the Chicago school of Advertising." It stressed finding "the inherent drama in the product and writing the ad out of that drama," said Advertising Age. "The art is in getting noticed naturally," they quoted Leo as saying, "without screaming and without tricks." "We try to be straightforward without being flat-footed. We try to be warm without being mawkish."

Leo attributed much of his influence to Theodore MacManus, father of "atmosphere advertising," who wrote a famous Cadillac ad in 1915. Running just once, in the *Saturday Evening Post,* the ad mentioned the car a single time, in tiny print at the bottom, indicating the company's sponsorship. Instead of hawking the car, it was an essay on leadership, dealing with image, character, and personality—a concept Leo adapted and expanded upon. Cadillac sales skyrocketed.

MacManus's copy, and Leo's which followed (for my uncle was

first and foremost a copywriter), veered 180 degrees from most ads, which were "bombastic, braggadocios, and, at times, pure bull. Hard sell used product features and claims, often exaggerated, to twist arms and pin the reader to the mat."

Leo's philosophy was different: "The best advertising . . . does not pound the reader or the viewer over the head with claims or proof. It merely lays the essential facts before him as a sensible, suspicious, sensitive and a fallible human being."

185

Dozens of Burnett campaigns illustrate the risk-taking, the willingness to challenge established convention by trying to win the reader with innovative, straightforward images:

An ad for the American Meat Institute stressed the "virility" of raw red meat by photographing it against a red background. Here was Leo's "inherent drama,"—"which we try to find without getting too kooky or too clever or too humorous or too anything—it's just natural."

He persuaded the Hat Corporation of America to run an ad with a photo of a man *not* wearing a hat—a shabby bearded type (clearly *not* executive material)—with the caption, "There are some men a hat won't help."

As early as 1967, Burnett promoted an antilittering campaign for Schlitz Beer by picturing an idyllic lakeside scene with the caption, "How would an empty beer can look here?"

To shift the Marlboro cigarette emphasis from quiet elegance to manly ruggedness (ads had previously been directed at the polo and steeplechase crowd), Leo came up with the cowboy image.

The Chicago school shunned New York's flash in favor of honest simplicity, relying, for example, on a shot of a frosty cake and minimal copy to sell itself, a finicky feline to push cat food, a sudsy mug of beer to whet the thirst. The inherent drama.

Leo's commitment to perfection was also legendary. He was tough on creative people because he was one of them. His co-workers measured his dissatisfaction, his LPI (Lip Protrusion Index) on a scale of zero to ten. After a disastrous creative review meeting, one poor wretch, asked how it had gone, was heard to reply, "God, it was awful. An LPI of 9."

Leo once killed a campaign by remaining silent for several painful minutes and finally mumbling, "I'm afraid what's wrong with it is that it is merely good." Several of the agency's major talents left the meeting and worked overtime for days to come up with a better campaign.

He urged his people to listen to "that little voice that tells you just how good that idea of yours is." A "creative conscience," he called it, an inner voice that would tell them if "it's a bum idea—or a phony idea—or somebody else's idea." Understanding when an idea could be better, he told them, "makes the difference between an enlightened professional and a so-so writer." When an ad was right, Leo knew it. And for these, he was quick to offer his highest commendation: "That's damn good!

I was sixteen before I ever met Leo. He had been a mythic figure, similar in some ways to Uncle Harry. Each Christmas, a gift would arrive for David and me, from Abercrombie and Fitch in New York or from an expensive Chicago toy store. Aunt Naomi, I suspect, ordered these from a catalog. One year brought glassed-in puzzles from England, where the object was to roll tiny pellets into holes or to hook colored rings onto a clown's bulbous nose. Another Christmas brought hand-carved wooden acrobats who linked to form a pyramid. As my interest in art blossomed, books on cartooning arrived, always with a ten- or twenty-dollar bill enclosed.

When David and I left for California in the summer of 1946, Aunt Naomi and my cousin Phoebe met us in Chicago (we had half a day between trains), took us to lunch and to the city's captivating Museum of Science and Industry.

Two years later, I finally met my uncle. I'd worked weekends setting pins at the Broadway Bowl to save money for a summer trip to New York. I hadn't planned a Chicago stop, but Greyhound put my luggage on a later bus, so I had a day's wait for it to catch up. I called Aunt Naomi, who directed me to a suburban train that would take me to the Lake Zurich station north of Chicago, where she would meet me and take me to the modest farmhouse (on 130 acres) where she and Leo lived.

I'd had a total of five hours sleep on the three-night trip from Santa Monica and felt like a walking zombie. Still, I devoured a generous meal and marveled at my aunt and uncle's new three-inch television, the first I'd seen outside a store window (an enormous glass on a wheeled stand magnified the image). I also got into a hot argument with Leo over my father's appearance the previous fall before the House Committee on Un-American Activities in its investigation of "subversion" in Hollywood. With piddling know-ledge but reckless bravado, I defended Pop and held forth on the imminent dawn of socialism—as Leo fumed and sputtered and grew apoplectic. Finally, he rose from his chair, blurted out that I should "go to Russia," and stomped from the room.

I soon collapsed into bed and immediately fell asleep. Later, apparently—I have no memory of it—in a daze, I strolled into Leo's study (where he was working), then into the master bedroom. Naomi awoke and guided me gently back to bed.

The next morning, Leo woke me at six. About the previous night's discord, silence. Instead, he provided me with big floppy hip boots and marched me around a muddy swamp he was converting to a lake. I was still groggy with sleep as we sloshed through the muck and bulrushes and batted away mosquitoes. Along the way, Leo supplied a running commentary on the varieties of trees he would grow (he ultimately planted twenty thousand), how the lake would develop its own springs, and what kind of fish would go in.

Here was the same relentless drive he brought to advertising.

Naomi had not wanted a lake. If Leo must have one, she asked, why didn't they sell the farm and buy another that already *had* a lake? Rumor has it the suggestion so infuriated Leo, who wanted to *build* a lake, that he barely spoke to her for two weeks.

On completion, he dubbed it "Lake Naomi." But my aunt got in the last word. She named the new dam that had made the lake possible "Dam Leo."

My mother, who visited the farm three or four times after she retired, reported an incident typifying his impulsive nature. Over dinner one night, she and Naomi had been discussing how pleasant a tree would look just outside the kitchen window. Leo overheard but said nothing. Mom and Naomi went on to talk about nourishing the tree, watching it grow tall, seeing it bud and sprout leaves.

Saturday morning, excited as a child, Leo woke them both at seven. "The men are here with the tree," he called out. Mom and Naomi roused themselves, stumbled into the kitchen, and looked out to discover a flatbed truck with a fully-grown thirty-foot maple about to be plunked into the ground. Instant gratification.

If he was compulsive, Leo also had the focus to quickly spot a phony. He hated deviousness. I got a taste of that indignation a year or so after the big Un-American imbroglio. Several friends had television by then, and guys on the commercials who won the girls invariably wore suits. I got it into my head that I needed a suit—desperately. But I was broke. I wrote to both Leo and Uncle Verne, requesting a loan of seventy-five dollars from each "to buy a suit." What I told neither was that I was buying *two* suits. My uncles were frequently in touch, my perfidy was unmasked, and I received a long letter from Leo, signed in his trademark royal green ink, fixing a repayment schedule and kicking me in the pants for failing to deal with him honestly.

The kick was justified. It took more such lessons to make the ethic my own, but eventually I caught on. Foot power.

⁓

Advertising, like most media, is an ego-driven business; so for newcomers at Burnett, it took a while to get used to the notion that Leo was attacking the concept, not the person. He was a demanding boss who ran "a sweatshop with a heart." His people worked long hours, as did he, but did so because he inspired a "consuming urge for excellence that was contagious."

He also inspired originality, but never for its own sake, and he was fond of quoting an old boss who said, "If you insist on being different just for the sake of being different, you can always come down in the morning with a sock in your mouth."

In his later years, Leo wrote little ad copy. Mainly he provided guidance, wrote memos, and offered "thought starting" ideas. While his "instant democracy" was final, Leo usually didn't need to exercise it. A creative give-and-take more often won the day. Everybody had a hand in decisions, and some faulted the agency for deciding campaigns by committee. "Could Hamlet have been written by a committee?" a critic asked, "Could the Mona Lisa have been painted by a club?" Leo replied with a question of his own: "Could a committee have created the Declaration of Independence, the Bill of Rights or the Constitution? Could a club have written the

Dan Bessie's uncle, advertising genius Leo Burnett. (Courtesy of Bachrach Studios.)

Magna Carta—cornerstone of freedom for the modern world? The answer of course is, 'Yes, a committee could and did.'"

Perhaps Richard Fizdale, recalling his first day on the job at Burnett, came closest to characterizing Leo's openness to new ideas and the people he hired to create them. In 1990, Fizdale was president and chief creative officer of the agency, but when he started, he was "an unrepentant hippie, with long, wild hair."

I was wearing love beads, a tie-dyed T-shirt, torn blue jeans and sandals.

And then, there he was in front me, almost 80 years old, short, slightly slouched, wearing one of his "freshly rumpled," blue, pin-striped suits, with a trace of cigarette ash on the lapel. I noticed his legendary lower lip, which was said to protrude farther and farther down his chin as his disapproval mounted.

I was panicked by Leo's lip. It wasn't just protruding, it quivered, as he looked me up and down, this refugee from the Woodstock generation.

How could I have known that, in describing my kind, he had written the following:

(And I quote): "Some of us find them frightening . . . all that roar and racket of their bikes . . . their music . . . the seeming wildness of their dress . . . (*Leo, I didn't own a suit!*) . . . their inexplicable terpsichorean modes . . . even their look, sometimes of bored and silent withdrawal.

"Many of us are simply bewildered by some of them. The beads. The hairdos. Like a Shakespearean road company in mufti. And the dark glasses.

"While business of any kind 'turns them off,' the business *I* am in apparently turns them off in spades."

As we shook hands, Leo was staring at the bell I wore around my ankle. He slowly raised his head, revealing a lip that undulated like a giant manta ray. Our eyes met. He spoke without a trace of rancor or disapproval, just loud enough for me to hear and never forget.

"You better be good," he said, and walked away.

⤙

While fine-tuning ad campaigns, Leo was tenacious. Even I had a small hand in one. On a summer visit to the farm, cousins Peter and Joe (Leo's sons) were there, along with Peter's wife Georgia. Naomi was serving lunch on the patio when Leo suddenly appeared, toting his immense portfolio. Out of it came a raft of mockups for Kellogg ads. Clearly chafing at the bit, he waited several minutes (while we all ignored him) until Naomi finally said, "You have something on your mind, don't you dear?"

Leo beamed, and the next hour was taken up grilling Joe, Peter, Georgia, Naomi, and me on the various ads: Which seemed more likely to win a reader? Which might turn consumers off? Why? Did they really make us want to buy Corn Flakes? Where they too far-out? (One featured a Freudian analyst holding a bowl of cereal and Leo wondered if it was perhaps a bit too "smart-alecky.") Actually, *all* of the ads were clever and engaging.

My feelings about Leo and the ad business were contradictory. On the one hand, it was easy to caricature him for my co-workers as a stereotypical capitalist, a short, potbellied tycoon who burbled when he spoke. That was always good for a chuckle.

On the other hand, I had a grudging admiration. Grudging, because, as with Uncle Harry, being Leo's nephew often brought admiring nods, and because while the animated commercials I worked on were (coincidentally) sometimes for his agency, it bothered me that he and I were political opposites. My talent contributed more than I was willing to admit to helping sell products, and that irked me. So even though joking about Leo meant that in a sense I was biting the hand that fed, I justified the contradiction. I was earning a good living and learning a trade.

Schizophrenic? Of course.

At the same time, feedback I got from people who worked with Leo painted another picture, one I initially ignored. He had an enormous influence, they said, in advertising trends. They also said he treated associates with respect, encouraging creativity and challenging them never to accept "good enough."

This was long before I made any real effort to discover *what* his philosophy was. At the time, I didn't give a damn about the "product loyalty" Leo espoused (I didn't even realize he *espoused* it), or his conviction that "if we do not believe in the products we advertise strongly enough to use them ourselves, we are not completely honest with ourselves in advertising them to others."

But Leo's wry humor usually made his point without beating fellow employees over the head. In a 1958 memo, expressing "an entirely personal point of view," he couldn't resist adding that "if any of us eats those nauseating Post Toasties or Wheaties, for example, in preference to the products of Kellogg's, I hope he chokes on them; and if any of us fertilizes his own lawn without first trying Golden Vigoro, I hope it turns to a dark, repulsive brown. If you smoke cigarettes and your taste is so sensitive that it discriminates strongly between 'our brands' and competitive ones, please, as a personal favor, don't put the competitive package in front of me on the conference room table, because it does things to my blood pressure."

The Marlboro campaign is a good example of Leo's dedication to the product. When Burnett took a brand considered slightly effeminate, a "woman's" cigarette, and gave it a masculine image, sales zoomed. Marlboros began appealing to even *more* women, women drawn to the tattooed he-men pictured in the ads. During the mid-1950s, "full, honest flavor" was pushed. Did my uncle and his associates seduce the smoking public? Of course they did. But few thought about lung cancer then, or about the heart disease that eventually killed Leo.

In 1970, cigarette advertising on television was banned. But during the 1990s, as tobacco companies shifted more and more of their marketing overseas, Burnett was still plastering buildings across the developing world with monster Marlboro broadsides. As late as 1994, the company Leo founded was taking credit (in an internal document) for helping to "neutralize" the effects of a Philippine government plan designed to reduce smoking by children.

Burnett finds a free-speech justification for continuing to advertise them. As long as any products—including lethal ones—are legally manufactured and sold, Leo's agency feels it has every right, in fact a *duty*, to advertise them in a responsible manner. Advertising bans they see as censorship. At the same time, Burnett promotes antipollution and recycling campaigns and fat-free products. It sponsors elder care, and Burnetters enjoy excellent company benefits and profit sharing.

The schizophrenia again.

I wonder what Leo would say. Would he continue pushing products that cause millions of deaths? That's impossible to know. He was fiercely loyal to the product, but he was also willing to be convinced he was wrong.

As a lifelong Republican, Leo was overjoyed when in early 1963 the GOP National Committee selected his agency for its 1964 presidential campaign. Even before a nominee was picked, Leo was burning up the phones to those close to potential candidates, urging that ads be started as soon as possible. Anticipating large commissions, the agency began strategizing. Though *Newsweek's* obituary for Leo erred in attributing the slogan, "In your heart, you know he's right" to him, he was deeply involved in the key planning.

193

Convinced at the time that Barry Goldwater was a stalking horse for American fascism, I was driving around Los Angeles with a bumper sticker proclaiming, "In Your Heart, You Know He's Nuts!"

But Leo's effort was premature; the bull elephants in the back room hadn't shifted their weight. Ultimately, a PR man pushed by Richard Nixon came on board, and his loyalty was to another agency. So, exit Burnett; enter Erwin Wasey, Ruthrauff and Ryan (Leo's employer of years before).

What Leo thought about this, I have no clue. Much of what transpired lies buried in Burnett archives, unavailable even to employees. But the $200,000 in commissions that Erwin Wasey rebated to Burnett to compensate for its time and effort must have smoothed quite a few ruffled feathers.

More is known about my uncle's reaction to his failure to win the account for Ford's ill-starred Edsel. In *The Burnettwork,* an agency publication, Aunt Naomi recalled Leo's disappointment, then added that years later, when Edsel came up in conversation, she'd remarked, "Weren't you lucky you didn't get that account? It was such a complete flop." Leo answered with quiet assurance: "Had we been awarded the account, the Edsel would not have been a flop."

And he probably felt that if the agency hadn't lost the 1964 presidential account, Goldwater would have won. He had that kind of confidence. While I doubt any campaign could have elected Goldwater, Leo would have approached the effort with the same dedication he brought to everything; for his attitude toward any job was grounded in the same ethic of hard work and honest conviction that drove the rest of the Burnetts.

With all his stuffy Republicanism, there was a democracy about the man. Following the morning we had trudged around his swamp together, the night after he'd told me to "go to Russia," he took me into Chicago on the commuter train, treated me to coffee and a Danish, slipped me a twenty-dollar bill, and put me in a taxi to the Greyhound bus which would take me to New York.

His democracy went far beyond family. "Leo often lunched at the counter downstairs in the Prudential Building," said a *Wall Street Journal* ad, celebrating the agency's fiftieth year. "It was a familiar scene: Leo standing behind a secretary, waiting for her to finish her sandwich and yield her place, so he could sit down and order. This was the distinguished advertising man, Mr. Leo Burnett, who could have had the best table in the city and the attention of five maitre d's for the asking. But Leo didn't like to be conspicuous. Besides, he had to get back upstairs quick—to get out the ads."

Even when I first knew him, Leo saw himself as an ecologist. I saw him as playing country squire. Perhaps I was mistaken, for during his later years, he became more and more concerned with ecology. Population, urbanization, and industrialization he saw as "the real culprits." And he recognized the interdependence of life systems and the environment: plants renewing the air, air purifying water, water irrigating plants, and man, as a part of nature, learning to work with it instead of trying to "master" it. A public interest ad in *Time* in November 1969 summed up his feelings:

> Mankind as a species needs esthetic as well as physical values— sweet rivers to walk by in solitude and serenity, and pleasant prospects even in the midst of industrial affluence. The constant din of urban life assails the ears relentlessly, and noise contributes its own ugly obbligato to the disharmony of our surroundings.
>
> "The world is too much with us, late and soon," as Wordsworth prophetically put it more than a century ago, "Getting and spending, we lay waste our powers."
>
> We have laid waste our powers for too long, not merely by ignoring the warnings of dead lakes and noxious air and ravaged countrysides, but also by periodically killing off our bravest and our best in senseless warfare.
>
> Now is the time for all good men to come to the aid of their planet.
>
> We have the technical skill and resources. We have a common

cause worth fighting for: a new kind of war to make the world safe for humanity against its own worst instincts.

Perhaps this mighty global struggle to restore the quality of our human environment may provide an effective and inspired substitute for national conflict and bloodshed.

Perhaps only a planetary view of man can guarantee our survival.

We have the weapons that enable us all to die together; can we not forge the tools that enable us all to live together?

Sounds almost revolutionary. Were Leo and Pop on the same track? Not likely. Leo saw population, urbanization, and industrialization as evils unto themselves. Pop would have argued that the drive for corporate profits, with but secondary concern for quality of life, was the seed from which these untrimmed weeds grew in the first place.

From his own father, Noble Burnett, Leo picked up a love of the outdoors and a respect for nature. In his ad for *Time*, he was passing it on. He and Pop saw different ways of achieving the same ends, but the ends were basically the same.

⁓

Much of what I learned about Leo came secondhand. That he was a terrible driver, that he once backed out of the garage without opening the door (leaving Naomi to explain to the carpenters), that he once jumped into a cab and said, "Prudential Building, fifteenth floor," all seem entirely believable. His mind was a beehive of perpetually buzzing ad campaigns.

Leo's mission was "to produce the best advertising in the world, bar none . . . advertising so interrupting, so daring, so fresh, so engaging, so human, so believable, and so well-focused as to themes and ideas, that at one and the same time, it builds a quality reputation for the long haul as it produces sales for the immediate present."

While his politics and his ability to find satisfaction in helping to sell products were anathema to me, I learned to respect his openness to ideas, his tenacious loyalty to what he believed in, and his willingness to give anyone the benefit of the doubt.

Leo brought integrity to his work. He was part of a vast creative

Leo (left) before he became a lion, with brother Verne and sister Mary (Mom) in St. Johns, Michigan, 1899.

process influencing hundreds of millions. He was honest in the way he went about it. And even with our sparse contact, some of that honesty rubbed off on me. His kick in the pants over the two suits paid off, and though if I'd seen him more often, we would have squabbled over dozens of earthshaking issues, I've come to understand that at heart he believed in people. We have that in common, and I believe that's a big part of what makes family.

I last saw Leo a year or so before he died in 1971. I'd been hired to animate a short film for a studio near Chicago and went back twice, once for consultation, then later that summer to do the actual work. Leo and Naomi were in their late seventies then. Though Leo worked at home three days a week, most jobs around the farm were handled by Esteban (I never knew his last name), a gentle migrant laborer who had knocked on their door ten years earlier, seeking employment. After working the farm most of each year, Esteban took off for a month or two to visit his family in Mexico. Two or three martinis had mellowed my aunt (one night when Leo was away), and she became reflective. Playing the loyal wife, she said, sometimes got to her. Much as she obviously loved Leo, there was a sense that the role had somehow restricted her life. She talked about how difficult it had become to manage the farm and about them both growing old. Without Esteban, she felt, they'd be helpless; they wouldn't be able to survive.

"Maybe I should shoot Esteban," she said, laughing. Then she thought for a moment and added with a mischievous grin, "No, maybe I should shoot Leo."

On his formal "retirement" in 1967 (he still went to the office four days a week), Leo made a speech to co-workers, acknowledging that they or their successors might someday want to take his name off the door and call the agency, "'Twain, Rogers, Sawyer and Finn, Inc.,' or 'Ajax Advertising,' or something." That would be OK, he said; but then he went on, speaking in the "medium low rumble that was the most imposing voice he could muster," to tell them when he might *demand* that his name be taken off the door:

> That will be the day when you spend more time trying to make money and *less* time making advertising—our kind of advertising.
>
> When you forget that the sheer fun of ad-making and the lift you get out of it—the creative climate of the place—should be as important as money to the very special breed of writers and artists and business professionals who compose this company of ours—and make it tick.
>
> When you lose that restless feeling that nothing you do is ever quite good enough.
>
> When you lose your itch to do the job well for its own sake—regardless of the client, or the money, or the effort it takes.

When you are no longer what Thoreau called "a corporation with a conscience"—which means to me, a corporation of conscientious men and women.

When you stoop to convenient expediency and rationalize yourselves into acts of opportunism—for the sake of a fast buck.

When your outlook narrows down to the number of windows—from zero to five—in the walls of your office.

When you disapprove of something, and start tearing the hell out of *the man who did it* rather than the work itself.

There was more, but that was the essence; and he vowed that if such a day came, he would "materialize long enough to rub my name out myself—on every one of your floors." And before he de-materialized, he would paint out the star-reaching symbol too; "And burn up all the stationery. Perhaps tear up a few ads in passing. *And throw every goddamned apple down the elevator shafts.*"

A 1990 article in *Forbes,* citing the agency's continuing success (billing $3.2 billion that year), went on to add that although Leo had been dead for twenty years, "employees, who call themselves 'Burnetters,' say things like, 'That's what Leo would have done' nearly every day."

Little wonder that some suspect the Leo Burnett Company is run by a ghost.

ELEVEN

birder

Dear Dan,
    *Sorry about the delay in getting back to you. I was in
southern India till late February and then almost
immediately went to Cuba for a week. Missed the whole
war [Desert Storm]! Why it is that everywhere I go
they've just had or are about to have a coup, insurrec-
tion or revolution?*

Love, Phoebe

*While Imelda and Ferdinand Marcos were deciding
what to pack, Phoebe Snetsinger quietly was making
history in another part of the Philippines last February.
On a mountaintop in western Luzon, some 300 miles
from Manila, she watched her 5,000th bird, the Philippine bullfinch.*

ST. LOUIS POST-DISPATCH, JUNE 5, 1986

Who in their right mind travels halfway across the world and
rises at 3 A.M. to slog through Hong Kong's Mai Po Marshes to sneak
a peak at a migrating Spoonbill Sandpiper? What normal person
starts a climb at sixteen thousand feet in the Peruvian Andes in order
to spot the Diademed Sandpiper-Plover? And would *anyone* spend
three days hacking through Mexican jungle trails to reach the mist-
shrouded habitat of a weird-looking bird called the Horned Guan?

My cousin Phoebe would. And she loves it. And she is a perfectly
normal sixty-eight-year-old woman with a sound, but intensely
curious, mind. She is also the mother of four grown children, the wife
of a retired poultry research expert (he's a topnotch magician and

ventriloquist, too), and she lives in the all-American city of Webster Groves, Missouri.

Two more items:

In 1981, when the superficial melanoma that had been removed nine years earlier recurred internally, doctors told her the cancer would metastasize within three months; within a year, they predicted, she'd be dead.

Nineteen years later, Phoebe has seen more kinds of birds than any person in the history of the world.

Phoebe is my favorite cousin. She instantly became my favorite when David and I stopped off in Chicago for a few hours between trains on our second trip to California, in 1946.

I was almost fourteen and Phoebe was sixteen. No girl I'd met till then was so soft-spoken, focused, interested in talking with David and me, and at the same time so "in the moment." Though I could never have articulated it in that way at the time, looking back, it's clear that others were flighty by comparison.

Off we went to the Museum of Science and Industry. An elevator took us deep into a simulated mine, where we boarded a coal car and chugged through a dimly lit tunnel. Later, we had lunch and chatted about matters now long forgotten. I remember a sunny day, laughter, and a friendly caring—from Aunt Naomi, too, but mostly from Phoebe. Here was another link in the family chain I felt missing since Mom and Pop's divorce.

I next saw Phoebe two years later. Homesick for friends in Poughkeepsie, I took the Greyhound bus east during the summer of 1948 and stopped off at the Burnett farm. Over sodas and sandwiches on the back patio, I sketched in my plan to return to New York after high school and become a painter. (Cartooning had yet to take a firm hold, and the image of Pop as a Bohemian writer in Paris in 1928 was magnetic.)

"What about college?" asked Leo and Naomi. I told them that I was thinking about not going; maybe art school. They clucked their tongues and pronounced this quite impractical. Phoebe became my favorite again. It was OK to be a painter, she said. It was even OK not to go to college if I didn't think I needed to.

The next time I stopped at the farm, Phoebe was away at college herself: Swarthmore. We didn't meet again for more than twenty years; I was busy discovering girls, learning the craft of animated cartoons, getting into left-wing politics, then starting my own family. When we did reconnect, it was during an overnight stop in Webster Groves on the way to Chicago. Rose, Joe, and Tim were along, we were in late and out early, and there was little time for more than a hug and polite chitchat.

In 1975, soon after Rose and I divorced, one of my first trips was an October visit to Missouri. Phoebe and husband Dave had bought a small farmhouse on 150 acres in the Ozarks, where Phoebe often went to be alone. Weekends, the family came out.

For five days, I traded Hollywood's anxious pace for the sylvan delights of paddling a canoe down a gentle river and discovering box turtles along oak-studded limestone ridges. The big excitement during my stay, an evening when Phoebe and I lay by a fire talking about my depressing love life (or lack thereof), and listening to the whispers of the gathering night. Suddenly, Phoebe sat up. "That's strange," she said. "What, what?!" I demanded, as I too sat up.

Far off, the blast of a steam locomotive. "That's the *second* train today," she said. "We usually only get one."

I snapped photos of distant deer, of socks drying on the line after the canoe ride, of the rusts and golds of a chill Missouri autumn; and I posed Phoebe and Dave—pitchfork in his hand—as Grant Wood's *American Gothic.*

Another three years went by. By then I'd met my future partner, Helen; but, skittish about too close a relationship, I left her behind and took son Tim with me when I went off to Phoebe's farm for a week in the summer of 1978. Tim poked into logs, rooting for copperheads (and had the good fortune not to discover any), set off a huge package of fireworks (legal then in Missouri), and barged into conversations with a fusillade of nervous chatter.

While she could tell my son he was being a pest, Phoebe had a way of combining her honest feelings with an understanding that he *was* fourteen after all and that it would pass. Looking back, I saw the same cousin I remembered when I was Tim's age.

Although Phoebe's passion for birds hadn't quite reached the rigorous pace it eventually would, she was already an avid birder, and her love of nature was at full tilt. ("Birder" is a term reserved for the diligent aficionados who seek out every species they can find and keep lists of what they've seen.)

While I was content to look on from a dry canoe, Phoebe plunged into waist-deep water in subterranean caves with Tim, who was in his spelunking phase. When he expressed curiosity about the planets, she set up her telescope so that he could examine Jupiter's Great Red Spot. When he connected with a party of St. Louis spelunkers to explore a narrow cavern, the kind you edge through on your belly and which claustrophobia happily keeps me out of, it was Phoebe's casual assurance that stayed my full-blown panic attack when Tim was unavoidably late for our rendezvous because an older man in the party had developed chest pains, and Tim and his companions of the "underearth" had to bring him out slowly.

For me, my cousin has been a lesson in patience; patience and focus. How Phoebe early on absorbed what it took me decades to discover, and how she became who she is, I've come to understand a little about. But even if I hadn't, that she *is* who she is seems enough.

⤜

During the late 1930s, I was busy learning to survive on the streets of Brooklyn. In suburban Chicago, Phoebe and her brother Joe were tramping around in Skokie lagoons, catching frogs and snakes and paying no attention at all to birds. Nor did they try to figure out what species anything was.

The Burnetts did little as a family. For Leo, the ad business was all-consuming—as birds would later become for his daughter. Phoebe's brother Peter, twelve years ahead of her, had his own interests. But Joe, eight years older, was delighted to have a tomboyish sister tagging after. He became her idol and role model. Though she saw him as an adult at the time, when years later she picked up a photo of him at the age when they had been mucking around after pond creatures, it stunned her, for he'd been a freckle-faced preadolescent. An amazingly tolerant brother then, Joe and Phoebe are still close today.

⤜

Nature and animals continued to interest her. She raised ducks and joined the local 4-H club—of which her future husband, Dave Snetsinger, was president. They went through high school together and married in 1953, after Phoebe's college graduation.

At Swarthmore, math and science absorbed her, and she thought about becoming a chemist, until she realized she was missing other opportunities, lost interest in chemistry, and discovered German literature. After graduation, she taught math and science for two years at a private girls' school near Philadelphia. She loved it and thought she'd eventually get back to teaching but never has, "since birds took hold of my life."

Back from a stint in the army in Korea (and after graduate school), Dave and the family moved to Minneapolis, where he became a professor of animal science at the University of Minnesota. In her mid-thirties by now, Phoebe had been a university wife and mother for six years. By 1965, with four small kids and badly needing some mental and physical diversion, a friend suggested she begin looking at birds.

She still remembers the fairly common Blackburnian Warbler spotted through field glasses that first fired her imagination. "My God," she thought, "that is absolutely beautiful. I had never seen anything like it, and at the same time, I realized that the bird had probably been in the trees in my own back yard every spring I'd been alive. It was as if a window opened up."

Two years later found the Snetsingers in St. Louis. As they were moving in, Phoebe discovered a Great Blue Heron, stuffed and mounted, sitting atop a garbage can next to the house. There could not have been a more fitting housewarming gift. She rescued the bedraggled creature, set it up inside, then promptly arranged for a baby-sitter every Thursday so that she could accompany local birders on their weekly outings. Before long she began augmenting local expeditions with birding trips to the West—camping and hiking trips "disguised as 'family vacations.'" She'd also joined the American Birding Association, was signing up for nature tours, and had begun planning travels abroad specifically to look for birds.

Phoebe was hooked for life.

I remember the day in 1981 when she called to tell me the doctors' verdict after surgery to remove the lump she'd discovered under her right armpit: malignant melanoma. It would spread to her liver, they said, or to her bone marrow or to her brain. She'd have a year—if she were lucky. I tried to mask my fear.

As usual, Phoebe had everything in focus. She'd been considering options, none optimistic; sticking close to the hospital, as her doctors advised; experimental treatments (with devastating side-effects), as the doctors also advised. These might prolong her life by months. And she'd have to put off a long-anticipated trip to Alaska.

But she'd also been thinking about another approach: doing nothing. She could simply take the massive doses of Vitamin C recommended by Dr. Linus Pauling and get on with her life. And besides, in Alaska there were dozens of birds she'd never seen. If she didn't go now, she'd probably never see them. This was clearly the direction in which she was heading, and like the rest of her family, I felt good about supporting her decision.

"You could just say 'fuck you' to the cancer, right? Say 'no' to the doctors?"

"Right. I could do that. I'm thinking about doing that."

"And just go on looking for birds?"

"That's what I'd do."

And that is what she has done for the past nineteen years. Off and on, I'd get postcards:

Dear Dan,

Home for a while . . . after a really incredible fall—Madagascar, Mauritius, Reunion, Seychelles, then home a week and off to New Zealand—wonderfully scenic, pleasant and easy country. Saw a wild Kiwi—*not* easy to do and a real triumph.

Dear Dan and Helen,

Just a quick note to update you. Back from a *fabulous* trip to Australia, New Guinea, and Fiji—but I left knowing I had a tumor, probably malignant, in my shoulder. Found it about the time Mother died in early July, but decided to go anyway—and glad I did.

During her first trip to Alaska, she discovered that birding took her away from thinking about the cancer. While it popped into her head almost daily, she learned not to let it run her life. When she returned from Alaska, she was feeling so amazingly well that she told me she was planning a trip to Australia. When she got back from Australia, she planned another trip, then another, and another after that (all made possible by a modest inheritance from her father, Leo). For nineteen years she's just kept traveling and gobbling down 12,000 mg of Vitamin C every day.

Phoebe's birding doesn't fit the stereotype of a tweedy dowager in sturdy shoes, armed with field glasses and a dog-eared copy of Roger Tory Peterson's *Field Guide to Birds*. Still, she's prepared. For a month-long trip, Phoebe goes through a familiar ritual: packing a few socks, cotton work shirts and pants, a canteen, binoculars, telescope, tape recorder, bird books, and gear for any weather, from balmy to treacherous. For a month, she'll need a large duffel bag; for a trip around the world, two.

Serious birding is not for sissies.

To see the Garnet Pitta, Phoebe and a group of companions fly to Jakarta then on to Borneo, bump along rutted jeep trails into a tepid jungle, then inch along the ground in a crouch through waves of ravenous mosquitoes. (Don't swat them, please; the sound might startle the birds.) Armed with a tape recording, they play the bird's high-pitched whistle. Nothing. Then again. Long moments, then someone spots an ice-blue eyebrow in a nearby thicket. The birders hold their breath, silent as an egret about to spear a fish. The Pitta appears, hops across the path, and then disappears. Phoebe and her comrades have come halfway across the world for three seconds of rapture. Wild with joy, they hug one another.

Now she is on a three-day uphill trek through the rugged mist-shrouded cloud forest of El Triunfo in extreme southern Mexico, then frantically racing, exhausted, farther uphill (after another party has spotted it) to catch a great view of the Horned Guan, a strange black and white turkey-sized bird with a striking red horn on its bill.

Now we find her on a tortuous climb along a razor-sharp ridge on Mindanao, hoping against hope she'll see the Philippine Monkey-eating eagle. As Phoebe and her friends watch, "an adult came soaring in from afar and cruised right past us with a monkey in its talons—an absolutely heart-stopping sight."

Phoebe, holding a stuffed doll
that looks like the endangered
Philippine monkey-eating eagle.

There was the time she survived a shipwreck on a coral reef off
Irian Jaya by hanging onto the capsized hull of an Indonesian
outrigger. And there is the incident dramatized so eloquently by a
profile in *St. Louis Life:*

> Somewhere in the dark lowland swamps outside Port Morseby
> in Papua, New Guinea, a middle-aged woman and her compan-
> ion sat huddled in the back seat of their rental car listening to
> five armed thugs calmly discuss how they were going to hack
> them both to death with their machete-like bush knives and then
> chop their remains into little pieces and throw those pieces into
> the marsh where no one would ever find them in a million years.
> It was near midnight. Several hours earlier at dusk, as the
> woman and her friend were returning from a sewage pond
> where they had been bird watching, they were stopped by a
> makeshift barricade across the road. Since that time, they had
> been abducted in their own car, taken for a long breakneck ride
> deep into the unfamiliar swamp, and with blade points at their

Phoebe changing socks after a canoeing and birding expedition, Missouri, 1979.

throats, subjected to horrifying abuse. And now the nightmare was going to end with the soft hiss and thud of the bush knives.

The woman, of course, was Phoebe. Her letter to me reporting these events was almost matter-of-fact, the abduction coming in at the very end. What was *important,* she said, was her sighting of the mysterious Kagu, an elusive bird few have seen in the wild, that she had spotted on New Caledonia weeks earlier. Citing her escape from the brutish Papuans, she told me how she and her young birding companion slipped out of the car, where their captors had briefly left them unguarded, then stumbled through savage wetlands for two hours in the dark, finally reaching the safety of a small village. "So much for the hazards of bird watching," she said in closing. (She also cautioned me not to tell her aged mother, my aunt Naomi, then still alive, about "this little adventure," because she'd worry.)

Phoebe has been back to New Guinea twice since then.

⌒

In 1985, the cancer returned; and again in 1990. Each time, a lump was removed and scans were done. There had been no spreading. Doctors don't try to explain it. Maybe it's the Vitamin C, or maybe a friend's joke hits the mark: "It's the constant travel," says her friend. "Jet-lag cures malignant melanoma."

Phoebe's "cure" seems to lie in setting and achieving short-range goals: one trip finds her chasing the Zigzag Heron; another, the Shoebill, a storklike bird; six more months and she'll reach a goal of five thousand birds. (When she did, daughter Carol plastered Webster Groves stop signs with "Phoebe is 5,000" stickers.)

That's how she does it—one step at a time. With a clear focus and patient determination.

When I brag to friends about Phoebe and about the vast number of "lifers" she's seen (birder shorthand for the first time you spot a new species), the question most often asked is, "How do the other birdwatchers know she doesn't cheat?" The answer, of course, is that they *don't*—not for certain. It's an honor system. But serious birders catalog new sightings, note information in their records, and dutifully report annual totals to the American Birding Association in Austin, Texas. And top birders know one another. They're often on the same trips, and anyone listing a "lifer" they haven't seen would be drummed out of the clan.

Birding, says Phoebe, is "an insidious pursuit. When you've seen the Elegant Trogon in Arizona, and then learn about all the other trogons and quetzals in the neotropics, Africa, and Asia, there is no stopping your imagination. And, of course, there is no end to this pursuit—ever."

My cousin is no mere "lister," as are some top birders, who, with middling knowledge, race from one spot to another, ticking off a new species after a quick peek. The real satisfaction lies in figuring out the birds for herself. She needs to have a mental image, to know what features to look for. Learning new species thoroughly gives her a "valid birding experience" instead of simply a list of check marks "representing birds that I could not identify if I saw them again."

By the time she's recorded a "lifer" in her card file, Phoebe has read everything she can about the species, written notes on important features, studied plates, photographs, or museum specimens—and finally, seen the bird to her satisfaction.

I know how she operates. I've been with her on brief outings, my trusty *Birds of North America* ready to whip out at the drop of a finch's feather. Phoebe spots a bird and tells me what it is. I check the book. She's right. She spots another. I check the book again. She's right again. By the time she's up to half a dozen birds, I pocket the book and realize that the twenty-five or thirty she'll see today (only one "lifer" when I've been with her) have long been intimate friends.

Phoebe's is a worldwide obsession. In America alone, sixty-eight million venture out specifically to look at birds. I enjoy them, too, and before we parted company in the fall of 1995, Helen dictated that I refill the rusty sink that waters the robins, jays, mourning doves, and woodpeckers outside our bedroom window on a daily basis; but unless I'm with Phoebe, I wouldn't travel half a mile to see a particular one.

The obsession seems pleasant enough—even necessary. Especially so when Phoebe tells me about observing a pair of rare Fringe-backed Fire-eyes in a Brazilian rainforest while chain saws roar nearby, or spotting one of the last thirty Mauritius Pink Pigeons, and the struggle of the Audubon Society, the World Wildlife Fund, and others, to safeguard their habitat. She's active in all these causes, everything from going to a "birdathon" in Hong Kong to raise money for the World Wildlife Federation, which wants to purchase a marsh near mainland China, to opposing plans for a golf course in a St. Louis park.

Anything for the birds—and thus for us.

The 1994 *Guinness Book of World Records* lists a variety of facts about birds: the largest nest, measuring nine and a half feet wide by twenty feet deep, belonged to a pair of bald eagles (*Haliaeetus leucopephalus*) nesting in St. Petersburg, Florida. The smallest egg is that of the vervain hummingbird (*Mellisuga minima*) of Jamaica. And the world's leading birdwatcher is Phoebe Snetsinger (*Femaleus WesbsterGroveious*), who by late in 1999 had logged 85 percent of the ten thousand or more known species. She promised husband Dave that she would slow down after reaching eight thousand. And she has. Just a bit. Maybe it's time. She and Dave are getting older, the kids are on their own, and he'd like to spend a little more time with her. Eight or nine months a year slogging through the eternally sucking mud of foggy wetlands might put a strain on any companionship.

Although other birders are hot on her heels, Phoebe isn't fazed by their pounding footfalls. She's in this for the sheer enjoyment and satisfaction of birding, not for the numbers. And maybe to prove something to herself—and to the cancer.

If she's home, she nests in Bird Central, the book-lined office just off her second-floor bedroom in the big old house in Webster Groves. Inevitably, she's planning the next trip—as from the corner, the stuffed Great Blue Heron, quietly molting, watches with a bemused tolerance of my dear cousin's mania.

I last spoke with Phoebe on the morning of November 9, 1999. I had called to check on how her "lifer" list stood, so that I'd have the latest count. The numbers were climbing, but she still had *so* many more birds she wanted to see. And she was excited, because she was leaving the next day for Madagascar. I smiled as I thought about her scrambling up yet another rocky cascade, catching a couple hours of sleep in a leaky tent, then waking before dawn to pursue some elusive and colorful species.

Alas, Madagascar would be her final journey. On November 23, after spotting the exceptionally rare Helmet vanga, my favorite cousin, Phoebe, who had been riding in a jeep with other birders, was killed instantly when the driver feel asleep at the wheel and the jeep overturned. Nobody else was seriously injured. Only Phoebe.

The news had me reeling for a couple of days. But then, I remembered Phoebe telling me more than once that something like this could happen. Given the choice, she would have much preferred to depart this life quickly, instead of from a lingering illness. Taking her leave while seeking more birds is, I believe, how she would have wanted it.

After the initial shock, I thought about rewriting this chapter, putting the whole thing in the past tense, but somehow that seemed wrong. Phoebe was always so alive. And I can't picture her dead, so I decided to leave it as it stands and as I knew her before that last expedition.

My cousin was a fearless woman—fearless in fighting the cancer, fearless in pursuing the birds. I celebrate all that she was. A snatch of dialogue comes to mind when I think about Phoebe, a line from a character in a buoyantly uplifting Australian movie, *Strictly Ballroom:* "If you live in fear, you live only half a life."

TWELVE

alvah: curmudgeon on the left

J. PARNELL THOMAS: *You are following the same line as
these other witnesses . . .*
ALVAH BESSIE: *I am following no line.*
J. PARNELL THOMAS *. . . which is definitely the Com-
munist line.*
ALVAH BESSIE: *I am using my own head, which I shall
continue to do.*
J. PARNELL THOMAS: *You are excused. If you want to
make a speech, go out here under a big tree.*
TESTIMONY BEFORE THE HOUSE COMMITTEE
ON UN-AMERICAN ACTIVITIES—OCTOBER, 1947

Alvah, you're a lovable pain in the ass.
MILTON WOLFF, COMMANDER OF
THE ABRAHAM LINCOLN BRIGADE

Pop was not always a curmudgeon. That started, I think, when
his dreams began to fall apart, when literary success began to elude
him and he was forced to make his peace with thMe political choices
he had made. While he never regretted those choices, while he
savored his role as a cantankerous rebel, he nevertheless thought he
deserved better than he got.

Thinking back on Pop's days in Hollywood is like watching late-
night TV. The close-ups are old friends. The players act out the same
scenes they did when I was a kid—in black and white mostly, with
splashes of Technicolor, as Fred and Ginger tap-dance across the
screen, or John Wayne wrestles a giant squid off some Caribbean
reef. Pinups of Betty Grable and Ann Sheridan on the wall of my
little room in Poughkeepsie dissolve into shots of David and me
gawking at Arab traders or Japanese soldiers crowding the Warner

Brothers commissary, or leggy messenger girls biking past in hip-hugging shorts.

Long before I read *Inquisition in Eden*, his acerbic memoir of those years, Pop filled my head (and anyone else's who would listen) with scripts about his movie days:

CLOSE SHOT: NARRATOR. IN BED. JANUARY 1943

He has his semiannual case of flu and is flowing from the nose, sneezing and coughing. The NARRATOR is trying to read Thomas Mann's *Joseph in Egypt* and is having an even worse time with it than with the cold. The phone RINGS.

NARRATOR: Yeh?
MALE VOICE: Alvah Bessie?
NARRATOR: Yeh.
MALE VOICE: This is Jake Wilk of Warner Brothers pictures.
NARRATOR: Cut out the crap!

He hangs up, picks up the book and tries to find the page, when the phone RINGS again. He lets it ring three or four times before he picks it up again.

NARRATOR: What the hell d'you want *now*!

It *was* Jake Wilk of Warner Brothers (whoever *he* was), and he wanted to know whether I would like to come to his office to discuss a contract for writing films.

For years, Pop had fantasized about writing movies. After meeting with Wilk, who offered a starting salary of $150 a week, Pop met with an agent recommended by a former classmate of his new wife, Helen Clare. The agent, Billy, called Jack Warner and arranged to meet him at the Stork Club that night. Then he said to Pop, "Tell me something about yourself."

There wasn't much to tell: Pop was drama critic for the Communist Party's *New Masses* (at thirty dollars a week), the only job he could find after Spain. He also broadcast for the magazine every Sunday morning (for free). And he'd been offered a month-long speaking tour for the International Workers Order, a mutual benefit insurance society and fraternal group, which would pay him a magnificent fifty dollars a week and expenses.

David, Dan, and Pop in Bucks County, Pennsylvania, 1940.

David, Eva, Pop, and Dan in Beverly Hills, California, 1946.

The next day, Billy called and told him to drop in at Jake Wilk's office to sign a contract. Then he reported a conversation at the Stork with Jack Warner that, writes Pop, "I would not have believed even if I had heard it myself." Claiming outrage at the $150 a week "the shit" working in Warner's New York office had offered Pop, Billy hit the ceiling when Warner told him that's what he had told Wilk to offer. "Bessie don't have to work for you for a lousy $150," exclaimed Billy. "He's the drama critic for a national magazine. He's got a house in the country. He's got his own radio program. He's got a best selling novel that would make a great picture. He's going on a nationwide speaking tour!" Warner allowed that he wasn't sure that he wanted Pop anyhow, since "I hear he's a red." "Warner, you guys make me sick," cried Billy, "The Reds are saving your goddamn moving picture business on the Stalingrad front tonight!" "You're right," said Warner, "I'll give him three hundred dollars."

Jack Warner would not always prove so magnanimous, and Pop's screenwriting bubble would burst within five years, but those years would include the second momentous event defining his life.

~

The Warner backlot was Wonderland when David and I arrived for a visit in July of 1944. Here were the sets and the stars that kept us glued to our seats in the rococo Bardavon Theater back in Pough-keepsie. In a private screening of *Robin Hood*, Errol Flynn leaped from a massive oak onto the Sheriff of Nottingham. We gunned down Zeros and Messerschmidts swarming over Burbank from the mock-up of a B-17, shook hands with Bette Davis, and watched a pulsing jitterbug being shot for *Hollywood Canteen*.

The summer was pure fantasy: Uncle Harry's Turnabout Theater; lunch at Lockheed Aircraft in Burbank (camouflaged against attack); a drive to Lone Pine, east of the Sierra, where a "mission" of the Civil Air Patrol took place. A squadron of 4–Fs and duffers too old for combat, the CAP flew off on weekends to scour the canyons around LA for military aircraft that had become lost in the fog. Pop wore sergeant's stripes and was the outfit's trusted "G2," charged with ferreting out subversive activities.

~

Dan, Pop, and David in Lone Pine, California, 1944.

Film studios were factories in 1944. Writers (actors, producers, and directors too) were on salary, assigned to pictures, worked nine to five, had their options picked up at the end of each year and usually got a raise or were dropped. Pop loved his first assignment, a rewrite of a script called *Brooklyn, USA,* and told the producer, Jerry Wald, he didn't see how it could be improved.

Outside Wald's office, his co-writer, Dan Fuchs, clued him in, telling him never to tell a producer that a script is good. "But it *is,*" said Pop, mystified. "Of course it is," said Fuchs, "But we've been put on to rewrite it, so it has to stink."

As I learned during my own forty years in film, Hollywood is still bogged down in the same self-serving nonsense born of fear. But in 1945, that discovery lay in the future. When I opened the big manila envelope and produced the eight-by-ten glossy for my sixth-grade class that Abbott and Costello had signed "to Dan and Dave," stardust still filled my eyes, and it masked the reality taking place at Warner Brothers.

The general consensus, down to the humblest technician, was

that a radical author who gave up New York for the movies had become a "Hollywood whore." At the writer's table, one of the Twins, Julius and Philip Epstein (with Howard Koch, they wrote the script for *Casablanca*) rose to toast Pop—with water: "Welcome to Warner's Concentration Camp," said the Twin; then, indicating the other writers, "Bessie, meet your fellow inmates."

At three hundred dollars a week, a private secretary, and the possibility of rising to a thousand-dollar salary ("What in God's name could anybody *do* with a thousand dollars a week?"), it was a pampered prison. As in any prison, Pop was warned by a parade of welcomers that even friends might stick a knife in your back. You could do good work, one director told him, but you had to play your cards right, learn diplomacy and politics. "You can't trust anybody," he said, "not even me."

In a dozen or so assignments at Warner's, Pop won credit on four pictures. I got a kick out of amusing my contemporaries by passing on his stories about them:

Northern Pursuit. Vast sums had been spent on a huge set for an abandoned mine. Pop told the producer it was too big for the half-dozen shots in the script. For this he was hushed up, told "that's how to get everyone fired," and that they'd simply write more scenes for the mine. During filming, Errol Flynn's inability to betray even the emotion of a gerbil on Valium over the brutal murder, by Nazis, of a fellow Canadian Mountie, was solved (after five takes) when director Raoul Walsh ordered the camera to zoom in tight, filling the screen with the actor's enormous eyes.

Objective Burma. Another Errol Flynn picture, about American paratroopers in Burma. Burma, however, was strictly a British operation, and Pop argued with producer Jerry Wald about it to no avail. At the London opening, the audience tore out seats and hurled them at the screen. The film was quickly withdrawn.

The Very Thought of You. From a Ben Hecht story that asked the question, "Should girls marry soldiers?" (since GIs might not return from combat). It premiered in Poughkeepsie, admittance with a war bond. Pop sent us VIP tickets. Rewriting a script that director Delmer Daves was unhappy with, Pop thought he'd get solo credit; and indeed, his draft brought wild enthusiasm. But when the film appeared, with "Screenplay by Alvah Bessie and Delmer Daves," he

217

learned one more lesson: as he turned his pages in—Daves had been rewriting *him.*

Hotel Berlin. An update of Vicki Baum's novel, *Grand Hotel.* Leonhard Frank, a refugee German dramatist served as technical advisor. When he and Pop weren't arguing about the current line of the Communist Party under Earl Browder, they were battling the producer over an inane story line: an underground leader falling in love with the mistress of a Nazi general. The producer, Lou, was adamant. With Leonhard Frank and his co-writer, Jo Pagano, Pop schemed to outflank Lou. At a story conference, Pagano started to tell Lou their new idea, then, knowing the producer wouldn't approve, chickened out. Pop leaped in: "The anti-Nazi underground leader *doesn't* fall in love with the mistress of the Nazi general . . ." (He could see Lou's face starting to purple.) "*But,*" Pop continued, shouting now, "he *pretends* to fall in love with her! In fact, he *seduces* her in order to get the secrets of the Nazi High Command!" Lou, beaming, sat back in his chair, slapped his desk and said, "I'll buy that! That I like!" Then, almost apologetically, he spread his hands and added, "All I wanted, boys, was the bedroom scene."

Pop's *Inquisition in Eden* is rich with Hollywood color: the day a Warner vice-president assembled every Jewish employee, marched in brandishing a rubber truncheon, "a prop for one of the anti-Nazi pictures we were making," and, smashing it on the table, demanded that everyone double their contribution to Jack Warner's favorite charity, the United Jewish Appeal (everyone reached for their checkbooks); the party at which Helen Clare, deep in her Martinis, batted her eyes at a PR man and asked, "What, precisely, does a labor relations expert *do*?" "My lovely creature," he replied, "it's very simple. The unions come to me and ask for more money. I say 'no'"; Pop's additional dialogue for *Action in the North Atlantic,* when, on arriving in Murmansk after a harrowing run through German U-Boats, an American seaman spots a husky Soviet stevedore (female), and says, "This is the first time in my life I ever wanted to kiss a longshoreman"; Pop and director Wolfgang Reinhardt writing Sidney Greenstreet, the fine fat British actor, into a remake of *The Amazing Doctor Clitterhouse* (*The Amazing Dr. Clitoris,* Pop called it), a ten-year-old film starring Edward G. Robinson. Their idea was scuttled by Warner's vice-president in charge of production (he of the rubber truncheon), who found their touching twist—Greenstreet falling in love with a pretty young girl—"Disgusting! Revolting!"

None of the credits mattered. As Pop and Helen Clare climbed out of their black 1940 Hudson in front of Grauman's Chinese Theater in March of 1946, expecting *Objective Burma* to win an Oscar for best original story, and as the crowds gawked to see if they were "somebody," his option had already been dropped.

The previous October, a strike by the Conference of Studio Unions boiled over when its picket line in front of Warner's was attacked by strikebreakers from the International Alliance of Theatrical and Stage Employees, armed with clubs, tire irons, and baseball bats. Warner employees threw blocks of wood and steel bolts onto the pickets from atop the sound stages, and the Burbank police cut them down with high-pressure hoses and tear gas.

The Screen Writers Guild contract gave its members no legal right to honor the line but did allow them to not go to work if there was a situation that might endanger life or limb. As chairman of the SWG chapter at Warner's, Pop, along with Howard Koch (*Casablanca, Mission to Moscow*), went down to observe the picketing. Jack Warner, looking on, decided that Pop and Koch were responsible for the entire strike.

Pop was beginning to think he'd been born under an evil star; two leaflets had been his only contribution to the strike. *Men in Battle* hadn't sold; *Bread and a Stone*, published a month before Pearl Harbor, was a dud. People were only reading newspapers. But as he sat in the Academy Awards audience, starting to doubt the possibility of saying much of importance in film, a fantasy was also forming that Bette Davis would tear open the envelope and announce (after a breathless pause) the Oscar for best original story, "Alvah Bessie and Lester Cole, for *Objective Burma*." He had his words picked out. He would march to the stage and say, "This is not my original story. It is Jerry Wald's. What is more, it is scarcely original. What is worse, there is not a word of truth in it, because there were no American troops in Burma, not even Errol Flynn." Then he would call Jerry Wald out of the audience, hand him the Oscar, and walk offstage to "the sort of reverberating cheers that would have to greet any such unprecedented display of integrity."

The Oscar went instead to *The House on 92nd Street.*

⌒

Pop was making six hundred dollars a week when Warner canned him, so for a time, he could still indulge in his big passion, flying. David and I went with him to Barstow off and on, where his friend Paul Pearce, a former actor straight out of an RAF movie, ran a small airport. Pop had begun teaching me to drive, and while he was practicing tailspins and Immelmanns, I was nearly tipping over his top-heavy Hudson on the gravel runway as I navigated wild hairpin turns.

And we still swam in the pool at Dalton Trumbo's antebellum colonial. Dalton worked nights, often in his bathtub, "sitting . . . cross-legged at a specially built writing table that spanned the tub, the water running in and out to maintain an even temperature, and a huge coffee cup on the table that was always full."

Even with projects for Columbia and other studios into 1947, Pop's savings and his war bonds quickly evaporated. His one decent paycheck was for *Smart Woman*, a screenplay for Constance Bennett; but the star bounced Pop over a scene he'd written, calling it "one of the most vicious pieces of Communist propaganda I have ever read." In it, a crusading young attorney has discovered that the local D.A. is a front man for gangsters. He confronts the man in a Turkish bath, warning him to turn over the names of the racketeers or he'll seek an indictment:

INT. TURKISH BATH
There is one other man in the room, a little fellow wrapped in a sheet, lying in a chair with an ice bag on his bald head, recovering from a hangover. His eyes are closed. The D.A. rises in high dudgeon [also in a sheet].

THE D.A.: (to the young attorney): You can't talk to me like that! I've been the district attorney of this county for the last twenty years!
(This last sentence is all that our little fellow with the ice bag has heard, and he too rises like a Roman Senator.)
LITTLE MAN: So, you're the district attorney, are you? Well, I've got a bone to pick with you.
THE D.A.: Don't bother me. Can't you see I'm busy.
LITTLE MAN: The woman next door to me keeps chickens. I came

Pop at Dalton Trumbo's ranch in Frazier Park, California, 1943.

down to your office to complain about it and your stooge gave me the brush-off.

THE D.A.: That's scarcely in my department.

LITTLE MAN: Is that so! Well, I voted for you, didn't I? (shaking his finger) I can tell you this! I won't vote for you again, and neither will my wife or my mother-in-law!

(He marches out of the steam room holding his sheet around him—though it slips momentarily, at the door.)

The scene, said Miss Bennett, discredited an elected representative of the people (the D.A.). It made no difference to her that the D.A. was *supposed* to be the heavy, or that the scene had come straight out of the original story she'd bought from Adela Rogers St. John, "a veteran Hearst sob sister." The scene was cut, and Pop was history. Worse, his agent reported that he was running into a "list" on which Pop's name had been placed.

Soon after, a handsome middle-aged man appeared at the Beverly Hills apartment Pop and Helen Clare were renting from director Edward Dymtryk. The man held a neatly folded subpoena, in blush pink, commanding Pop to appear in Washington D.C. on October 23, 1947, where the House Committee on Un-American Activities was probing "Communist influence in the motion picture industry." (Remember that sneaky line about kissing a Soviet stevedore?)

We didn't own a television in 1947, so in order to witness Pop's appearance before the Committee, I had to catch the big blue bus into Santa Monica, where the Criterion Theater showed newsreels of the hearings.

The circus performed for two weeks. A thousand sighing secretaries mobbed the House caucus room to get a glimpse of Robert Taylor. Gary Cooper, pressed to name scripts tinged with subversive ideas, couldn't name any, "because most of the scripts I read at night." Ayn Rand, at Warner's during Pop's tenure, testified that *Song of Russia* (MGM, 1944) was Red propaganda because "there is a park where you see happy little children in white blouses running around." Actor Adolphe Monjou, modestly admitting he was an authority on Marxism, vowed he'd move to Texas if the Communists took power, "because I think the Texans would kill them on sight."

While Investigator Robert Stripling, Chairman J. Parnell Thomas, and first-term Congressman Richard Nixon treated the "trained seals" (as Pop called them) with deference and respect and let them hurl gossip and innuendo at anyone they cared to, the atmosphere shifted rapidly the moment Pop's friend and fellow writer John Howard Lawson took the stand.

Lawson wanted to make a statement. Denied. Two questions asked of him set the pattern: Was he a member of the Screen Writers Guild? Was he a member of the Communist Party? He cited the First Amendment: if Congress can't legislate in the area of free speech, neither can it investigate. Lawson, Trumbo and Albert Maltz, who followed, attacked the Committee; it had no authority, they said, to pry into private association or personal belief. Like Lawson, Trumbo was forcibly removed from the stand, shouting, "This is the beginning . . . of American concentration camps!" (Three years later, the McCarren Internal Security Act provided for the setting up of just such camps for individuals deemed a threat to the United States.)

223

The next name called was Alvah Bessie.

Pop cut a dashing figure in the double-breasted pinstripe he'd bought for the occasion. Stripling quickly dispensed with the pre-liminaries. "We'll move on to the sixty-four-dollar question," he said. "Mr. Bessie, are you now, or have you ever been, a member of the Communist Party?" Studied indignance rising in his voice, Pop waxed eloquent:

> Mr. Stripling and gentlemen of the Committee. Unless it has
> been changed since yesterday, in our country we have a secret
> ballot, and I do not believe this committee has any more right to
> inquire into my political affiliations than I believe an election
> official has the right to go into a voting booth and examine the
> ballot which has been marked by the voter. General Eisenhower
> himself has refused to reveal his political affiliations [Ike had yet
> to declare as a Republican] and what is good enough for General
> Eisenhower is good enough for me.

Well! This brought down the gallery. Humphrey Bogart was impressed. So were Lauren Bacall, Danny Kaye, Ira Gershwin, and the dozen or so others who had chartered a plane to Washington to support Pop, Ring Lardner Jr., Lawson, Trumbo, and their fellows, initially called the "unfriendly ten." (Ronald Reagan, Walt Disney, and Jack Warner were among the "friendly.") Pop impressed me, too, as I sat alone in the nearly deserted theater that Saturday. He impressed me in spite of Stripling's comment that the Committee had determined that the Communist Party was not a political party, "but is, in fact, the agent of a foreign government."

The gigantic image of Pop on the big screen typifies the contact we had, a connection held together through brief visits or filtered through the media. During the next two years that was how it was. I'd hear him being interviewed over the old Philco, or look on from the third row of a huge audience, as on stage Pop auctioned off a necktie he'd bought in Barcelona in 1938 to raise money for the "Hollywood 10." Not that he wasn't there; he was. But he was usually bogged down with a dozen distractions. Like his letters from Spanish trenches, the connection seemed peripheral.

I got some static over Pop's appearance: from former schoolmates in Poughkeepsie when I went for a visit in 1948, from a high school PE teacher, and from Jefferson Machamer, a cartoonist whose girly gags for *Colliers* were famous in the 1940s, and from whom I'd taken drawing lessons. When I walked into Jeff's office, he rattled the *Los Angeles Times* at me and demanded, "What's this about your father!" Following my semicoherent reply, he wisely figured out that at fifteen I probably couldn't tell the difference between a Communist and a proctologist and groused that I was a dupe. David, then thirteen, got into fistfights when other kids called Pop a traitor to his country.

"Your dad's a brave man," said Nan Olman, my high school art teacher. And others were sympathetic: on his return from Washington, Pop found a kosher salami and a bottle of Courvoisier from his good friend, actor Lee J. Cobb. At the Beverly Hills post office, he handed over a five-dollar bill for stamps. It brought a *ten* in change. When he protested, the clerk winked and whispered, "to help out."

In the beginning, it seemed like everyone was supporting the "10." The night before he flew to Washington, Pop took David and me to the Shrine Auditorium, where Gene Kelly hobbled out on crutches—he'd broken an ankle, dancing—to chair a gathering of seven thousand. As the hearings ended, John Houston, Lucille Ball, Groucho Marx, Judy Garland, Frank Sinatra, Rita Hayworth, Leonard Bernstein, Burt Lancaster, and a long list of others spoke their piece on a radio program, "Hollywood Fights Back." There was a concert with Paul Robeson, one of Pop's heroes and a friend from New York theater days. (Pop often got weepy when he talked about Jesus, Lenin, Robeson, Jeanne d'Arc, and others whose deeds for the common people seemed to him larger than life.) Later, we went to a rally at LA's Gilmore Field. As the chairman recalled the titanic gridiron battles fought on this turf, he turned, and with a sweeping gesture, introduced "our team." Led by Pop, the "Hollywood 10" marched on to a deafening ovation—as I swallowed hard. When contributions were called for, we all waved dollar bills in a "sea of green." And when, "Charlie Chaplin gives $1,000" was announced, the crowd went wild.

But most of the big names soon tucked their courage away, along with much of liberal America, which rolled over and played dead as the Cold War took hold and a pressure to conform frosted the land. The day after the "10" were cited for contempt of Congress, the major producers announced they would discharge or suspend without pay any in their employ "until such time as he is acquitted, or has purged himself of contempt, and declared under oath that he is not a Communist." Some, like Bogart, quickly issued public retractions of their support. Others, like Edward G. Robinson, appeared before the Committee voluntarily to quash rumors that they were disloyal. Still others were subpoenaed themselves. Most simply shut up.

Over the next months, Pop came to Santa Monica every Sunday to continue my driving lessons. Terrified that my grinding shifts and jerky turns would send his clunky Hudson into a palm tree, he wore a perpetual scowl, growled at me to "stop riding the brakes," and in between, filled me in on legal action in defense of the "10"; or he'd tell me about the hard time he was having finding work.

One producer, Hal Chester (one of the original Dead End Kids), refused to be intimidated and turned up three jobs for him during 1948. "Of course," he said, "I can't pay you six hundred dollars a week." Over the next two years Pop brought in a total of forty-two hundred dollars. As in Woody Allen's *The Front*, scripts or treatments he wrote were sold with someone else's name attached. He outlined a novel, but the publisher wanted to see one hundred pages, which Pop, more and more depressed, felt incapable of turning out. He was scraping by on loans. (Among his effects, I found a list of debts outstanding in 1951: Gene Kelly, five hundred dollars; Dorothy Parker, one hundred dollars; Albert Maltz, five hundred dollars. Clifford Odets and John Garfield, he'd managed to repay.)

He consulted a psychiatrist about his depression. Years of "deep analysis" were required, the man said. This motivated Pop to begin his autobiography, which started at age one. He worked at it for five days, then became so disgusted that he gave up. His discovery two years later that the analyst was an FBI informer, six of whose patients turned up as "friendly" witnesses, was an aside. Somehow, starting to write about himself, snapped Pop out of his depression.

Finally, the time came when there was, literally, nothing to eat in the house. He *had* to earn money, but he had no skills aside from writing. He got an idea for a story, and he decided to approach "the Biggest Star of Them All." So he called Charlie Chaplin, arranged an appointment, and arrived at the appointed time "with a dry throat and a pounding heart."

Pop's idea was an updated version of *Don Quixote,* with Walter Houston playing the Knight of La Mancha and Chaplin as Sancho Panza. He would set it in modern Spain, under dictator Francisco Franco, "and what would drive Quixote mad, instead of the romances of chivalry of the 16th century, would be his belief in the clichés of the now worldwide American credo, which I had learned at my father's knee: 'A man is judged by the appearance he makes,' 'Woman's place is in the home,' 'Work hard enough and you will succeed,' 'It's not who you are but who you know,' etc., etc., *ad nauseam.*"

Chaplin was intrigued, but told Pop he'd be crucified if he tampered with a great classic; added to which, "I like the things I do to be my own." Pop could hear his salesman father's voice intoning another all-American cliché: "Never take no for an answer. Sell yourself! Put your foot in the door and don't take it out." But he had none of Grandpa Dan's bravado.

Tea was served. Chaplin read him sections of *Limelight,* which he was then completing, and invited him to watch while he played tennis; then he showered, put on a robe, and walked Pop to his car. "I climbed into the Hudson, and he shook hands with me and turned and walked rapidly away. I looked into my hand; there was a bill folded up in it—a $100 bill."

The one hundred dollars, which Pop added to his list of debts, didn't last long. Desperate, Pop called on his friend Lee J. Cobb. (Also a flyer, we had once come down through a hole in the clouds in Cobb's *Beechcraft*, barely avoiding a crackup with another plane that was ascending.) Cobb said he wasn't solvent, but if it was a matter of eating, Pop could send Helen Clare and Eva to his house for a meal or buy groceries and send him the bills. Pop wanted a loan. Cobb wouldn't give it to him. Pop got angry and called his friend a dirty name. Cobb's face filled with sadness. "I forgive you," he said, then, as Pop started to leave, Cobb added, "You're a revolutionary, you know. Go on being a revolutionary. Go on being an example to me." Pop walked out and slammed the door.

Trumbo had predicted it. Soon after the subpoenas were issued, Pop, Helen Clare, and Eva had driven out to his ranch in the Tehachapi Mountains north of LA. Over cocktails, Helen Clare asked of the impending hearings, "Do you really think we'll lick them to a frazzle?" Dalton took a long sip of his drink and said, "Of course not. We'll all go to jail."

In the winter of 1950, Pop came to see me in *Stage Door*, the senior class play at Santa Monica High. So did a talent scout for Paramount Pictures. Pat Paulo, playing opposite me (she'd been featured in *Life* as a California beach bunny), went for a tryout with me in tow. Pat got a contract, but I was told that my face was "too wide for the screen." At the time, I thought it had to do with Pop. Later, I realized it was my mediocre acting.

Pop's case had been tied to those of Lawson and Trumbo. Tried first and found guilty, their appeals eventually went to the Supreme Court, which denied a hearing by a five to four vote. Protests from Picasso, George Bernard Shaw, Vittorio De Sica, and from film industry groups around the world, fell on deaf ears. In July, Pop and his fellows left for Washington—trial, sentencing, and jail, a forgone conclusion. Along with Helen Clare and Pop's friend, actor Ned Young, David and I (holding a long banner which demanded, "Free the Hollywood 10"), joined three thousand others seeing him off at

Seeing the "Hollywood 10" off to jail, Los Angeles, California, in June 1950.

the LA airport. To Pop's astonishment, Lee Cobb's melancholy face appeared in the crowd behind the police lines. Three years later, he joined the parade of informers. As Pop hugged us, then started for the plane, David said, "Don't let them push you around, Pop." I was trying to ignore a screaming headache. On the way back to Santa Monica, Ned had to pull to the curb so I could heave my dinner.

The next day, I drove the Hudson into Hollywood to turn it over to the Screen Writers Guild; Pop had taken a loan on it that he'd been unable to repay. The day before, he'd driven it to our house. We sat talking, and David and I promised to write and to visit Helen and Eva. He'd had a few drinks, so as I drove him back to Beverly Hills, he rambled on about his days as an actor, talked about the senior play, and told me that he had a crush on Pat Paulo; and he ruminated over what lay ahead: "I don't want to go to jail, you know." "I know," I replied, "but you'll get through it OK. A year isn't really so terrible." "No, it's not a long time," he agreed. I don't think he believed it.

> Federal Correctional Institution, Texarkana, Texas/
> 25 November 1950
>
> Dear Dave: Or should I call you Sophomore B President, or Quarterback? Very happy to have yours of the other day, with the clipping about your exploits on the football field. . . . I take it next fall you will be on the first string—if you don't break your neck in the meantime. . . . My cold is all better, and as you may have noticed from the typewriter, I am no longer driving a truck. I am now the clerk in the store-room . . . and with this machine I type receiving-reports, inventories, etc.
>
> Dear Dan: I had a brief letter from you from New York on October 31, then, before I turn around, you are back in California. . . . Good to know you got something out of the short time you spent at the Art Students League. Did you get my last to you . . . ? With all the stuffy, fatherly advice? I won't be home as soon as we had hoped, but you must not worry about me; I am OK, if somewhat lonely for my kids.

He was trying his best, even from prison, to guide us through a hard year. With David working to fit in at Santa Monica High and me trying to decide what to do with my life, he made a big effort to keep up *our* spirits as well as his own:

> 4 February 1951
>
> Dear Dan, you irresponsible wretch. How DARE you lose that poem I sent you? And which one was it? I've sent four to you guys altogether. (All right, I forgive you.) Your cartoon of me is a gross libel. I do not look nearly as dilapidated as you seem to remember me. But that is not your fault either. And not only

have I lost 'some' of the 'stomach weight' but *all* of it. I am
myself again, if not 'dashing;' just sitting.

Your father, Alvah Bessie 5855–TT

Texarkana didn't turn out to be the "big house" I had joked about
in a letter, and after a few months, his duties took him outside the
walls. Del, a big, dimple-cheeked con man became his best buddy,
supplied him with chocolate, and turned up years later when Helen
and I were struggling to find investors for *Hard Traveling*, offering to
shill for us as a fund-raiser. We declined, remained friends, and began
to see why Pop liked him so much.

Pop read seventy-five books during his ten-month stay (two off
for good behavior). He wrote poetry, started work on what would
years later become a funny reminiscence of his teens, crafted marvelous wooden boxes from spent matches and LePages glue, and got to
know a lot about men whose lives he'd barely touched—young
blacks and southern whites, mainly, doing time for everything from
forgery and moonshining, to drug addiction.

In his last interview before he was released, one of the prison
officials told him, "Bessie, I've read your testimony and the others';
I've looked up the Supreme Court decisions in similar cases, and I've
studied a lot of American history since you came here. And I want to
tell you this: I understand you're some sort of radical—and I don't
hold with such ideas—but from what I understand of the American
democratic tradition, you *are* here on a bum rap" (From *Inquisition in
Eden*).

~

Pop's life after prison is a montage, his infectious patter narrating
every scene. Some shots are exciting; others, packed with frustration.
The first years are rough.

April 1951. Trumbo and a few others are writing on the black
market when David and I meet Pop at the airport. Lacking important
credits, his movie career dead, Pop lands an assistant editor's job on
The Dispatcher, house organ of Harry Bridges' dockworker's union in
San Francisco. The work is often dull and demanding, but Eva and
Helen Clare have to be supported. The job pays $125 a week, not
enough to cover the bills.

January 1952. Pop meets me at the ship when I return from a

forty-day trip to the orient, working as a galley hand on the *President Wilson*. A chain-smoker, he approves of the lighter with an embossed tiger I bought for him in Hong Kong. McCarthyism is in full swing, and my being the only crewmember strip-searched for narcotics is no coincidence. I hang around the city for a few weeks, working nights loading Folger's coffee into freight cars. When I walk into Bruno's (where union officials meet for lunch) sporting my brand new longshoreman's cap, Harry Bridges guffaws, and in his thick Australian cracks, "It'll tyke more'n that t' myke a woiker outa you." I do *not* appreciate Pop's laugh.

While he edits *The Heart of Spain* that year, an anthology of Spanish Civil War writing issued by the Veterans of the Lincoln Brigade, a teapot-tempest swirls around the efforts of Pop and others to include authors such as Orwell, Malraux, and Hemingway, whom the vets deem politically incorrect.

January 1953. Pop drives to Los Angeles for my wedding to Rose Kuras. I have adopted his politics by now, even as his own commitment to the Communist Party (unbeknownst to me) has begun to slip.

June 1955. Another subpoena; this, from the Senate Judiciary Committee, probing "strategy and tactics of world Communism." Winston Burdett, CBS reporter and a friend from his days on *The Brooklyn Eagle*, shows up to testify that Pop had been the main influence in getting him to join the Party. Asked to identify a flock of people he'd known on the *Eagle* as Communists, Pop takes the Fifth Amendment.

A month later he's in Santa Monica right after my daughter Ann Lisa is born and jokes that Rose and I should call her *Victoria* Ann Lisa, because then her initials will match those of the Veterans of the Abraham Lincoln Brigade (the group made up of the American volunteers who had fought in Spain).

Helen Clare has been drinking heavily since before Pop's time in jail. She is miserable in San Francisco and unfulfilled as a writer, and she and Pop have grown apart. Communication finally breaks down completely and they divorce.

1956. David is in the army in Korea, near the 38th parallel demarcation line (after the war). Officers harangue the troops about imminent reinvasion and keep them in a state of perpetual tension by racing them downhill, screaming and yelling, bayonets fixed, while edgy Chinese look on from watchtowers.

By the time Pop visits Rose and me after the birth of our first son, Joe, I have begun working in animated cartoons at MGM.

Pop also has a clever screenplay on the market. *The S Bomb* concerns a stripper who turns out to be the one telepathic earthling an alien race is able to communicate with (attempting to warn our silly little planet about the danger of atomic testing). It doesn't go anywhere.

With one of *my* big toes testing the Hollywood waters, Pop starts writing me about the chance of reinventing his movie career. Dutifully, I make inquiries about job possibilities. There are no takers. And while he's busy wishing up an assignment to rescue his finances, another of his dreams has been falling apart.

The Soviet Communist Party had held its 20th Congress in 1956, with Nikita Khrushchev's secret speech about Stalin. Early in 1957, Pop writes a letter to the American Communist Party, declaring that "after twenty-one years of organized activity, I am now an unaffiliated radical." The American working class, he says, "is further today from an acceptance of our ideas than it has been at any time in our history." The Party will get nowhere unless it can "prove that we are part of the mainstream of American life, instead of fancying ourselves as the 'vanguard' of a class that has rejected us." His ideas haven't changed, he adds, and if it comes to defending his beliefs, "I would not hesitate to accept imprisonment for them, as I accepted it in 1950."

His writing continues. That same year, his didactic but skillfully crafted *The Un-Americans* is published. Outside the Left, the few who bother to review this semiautobiographical novel do so mercilessly. Worse, reduced membership on the docks forces the union to cut expenses, and Pop is again out of a job. But not for long.

"Alvah, without you I am a myth." This, from nineteen-year-old Barbra Streisand, to whom he gave an elaborate buildup when he introduced her from his backstage booth at San Francisco's fabled *hungry i* nightclub. (She gave him an antique necktie box after her three-week stint.) Woody Allen, then equally unknown, and sympa-

Pop working as
backstage announcer
and light man at
San Francisco's
"Hungry i," 1956.

thetic to Pop's blacklisted status, was even more effusive, and vowed to give him a leg up as soon as he made it big himself.

Pop's seven years as light man, stage manager, and disembodied voice announcing the acts at the brick-lined cabaret and watering hole were a mixed bag. Grumping about the eighty dollars a week Enrico Banducci paid him, tossing caustic barbs at acts he didn't like, and resentful at the come-down, Pop was nevertheless completely at home in the milieu, and among the characters at the "i." He loved dropping names. A father-confessor to Kaye Ballard, he hobnobbed with Bill Cosby and Nichols and May, introduced Mort Sahl and Dick Gregory, ghosted screenplays for Lenny Bruce (none sold), and clipped columnist Herb Caen's "Baghdad-by-the Bay" whenever his name appeared.

"Professor" Irwin Corey, "The World's Foremost Authority," got him the job. In his baggy pants and tattered coat, the pint-sized Corey traded insults with everyone and bombarded women with sexual innuendo. Holding the stage until Pop threatened to drag him off, he also interceded with Banducci over Pop's weekly salary, until it finally edged up to $110.

Visiting him at the "i," I'd watch him amble on stage to adjust the mike. He'd flash a condescending smile and bow if some drunk suddenly started to applaud, then duck off to dim the lights and fade up a baby spot as he intoned, Moses-like, "The *hungry i* is pleased, proud and absolutely *terrified* to present the one and God help us the only . . . Phyllis Diller." He got a kick out of watching Sahl or Corey shake up audiences mired in the complacency of the fifties, and was on hand the night Jonathan Winters cracked up, began weeping, and told the audience his wife had left him. He motioned Pop to dim the lights. Then he flicked on a cigarette lighter and left the stage, mumbling, "It's Halloween, kids." At dawn, police found Winters climbing a mast on the gold-rush schooner *Balclutha,* docked at Fishermen's Wharf, ranting that he was a man from Mars.

Happily, night work left Pop free for a day job. For the *People's World,* the Communist Party's west coast weekly, he wrote features, film, book, and theater reviews (even though he'd quit the Party a year earlier). When few letters to the editor came in, he'd write them himself, often attacking one of his own stories to bait the readers. When nobody replied to that, he'd write another, vilifying the letter-writer, and perhaps signing it, "mother of three, Petaluma."

On visits to the *People's World,* I first heard Pop referred to as a "curmudgeon" by editor Al Richmond. But the paper was an outlet; Pop could tear apart what he didn't like (though he mostly reviewed what he *liked*) with critiques that cut to the heart.

Auntie Mame, he called "a corny vaudeville joke." The dialogue, he felt, loaded with such (then) risqué words as "bitch, lesbian, nympho-maniac," was the sort of thing that "titillates middle-class audiences." What could be more amusing, he asked, sarcastically, than a ten-year-old boy "watching with wide-eyed amazement the antics of his father's crazy sister and her drunk 'First Lady of the Theater' friends." Eve Arden (in the title role), he said, "doesn't even bother to stay inside the character for more than five minutes at a time."

By himself, Pop enlarged the paper's staff by four. "David Ordway" was the film critic (my brother David went through basic training at California's Fort Ord); "Jonathan Forrest" did book reviews, along with "N. A. Daniels" or "William Root." Under his own name, he wrote features on Spain, Hollywood, or the blacklist.

In 1960, Pop left the *People's World,* and in 1962, when a new manager was hired and "decided to replace a number of the staff with his own stooges," the *hungry i* left him. At the club, Pop's face, that of an aging basset, frequently got him mistaken for the British actor Sir Cedric Hardwicke. For seven years he scrupulously denied the allegation when some patron claimed to recognize him. But just days before he left the *"i,"* a man stepped up and said, "Your face's familiar."

> "Hardwicke," I said, not even taking the trouble to practice my phony British accent.
> The fellow reached in his pocket for pen and paper, then thought better of it. He said, "Are you up here to make a movie?"
> "Just the weekend," I replied.
> "I've enjoyed your pictures so much."
> "Thank you."
> He bought his ticket and went into the showroom, and I've been wondering ever since what he felt when I came out on the stage between the acts with the comedian's props, laid them on the piano, and raised the mike to the right height.
>
> from *Inquisition in Eden*

If he barely eked out a living, he was still a celebrity on the Left. In 1961, East German television hired him to dramatize *The Un-Americans.* Since no one accepted East German marks, he had to spend the money there. From Berlin he went to Moscow, where he met his greatest living heroine, Dolores Ibarrúri (La Pasionaría), leader in exile of the Spanish Communist Party.

Pop's affection for things Spanish—and his love for the French—combined in Sylviane Molla, a vivacious Casablancan of both derivations. They married in 1963. Sylviane cooked gourmet meals, kept a spick-and-span house, fed Pop's ego, exhausted herself supporting them both as a multilingual secretary during long years when he earned almost nothing, and endured his grumps (and he, hers). "She is the only woman who has ever understood me," he often said. Sylviane doted on his gentle love, basked in his reflected glory at endless appearances reaffirming his status as a martyr of the literary Left, and soothed the guilt he professed over his inability to support her. While his concern over her demanding job was genuine, that very job left him free to keep at his writing and his voluminous correspondence.

"He was not always easy to live with," Sylviane told me after he died, "but I loved him, and I still miss him."

By early 1962, David had moved to San Francisco, and was working as a physical therapist. The blacklist had been cracked. Trumbo and Ring Lardner Jr. were working under their own names. Others were working, too, and Macmillan gave Pop a contract for *Inquisition in Eden*, which came out in 1965. Meanwhile, we kept up hot political arguments through the mail, for I hadn't quite soured on the Communist Party.

Part time, I was collecting campaign buttons:

> Dear Pop,
>   I *don't* have and have *never* seen a button which says, "J. Edgar Hoover is NOT a queer." If I turn one up, I'll send it. Do you want one that says, "Copulate for coexistence?"

When Marilyn Monroe committed suicide in 1962, Pop, furious and brokenhearted over what he felt Hollywood had done to a woman just realizing her creative potential—and on whom he had a crush—began making notes for *The Symbol*, which Bennett Cerf published in 1966. Assumed to be the inside dope on Marilyn's life (which Pop hadn't intended), it was widely panned as "tasteless titillation," or "the junkiest literary insult of all seasons."

A few critics understood what he was trying to say:

> . . . his dialogue is as real as the shutter, the scream, the curse and cliché of inarticulate and passionate people. Most of *The Symbol* is frankly concerned with the hoaxmakers and celluloid rainbow chasers peddling their fleshpots of gold on the far side of paradise.
>
> Sibyl Farson, Worcester, Mass. Telegram

> Mr. Bessie's deep knowledge of the métier is everywhere in evidence. We have an exciting addition to the small number of those good books about our mythic creatures.
>
> Wirt Williams, *The New York Times*

And Hemingway's former wife, Martha Gellhorn, reviewing for the *St. Louis Post-Dispatch*, called it "a superb feat of the imagination . . . a magical achievement. There is not a cardboard figure or a canned voice in the novel."

The excitement of receiving a large paperback advance (a million copies were printed) helped bring on Pop's first heart attack the next day, but also bought a couple years of financial security. Probing many of the same social issues he dealt with in *Dwell in the Wilderness,* and *Bread and a Stone, The Symbol* dealt with an individual struggling to make sense of a way of life she felt was destroying her but couldn't live without. Growing up in the Bessie family, loathing his father and the world he represented, and adrift in political rebellion, Pop found it easy to write about loneliness and alienation.

In *The Symbol,* he was still shucking off the nightmare years and getting back at the "hoaxmakers and celluloid rainbow chasers" who had slammed the door on him in 1947.

The scenes keep playing. He's dismissed from his last fulltime job, PR man for the San Francisco Film Festival, run by "a monster . . . who is permitted by his father to run six movie houses"; he meets Spanish director Jaime Camino, who becomes a close friend and flies him to Spain in 1967 to write *Espana Otra Vez,* the story of an American vet returning after the war. The film becomes Pop's first produced feature since Hollywood, and amazingly, even with Franco still alive, it is Spain's Academy Award nominee for 1968. Pop, a perpetual ham, writes himself a part. Later, he writes *Spain Again,* chronicling his return to the battlefields of 1938 and his search for the grave of Aaron Lopoff, his comrade who died there. The search is futile, but friends in Barcelona promise to keep looking. After returning home, a letter arrives saying that bodies originally buried in that area "had been removed" from a mass, unmarked grave. "I was puzzled by that phrase," he wrote, "until I remembered that other Brigade men who had visited Spain since the war, and searched out isolated graves of men who had died in action and been buried on the spot, invariably discovered that the local peasants had been caring for those graves for over 20 years, and placed fresh flowers on them regularly."

On the fringes of the industry now (directing animation), I got Pop assigned to a screenplay for a TV commercial company I was working for that had larger ambitions; and when I opened my own small studio, he wrote scripts for my educational films. His quick mind spiced the dullest projects. Example: a ten-minute film helping parents of retarded children learn how to toilet train their kids. He came up with the notion of comparing the formidable task of teaching a penguin to roller skate to teaching toilet training. He griped about the job to fellow "Hollywood 10" member Adrian Scott. Though Scott was mortified that Pop was reduced to such work, I tried to smooth Pop's feathers with the notion that the film made from his script, for which he earned five hundred dollars, was of far greater value than most of the zillion-dollar glitz being churned out by the big studios. He understood, but his pride wouldn't let him admit it.

In 1973, Dalton Trumbo became too ill to continue work on *Executive Action*, a screenplay about the murder of John Kennedy that I was co-producing, so I got Pop hired to create additional scenes; he was thrilled to appear in a still photo used in the film, posing in a Panama hat as a right-winger operating a seedy outfit called the "World Campaign against Communism."

And though I loaned him money (so did David), as he had loaned me money during my own harder times, neither of us was setting Hollywood on fire. While I was directing medical films to be shown in doctor's offices, *The Symbol* had been bought for television. And the small sum he earned for this sparked Pop's hopes (for a time) for a return to films. Hired to write the screenplay, the creative differences with the production company drove him up the wall. By the time *The Sex Symbol* was released as an ABC Movie of the Week (1974), he was pushing me to find more work, "because once the SHIT SYMBOL is seen on 17 September (IF it is seen, that is) and I have a solo credit on it as writer of teleplay AND novel, NOBODY will hire me but you, dear Number 1. I shudder to think of what it is going to look like now."

Outraged by the carving knife that producer Douglas Cramer took to his screenplay, Pop disavowed credit and wrote critics that he'd "never again sell anything I have written or may write in the future to commercial television." An empty threat; the networks weren't exactly camped outside his door.

As he predicted, *The Sex Symbol* was panned from Maine to the Mexican border.

Later, with another Spanish Civil War vet, Pop and I collaborated on a screenplay about Jim Lardner (son of the humorist, Ring). Lardner was the last American to volunteer with the Lincoln Brigade, and probably the last to be killed, on the very night before the Lincolns were withdrawn. Jane Fonda (we'd written a love story into the script) showed interest, and for a few weeks the flame of Pop's triumphant return to Hollywood flickered again. Unfortunately, it quickly died: "Fonda is nuts if she can say—in one and the same breath—that the love story gets in the way of the main story, and that it is 'too political.' It is either one or the other. Hemingway's 'love' story sure did get in the way of the Spanish war in *For Whom the Bell Tolls* . . . Let's start looking for another actress" (Letter from Alvah to Dan Bessie). And so it went.

By the mid-1970s, the radical thirties and the blacklist fifties had become historically hot. One by one, the "Hollywood 10" were dying off, and Pop was frequently in demand by the media. He was still smoking and didn't give up his two packs of Camels a day habit until after his second heart attack. He and Sylviane were living in a tidy tract home in sunny Marin County by then. An admiring circle of friends dropped by, they had a swimming pool, and Pop installed a generous wine cellar in his garage—which I discovered on one of my visits (soon after he wrote to complain about how broke he was).

In 1980, Holt Rinehart and Winston published *One For My Baby*, a lightly fictionalized account of Pop's years at the *hungry i*. It sold poorly, but when Pop tried to buy up the remaining copies, he discovered that Holt had shredded them—in violation of his contract. The National Writer's Union sued on his behalf.

In 1982, he paired his best short fiction from the 1930s with a novella combining his comic adventures as a teenage herpetologist, which included a revealing look at his feelings toward his father. David raised money (Woody Allen contributed five hundred dollars) to bring out *Alvah Bessie's Short Fictions/The Serpent Was More Subtil.* Except for editing *Our Fight*, a second anthology of Spanish war material, and over which, at age eighty, he was again quarreling with the Lincoln Brigade vets, this was to be his last book.

Before these final efforts, in May of 1979, Sylviane's savings made possible a final trip to Europe, where Pop was on a pilgrimage to visit places associated with another of his great heroic figures,

Jeanne d'Arc. Always a romantic, he'd probably script it something like this:

EXT. COUNTRYSIDE NEAR CHINON, FRANCE

A stark day. Black, ominous clouds. A steady drizzle falls to the horizon as a tiny Renault approaches the ruins of the château where five hundred years before, the Maid of Orléans had rooted out the disguised dauphin and talked him into giving her an army to drive the English back across the channel.

A bald man of seventy-two and his handsome dark-haired wife—she's driving—slow to take stock.

BALD MAN: This is terrible. It's been like this all morning. It's going to pour any minute. Anyway, it's probably closed—or they've taken off for a two-hour lunch. You know the French.
HANDSOME WIFE: Stop bitching.
BALD MAN: But we've come so far. I've waited fifty years to visit this place.

Slowly, the clouds part. Shafts of light slant through—then the sun appears. The sky immediately above the castle clears. Pop and Sylviane park, climb out of the Renault and hurry to the gate. A bored attendant collects their thirty francs. They visit for two hours. Pop examines the rubble of the great hall where Joan recognizes the dauphin. He climbs the crumbling stairway to the ruined turrets. His eyes are moist, recalling her martyrdom. As he and Sylviane climb back into the Renault, as if on cue, the clouds move in. Gloom descends and the rain comes down in buckets.

"She did it for you, you know," says Sylviane. Pop raises a questioning eyebrow.

"Joan, of course," adds Sylviane.

Pop is too choked up to respond.

⌒

Years before he died, the University of Wisconsin asked Pop to donate papers from "my so-called literary estate." Though he sent them a dozen boxes, it fell to me to complete the job.

The collection was massive. He kept everything: a list of every address he lived at; another, of organizations he belonged to since age fourteen; get-well cards following his second heart attack; a log of every airplane flight he ever made—with dates, distances, destinations, and the names of the airlines. I found a book he stole from me in 1967 ("borrowed," he'd say). I sorted and categorized for weeks. There were film and book reviews back to the 1920s; articles from publications as diverse as *The Nation, Literary Gazette* (Moscow), *Rolling Stone,* and *Pets of the World;* tear sheets of a couple dozen short stories, and a hundred or more feature pieces: "Tragedy of Negro Doctors" (1942); "Sick Comedians" (1960); "Bette Davis: A Life-Long Love Affair" (1978). One story featured his pet iguana, Jaime. I discovered hundreds of letters, debating, discussing, reporting, cheering up, dressing down, suggesting film ideas, or complaining about the state of the world; communications with Studs Terkel, Melina Mercouri, and Jules Dassin, a dozen Lincoln vets, authors, editors and publishers from Paris to Tokyo, and to all of the "Hollywood 10." As astounding as was the volume, more astounding was that he did it all *sans* computer, pecking away with two fingers at up to eighty-five words a minute with a high degree of accuracy.

In his eightieth year he was still a rebel, appearing on college campuses to speak about Spain or Hollywood, protesting Marin County utility rate hikes, or chopping Ronald Reagan down to size in a Letter to the Editor, characterizing the president as a "crinkly-eyed 'charismatic' ham who is always 'on' and whose copy-book philosophy dates from the time of McKinley."

⌒

I last saw Pop the day before he died. Helen and I had stopped at his house on our way north of San Francisco for a weekend away from the pressure of trying to get *Hard Traveling* distributed. An ambulance was parked in the drive. Chest pains had kept him awake all night, and paramedics were hovering about. We followed to the hospital then waited while he was checked and got a dose of oxygen. Immediately, he became his feisty self.

"I want to go home," he said. He wanted to go to Greece, too, he later told Sylviane. (Another lifelong dream.) Shortly after Helen and I got home the next evening, we got a call saying that Pop had died of a massive heart attack. It was July 21, 1985.

The following day, word came that the Writer's Union had won

Pop as I like to remember him, San Francisco, about 1970.

its damage suit on Pop's behalf against Holt Rinehart and Winston for shredding the remaining copies of *One For My Baby*. He couldn't cheat death long enough to savor the victory, or to visit Greece—and he'd long since resigned himself to forgoing the doctor's career his father had denied him. But he would have gloated over that last literary triumph. And in a way, he got even with Grandpa Dan; years before, Pop had made arrangements to donate his body to the medical school at the University of California.

Long after he died, whenever the phone rang, I expected to pick up and hear that sardonic yet vulnerable voice wanting to know what was new, how I was, how "Ochichona" (big brown eyes)—his name for Helen—was, and when we were coming to visit. There would be the crusty edge, of course, the peculiar combination of someone who "hated men, but loved mankind" (David's words). There would be the infectious raconteur, the self-involved, loquacious personality who never stopped feeling that he had to entertain.

But mainly I remember the other side.

If AT&T *had* somehow managed to put him through from the Great Beyond, I would have told him what I never did in so many words: "Pop, when you wove Ed Sloan out of Harold Frisbie's cloth in *Bread and a Stone,* you created a character that never fought in Spain, never wrote movies, never spat in the eye of small-minded congressmen, never left behind a rich literary legacy or got a chance to play a small but important role in the history of his time, as did you. But you had the ability to transcend the huge personal and intellectual gulf that separated you from Sloan; you somehow conveyed his essential decency. You understood that like most people, all he wanted was a chance. That's a gift. That's the measure of your humanity and your craft. With all the grumbles over what you think your time on Earth *should* have been, I celebrate who you were, a man who never let go of his dedication to trying to make life better for everyone."

While Helen and I were filming *Hard Traveling,* Pop's health was on a downhill slide. He tried not to talk about it (too much). And he vowed more than once, "I won't die until the picture is finished." And he didn't. He saw it three times, and at each screening, when I peeked to see his reaction, tears were streaming down his face. A sentimental curmudgeon to the end.

THIRTEEN

love and posters

Being stoned is like walking into a symphony concert without knowing you bought a ticket.
EVA CHRISTINE BESSIE WILSON,
FROM HER UNPUBLISHED AUTOBIOGRAPHY,
RED DIAPER BABY

What started less than a year ago as a San Francisco graphic gasp now has the makings of a national revolution. Wes Wilson . . . started it all . . . by designing his wedding invitation á la acid-art nouveau.
THE VILLAGE VOICE, DECEMBER 22, 1966

Wes Wilson began creating posters for Bill Graham's folk-rock happenings at the Fillmore Auditorium soon after he and my half-sister, Eva, married in 1965. The graphics spawned by their wedding invitation were ripped from walls and telephone poles, to reappear in student pads across America. Graham complained that after tacking up 150 posters along Berkeley's Telegraph Avenue, and then stopping for a cup of coffee, when he drove back down the street, only three were left. At San Francisco State College, the advertising office of the student newspaper was broken into, and the posters covering the walls—nothing else—were stolen. Within a year, museums were starting to collect them, half a dozen artists besides Wes were soon creating their own versions, and the Fillmore alone was distributing three thousand posters and six thousand handbills for every dance.

Seldom directly political, the art created by Wes and his contemporaries, Mouse, Alton Kelly, Rick Griffin, and Victor Moscoso nevertheless reflected the generational shifts taking place around the war in Vietnam and the death of hope triggered by the murder of John Kennedy. At first, the posters were created simply to advertise; but to the mobs of young people rocking the night away at the Fillmore or the Avalon Ballroom, the fantastical designs said something more. They were, as writer John Thompson says, part of a "cultural explosion in the mid-sixties, when the baby boomer generation rose phoenix like from the ashes of World War II, coming to age with a roar of creativity."

Wes and the others were expressing *visually* what Janis Joplin, the Grateful Dead, and the Quicksilver Messenger Service were *musically.* Not just trippy designs to help Bill Graham line his pockets (though they did that, too), the posters turned out by Wes and his fellows "were widely accepted as radical manifestos of a revolutionary spirit."

Revolutionary is as revolutionary does. I had my own political agenda. And while moved by the insurgent nature of the art and the music, I was never a part of it, being too long saturated with Van Gogh's sunflowers, Kate Smith singing "White Cliffs of Dover," and other aspects of an eclectic cultural bequest from Mom and Pop.

The blend of religion, rebellion, and psychedelics that reflected the sixties hit its stride in one of Wes' early posters for the Family Dog, a "metaphoric association of free spirits" that originally presented vanguard groups such as The Charlatans, The Great Society, and The Jefferson Airplane. It shows the group's adoptive father, a supremely cool, pipe-smoking Indian with a top hat, and a legend on his chest—a legend that took hold of so many—Wes and Eva among them:

> MAY THE BABY JESUS
> SHUT YOUR MOUTH
> AND OPEN YOUR MIND

Watching a colicky infant sister having her diapers changed is less than a thrill for most ten- or twelve-year-old boys, so when David and I arrived in California in 1944, we did what any ten- and twelve-year-olds did: we gawked, told Pop and Helen Clare that Eva was "kinda cute," then ducked out in favor of more Huck Finn-like excitement, such as catching tree frogs in the backyard.

Helen Clare, who, says Eva, "looked like a cross between Bette

Davis and Tallulah Bankhead [and] talked like both of them," started out to become a concert pianist, then went to New York in the 1930s and broke into publishing. Pop won her, Helen Clare once told me, with his "deep books" look. While the promise of intellectual gymnastics may have dazzled her, I suspect Pop's pursuit was inspired less by the prospect of sparring over Marx or Kafka than by the bedroom possibilities he saw in this gorgeous blonde, who also happened to be a witty match for himself.

Eva, who ascribes psychological motives to much of Pop's radicalism, wrote a reflective and often revealing account of her childhood with Pop and Helen Clare, her marriage to Wes, their days in San Francisco and Marin County, and the beginning of a new life in Missouri. After her teens, I had connected with Eva infrequently. Twelve years, long miles, and a hundred interests separated us, so her memoir, *Red Diaper Baby*, helped me to understand some of the confusion she felt while growing up.

Helen Clare was thirty-five when Eva was born. Maybe because this would be her only child, and maybe because both she and Pop displayed such limited parenting skills, my sister was endlessly indulged. While Helen Clare played piano and doubled as the wicked stepmother, Eva, as Cinderella, directed Pop, as the prince, in family skits. She went to nursery school with Natalie Cole and Peter Stark (grandson of Fanny Brice). Peter's mother, she saw as bright and cheerful. By comparison, Pop and Helen Clare were sad and worried, their faces "etched with pain." While pressures of the Hollywood blacklist played a role, Eva felt it was her laissez-faire upbringing (as well as her parent's depression) that led to her retreat into fantasy, where demons could be vanquished—and also helped create a "hard stone" of both guilt and personal safety. She was never spanked. Everything was "explained."

I saw Eva as a spoiled kid whose parents didn't know how to handle her. In her own child's mind, the line between the real and the make-believe became increasingly blurred, and she often had a hard time figuring out up from down. She remembered coming down a long, winding, brass-railed stairway at Christmas, presents spread across the living room, beneath a tree that stretched to the ceiling. "There was even a note in the tree from Santa, saying I had been good all year. The little stone melted. I wasn't sure if I had passed the test each year."

When Pop flew to Washington to appear before The Un-American Committee, Helen Clare told Eva how Galileo had resisted the powerful in his day. Pop, she said, might have to go to jail. When he did, they moved to a cheaper apartment and made ends meet with gifts (some anonymous) from sympathizers. Pop became Eva's hero. She played songs from the Spanish Civil War and marched around the living room holding up his photo.

Helen Clare's drinking increased; friends fell away. Those that remained, like actor Ned Young, who Warner's had been grooming as a new Bogart, took the Fifth Amendment; and though they didn't go to jail, they were still blacklisted.

Ten months after Pop entered prison, Helen Clare, Eva, David, and I met him at the Los Angeles airport. He came down the ramp looking tanned and fit. Even though the daisies Eva had planned to strew in his path had wilted and fell instead in a sorry clump at his feet, Pop still thought it was wonderful. "*Everything* I did was wonderful," she said.

Pop toyed with several job possibilities: selling encyclopedias or expensive sports cars; but when an offer came through from the longshoremen's union in San Francisco, he grabbed it. Eva didn't want to leave her friends, or David and me, "who were more like uncles," or the warm, safe beaches of Southern California, "But it was an adventure, and I could enter my inner world and pretend some more. I could *always* do that."

Certain things couldn't be pretended away and were obvious to even a seven-year-old. Though she saw Pop as Galileo, the shadows around her parents' eyes seemed to be deepening. The cheerful lawns of Beverly Hills gave way to houses all crammed together, "tall and skinny, like old dowagers." San Francisco friends had messy apartments, "crowded with books and gloomy paintings." "Real people," Eva thought, didn't have books on Franco's Spain "filled with pictures of pregnant women hanging by their arms and legs," dead babies, and other horrors. "Real people" had *few* books or maybe leather-bound copies of the classics. "Real" fathers came home and pruned roses; Pop came home and "typed, typed, typed."

His job didn't pay enough to pay the rent on their sunny apartment next to Sutro Forest, so they moved to a dark flat in the Haight-Ashbury district. When Eva groused about the ugly neighborhood, Pop barked, "The people who have to live here don't like it, either!"

Helen Clare was also feeling the strain. She suffered from "heat prostration," saw lights flashing before her eyes, and kept drinking, which aggravated her hypoglycemia. Pop spent nights at writing that he hoped would add to their income. There were few squabbles, just tension, a tone of voice, and code words when Eva was listening. By nine, Eva felt the marriage falling apart (as did I, when I hitched up from Santa Monica on visits), and though it had never been stated, she was so sure Pop and Helen Clare would divorce that she began rehearsing how to tell her friends.

Pop making light of the 1950s war scare "devised by the government to raise the people's support of the military and hence the prosperity of the economy" didn't calm Eva's jitters over air-raid drills in school, panic at the Rosenberg's execution, or her terror that atom bombs might wipe out San Francisco at any moment.

By eleven, she found a refuge from her nightmares: Helen Clare had taken her to the San Francisco Ballet's annual performance of "Nutcracker," and, striking with "the intensity of Promethean fire," Eva knew that more than anything in life, she wanted to dance. Here was the combination of music, purity, fantasy, and radiance matching the daydreams that helped her to escape from her parents' crumbling marriage and from Pop's intensely political world. When Pop and Helen Clare finally separated in 1954, much of America was awash in a bland sameness. Mom, apple pie, and ponytails dominated television, even as on that same tube millions watched the Senate censure Joe McCarthy.

At home, Helen Clare, working now as a registrar at the California School of Fine Arts, continued her charge account at I. Magnin, bought the finest cuts of beef a slim budget allowed, sent the laundry out, and had a woman in to clean the apartment. Pop's letters after the divorce reflect his complaints, but also his hardworking attempts to keep his mounting bills paid and help Helen Clare and Eva maintain a lifestyle far more elegant than the $125 a week he was bringing in. They went to the ballet, the symphony, and to art museums—in taxis. And, while Helen Clare kept telling her they were "poverty stricken," Eva also recalls eating filet mignon and feeling "as confused as it's possible to be."

Early in 1956, Eva entered the San Francisco Academy of Ballet. "And I was a good dancer. The cross was, I had big breasts in a world of flat-chested bean-poles."

Though she'd begun to emerge from her cocoon, this was also the beginning of a long emotional estrangement from Pop. He tried to understand, but Eva hid her feelings. Marxism was no substitute for *Carousel* or *The Song of Bernadette*. Pop and Helen Clare, she reasoned, were sad because "they had never seen the Virgin Mary like Bernadette had." And she still saw herself as Cinderella, longing for a handsome prince.

With Pop working at the *hungry i*, Eva founded the Kingston Trio fan club, went boating with the Trio's Nick Reynolds, and hung out with a lively, artistic crowd. The "in" circle read Camus, Thoreau, and Kerouac, haunted the Coexistence Bagel Shop, refused to salute the classroom flag after Caryl Chessman was executed, and (if their parents could afford it) began therapy. By the time she graduated from Lowell High School, Eva thought of herself as a "full-blown Beatnik."

By college at San Francisco State, ballet was losing its appeal, and Eva found life increasingly absurd. With Helen Clare, she came south to Santa Monica for a visit. Cocksure of myself in those years, I suggested that if she wanted to "meet a healthy, non-neurotic boy," she should join a Marxist youth group. "I didn't stay long," writes Eva.

A string of disappointing suitors followed. She fended off older men trying to bed her, searched for a "bohemian ideal" at North Beach's Cafe Trieste, and fell in love with Blaze, a wild romantic who dabbled at painting and scoffed at paying work (which he was forced to take now and then in order to eat). They spent weekends in his sparse room, foggy mornings at the beach. Pop and Helen Clare were terrified that Eva would catch syphilis or gonorrhea—or become pregnant.

Blaze wanted her to hitch to Acapulco. Instead, they hitched to Sausalito. He threatened suicide if Eva left him, disappeared into religious retreats for days, then showed up again "filled with light and love," insisting they get married.

She didn't want to marry Blaze; she wanted to explore with him, "roam the city at night, pretending to be the people in *Black Orpheus*, and watch the sunrise from the top of Nob Hill." And his madness was getting to her. She wanted someone with soul, but also someone who matched what she saw as her own increasing stability. "All the souly people I knew were unstable. The stable people, with the exception of a few college professors, lacked soul."

When the news of John Kennedy's assassination was flashed, Eva, heartbroken, ran to Blaze for comfort. He'd vanished again. This was the kick in the pants she needed. Gradually, she began to spend less and less time with him, and more and more with Wes Wilson, a man who had just moved into the same building. With his dark hair, high cheekbones, and aquiline nose, Wes looked like a character from the Renaissance. He paid for her coffee and opened doors. "He was the first beatnik artist," she writes, "who was *also* a gentleman."

Breaking off with Blaze accentuated his bizarre behavior. He'd show up at all hours, pleading with her to come back, attack Wes with his fists, or Wes's apartment walls with karate-kicks. Eventually, he walked into the psychiatric wing of San Francisco General Hospital and said he needed help. "Relief," wrote Eva, "I no longer had to be the keel on our sinking ship. I had steered it into a calm, warm bay. I could rest."

Almost immediately, she began living with the gentle and immensely talented artist who had stepped out of a Botticelli. A beatnik Romeo and Juliet is how she saw Wes and herself.

⌢

They found a charming apartment with a picture-perfect view of the Golden Gate Bridge just above Haight-Ashbury and bought a Volkswagen bus. Wes had shelves of philosophy books. Eva had novels. Wes worked as a printer, and Eva got a job with filmmaker James Broughton. It was 1964: early Dylan, early Beatles, days at The Blue Unicorn and other pre-hippie joints serving coffee and poetry. They met Fritz Pearls on a trip through Big Sur, psychologizing as he "held, stroked, and hugged his patients. He practiced therapy everywhere; in the restaurant, nude in the pools, or sitting by the sea."

When they married in October of 1965, Pop brought Eva down the aisle, muttering, "This is an archaic tradition, giving the bride away." Eva loved it. Wes's father, a right-wing Republican from Stockton who hated Pop's politics, didn't show up; he sent a Bible as a wedding gift. David was there, along with Rose and me, and when we walked Wes and Eva to their VW after the ceremony, someone had scratched on their "Get Out of Vietnam" bumper sticker, the single word, "Why?"

> I was born stoned. Music activated it more. Or directed it
> upward, charging my batteries with super. I am a hi-fi person. I
> think I might have been called hyperkinetic. But with a natural
> grace that made it more pleasant than unpleasant. Thank God.
> From *Red Diaper Baby*

For me, the mid-sixties mean left-wing politics and looking for work (animation is in the doldrums); for David, mending from the rupture of a second marriage; for Pop, a contract for *The Symbol*; for Wes and Eva it's a time for raising kids, for endless discussion of life, endless lovemaking, getting stoned, and a time for the new musical wave, rock concerts. Chet Helms arranges the dances, Wes draws the posters, and everyone goes to the Fillmore and has a blast. The Family Dog is born; Bob Dylan entertains, along with The Butterfield Blues Band—and The Beatles. (Wes does a poster for their last concert, which takes place at San Francisco's Candlestick Park.)

Feeling herself carried along on a tide of energy, "riding the waves, loving the current and the flow," Eva sees Van Gogh's *Starry Night* in the sky whenever she drops acid.

It's 1966. San Francisco is becoming the center of New Age culture. Continuing the diary she began in 1955, Eva is high on pregnancy (acid can wait until later). She muses about Wes and other women but then decides they believe in free love, and that "love for others does not destroy the love we have for each other . . . I cannot be limited to one man, to the straight structure of marriage." Eldridge Cleaver has moved in above them, engaged to their landlady, who is decorating his room with African wall hangings and a zebra-skin rug. The Black

Poster by Wes Wilson for Bill Graham Presents program. Courtesy of Bill Graham Presents.

Panthers meet weekly (beginning at 2 A.M.) and play Flamenco at full blast.

Some of their friends become famous: Peter Kraemer of The Sopwith Camel (Eva's boyfriend for a time), a singer friend of Wes's named Janis Joplin. The watchword seems to be, "Drop out, tune in, and turn on."

But not everyone is in the same space:

June 15, 1966

> Last night we dropped in on Maria and Francisco. They are utterly missing the point of the Aquarian Age. Posters of Chairman Mao decorate their apartment . . . We told them of our plan to get a home in the country and they accused us of attempting to "escape from reality." . . . They are where my PARENTS were in the 1930s.

That same month, Eva graduates from San Francisco State with a degree she considers meaningless. Wes continues turning out posters—for Bill Graham now, who takes over the lease on the Fillmore "with money [and a] New York business consciousness." Media quickly catch up with the graphic changes reflecting the revolution in lifestyle. Wes creates posters, says *Life*, "whose wiggly typography melds into stylized images of girls akin to pre-Raphaelite vamps." San Francisco's *Examiner* goes farther:

> Not since Monparnasse has serious art . . . served commercialism with such coruscating originality. And what is entirely new . . . is its pyrotechnic calligraphy, particularly in the work of Wes Wilson, where lettering itself takes on the music's beat.

In August, son Colin is born. When *The Symbol* comes out, Eva decides it is "wooden" and that Pop's "visions of Marilyn Monroe and the fact she was destroyed by Hollywood are only true superficially. People are never destroyed by anything other than themselves."

Time comes calling for a story on the poster revolution and commissions a cover by Wes. *Newsweek* has to have one for their international edition. High on his fame, Eva is at the same time guarding her private thoughts. Wes, she says, is jealous of her diary, and they avoid conflict by spending time in separate activities: for Eva, theater and Anais Nin; for Wes, his art.

Wes and Eva, with their children, Colin and
Theanna, in Marin County, California, 1972.

Early the following year, they move to Mill Valley, for "a quiet
life." The *Time* article is about to appear, and they are invited to a
formal party at the home of a wealthy executive, where "people stand
around, drinks in hand, admiring expensive things" and where "we
were the conversation piece."

The war in Vietnam is heating up, and when eagle-eyed editors
discover a peace symbol lurking in the image Wes has created, the
Time cover is rejected. More rewarding is the first Joint Show of the
"Big Five" poster artists at a swanky San Francisco gallery, brokered
by Norman Moore, inventor of the microwave oven.

Later, Eva and Wes play roles in James Broughton's short film,
The Bed. In luminous shots taken in a sylvan glade, naked men and
women bounce on and off an ornate brass bed with a satin quilt, in

Wes's poster for a 1966 performance in San Francisco's Filmore Auditorium. Courtesy of Bill Graham Presents.

an improvised mock orgy. Eva, in a multicolored bodysuit, slithers down a tree toward a smooth-cheeked virgin male. (Unaware of their participation, I saw the film years later and, suddenly startled, recognized them both.)

Soon to move farther into the boondocks, farther from the Haight, Wes and Eva find that the culture still manages to intrude. When Wes, following his participation on a radio panel that includes Andy Warhol, invites the artist to come by, he never expects him to show up. But when Warhol *does* suddenly appear with his entourage, Wes, in flannel pajamas, is about to go to bed. Helen Clare is baby-sitting. Eva is at a play rehearsal. Warhol strolls in, sits (wordlessly), while his groupies roam the funky house. Ultra-Violet snaps the back of Wes's pajamas. Nico, long, slinky, heavily made up, puts on her own record and loses herself in the sound of her own voice. Wes, eager for creative feedback, shows Warhol to his studio. An art magazine on a table features a photo of a button proclaiming "Pop Art Stinks." "It does," says Warhol. Helen Clare, bewildered by Wes and Eva's life-style, keeps peeking out of the upstairs, appalled by the odd group. An hour or so of this quirky activity, then Warhol and his clan bundle into his limo and depart.

Transitioning through the sixties, Wes and Eva hold a house-warming with a naked party that "didn't turn into an orgy, but it was fun anyway." Eva decides that "intensely creative men like Wes often cannot tolerate their women to be creative, too," and thinks perhaps she shouldn't be married. LSD is part of the scene, and Christmas Eve at the Broughtons' finds Alan Watts trudging around in a long robe, talking about the "spirit of the age, the coming together of people of divergent backgrounds, the renaissance in art and music."

The summer of 1968 bring Wes a five thousand dollar award from the National Endowment for the Arts. He and Eva use it to purchase a big, old rambling house. But the poster boom is softening. Wes has broken with Bill Graham over the small royalties he's been receiving. His last poster features a huge serpent oozing around the Fillmore, a dollar sign in its mouth. Along with the NEA award, they keep their heads above water by sales of Wes's originals to museums and private collectors and by Eva's waitressing.

At The Old Viking, she dresses as a Swedish beer maid and

BE, so they should not be offended if someone reminds them of that fact."

With long, silent gaps, the bickering will go on for years.

There are plans for a commune, finally realized in their old Victorian, with the Wilsons shepherding a curious collection over the next three years. There is Ron, a macho punk, who orders his several girlfriends around; David, a fine poet, "hypersensitive to the point of extinguishing. He may be the reincarnation of Rimbaud . . . One night, I heard Ron in the kitchen, asking David if he wants to kill him. I think we need a healthier gang here."

"Steppenwolf" moves in and resolves his hostility toward the Establishment by building "exploding magnesium bombs to weld cable cars to tracks." Victor Moscoso (one of the "big five" poster artists) and wife Gail move in, then Midnight, a "nymphette," who "absorbs all the male energy . . . Hippies, writers, musicians, businessmen pass through to her basement room. Then they use the toilet and leave." She exists on Diet Pepsi. The Moscosos exit, to be replaced by a chubby dropout from New York who sweeps through in flowing gypsy robes, munches burdock root and seaweed, drenches the house in incense, and studies the sitar.

Eva quits work at The Old Viking, and they are months behind in their bills when her second pregnancy begins to show. Wes goes on trying to perfect his melded glass technique but has yet to achieve what he wants. Eva's diaries overflow with ruminations about the past and the present: long childhood nights wondering when the fascists will break down the door and drag Pop and Helen Clare and her off to a concentration camp, life "as a series of experiences imposed upon me by the universe," concerns about Helen Clare's heavy drinking. "I must banish her [from the house]" Eva writes, "until she's joined AA."

The restless search for meaning goes on. Eva has "accepted Jesus as my personal savior" and is semi-content with her role as "hippie housewife" when daughter Theanna is born:

> So here I am, big ol' Victorian house, set in redwood trees, in the
> magical, mystical land of Lagunitas, still riding on the high left
> over from the experience of fame, LSD, and the Haight, still
> living in the current of the energy wave created by the explosion
> of hippiedom, my house filled with people named Midnight,

suffers the owner's fat, hostile wife (who cooks) and the man's Saturday night ritual: getting drunk, then storming into the kitchen insisting that marijuana is being smoked. Eva pokes her head out, sniffs the patchouli oil, Swedish meatballs and onions, and assures him it's merely a strong scent. What she *doesn't* tell him is that his own daughter has been turning on.

Wes lands a wealthy patron and is able to concentrate on developing a new art form, melting colored glass to create vibrantly original images. Helen Clare, after a brief emotional collapse, begins teaching English as a second language. Eva spends hours with her diary, rehashing her life, her feelings about Wes, other men she knows, and about her mother, a person who "has a mind which has always been ahead of its time and unfulfilled."

Her relationship with Pop and his wife Sylviane is another matter. Chiding Eva for her "rudeness" toward Sylviane, disparaging the "love generation," and calling her "one of the most conventional people I know," his letters parry the New Age consciousness she throws in his face. All the forms of rebellion by her generation, he writes, "from the drug use to the alcohol and sexual promiscuity and sexual 'inversion' are forms of 'escape,' and rejection of this society . . . which MY generation went through (a part of it, that is) in the 1920s after World War I had disillusioned us all. We drank. We fucked. We ran away to Paris with or without money. We smoked hashish, opium; you name it, we did it. We drowned ourselves in jazz-music; the style then, Negro music; we went to Harlem and danced all night and tried to BE black because they were so 'uninhibited,' etc."

It is her generation, Eva replies, "that *externalized* the *internal* revolution which is RELIGIOUS, SPIRITUAL IN NATURE, and is going on in the minds and hearts of Truth-seeking men and women all over the world. It is so much DEEPER and SERIOUS than any press-invented label, than bohemia, which reminds one of the beat era, which I never liked—it was too depressing—and more intense and meaningful than non-conformity or rebellion." Pop is sarcastic to her friends, she says, asking them, "What tribe are you from?" or "Are you Frank Zappa?" He replies that "if I asked your friends what tribe they were from, it was because they were wearing long hair and head-bands like Indians, and it is Indians they would like to

Lash la Rue, Yerba Santa, not to mention Midnight's friend, Gut, nursing my daughter and trying to keep my son from biting her, while he pretends to kiss her, and Wes is doing glass alchemy in our basement.

As the sixties wind down, passages creep in that seem to reflect a different insight. Love affairs, she's decided, are a "distraction from real spiritual progress." Hippies by the score, she writes, are flocking to Hawaii, a paradise, only to discover that they are "the same old screwed up selves they were on the mainland. After months of beach, sex, dope, sun, there comes the reality of being without a shelter, nothing to eat but mangoes, and a desire for security. Security and joy. Inner things we all search for everywhere."

My sixties have been different. I rarely see Wes and Eva, usually on one of their trips to visit friends in LA or on their way south to take Colin and Theanna to Disneyland. Except for an occasional sarcastic remark from Pop, a flyer advertising a show at which Wes's work appeared, or an occasional visit when I travel north, I know little about what they are doing. Only Eva's diary finally tells me about an exhibition of Zap Comix at the San Francisco Art Institute, where Eva felt "embarrassed that the fine talents of Victor and so many other artists were being used in the service of adolescent pornography. Dope lawyers and entourages of ladies, very hip, elegantly dressed in silks, fringe, and satin, stand around viewing Minnie and Mickey Mouse in all possible sexual positions."

Still feeling spiritually incomplete, and influenced by her friend Liz Epstein (whose father and uncle co-wrote *Casablanca*), Eva visits Jim Jones's People's Temple. Jones's charisma gets to her. His "Taurus style" she finds "earthy, sexual, and domineering." She cries for most of the four-and-a-half-hour ceremony and feels immense love for everyone.

She is almost ready to follow. Wes, however, is unimpressed, and Eva's rapture soon dissipates. Ultimately, she decides that Jones is "too political." And though her friend Liz spends several years as a member of his flock, she leaves before the final Guinea tragedy at Jonestown. The night after her last visit to People's Temple, Eva and Wes go to the opening of Winterland. It is an immense contrast. On stage, The Jefferson Airplane, The Grateful Dead, and Quicksilver Messenger Service entertain. Backstage, jaded groupies snort cocaine. At the end of the evening, they learn that Janis Joplin has died. Eve remembers her from 1964, "in the Goodman Building where Wes and I lived briefly, leaning against her door, smiling warmly. That lady was real; a self-made soul singer. Real, but foolish.

More than pretty, she had guts. Lord, be with her."

Eva has somehow held on to a gut-level reality during the upheaval of the sixties; raising her kids while being a practical help and an emotional support to Wes, who is making his own special contribution to the world of art. Despite the protestations in her diaries, her early years have clearly supplied her with enough emotional strength to blunder through.

Much to their relief, the communal birds finally take flight, and the Wilsons begin to live a more "normal" life. By the early seventies, many of Wes's poster buddies have "gone commercial," which Eva considers "impure."

Her letters to Pop chastise Sylviane's *Better Homes and Gardens* lifestyle. His wife, she says, has been "insulting of our house, our neighborhood, the way I am, Wes's art, and so have you and an apology is in order from both sides if you ask me." Sylviane's materialism and her own idealism are incompatible, she writes. "She's straight, I'm hip, and never the twain shall meet; in this lifetime, anyway."

It's 1973. Helen Clare is threatening suicide if she can't visit her grandchildren more often. Wes has a major watercolor show. Eva is reading the *Bhagavad Gita.*

Ten years into their marriage, son Jason is born. After years on the glass project, Wes is still unable to solve many technical problems. Eva is feeling sad and insecure. The attempts to make peace with Alvah and Sylviane, though, have been inching forward, and David and I join the rest of the family at a huge banquet at Spenger's Fish Grotto in Berkeley. Sponsored by the Veterans of the Lincoln Brigade, Pop is guest of honor on his seventy-second birthday. Governor Jerry Brown wanders in, spots the militant posters, realizes this is a radical gathering of some kind, offers a brief polite hello, then diplomatically ducks out.

August 1976. The Wilsons detach from Marin County, which, Eva feels, "is rapidly becoming a Babylon of self-indulgence, and we are no exceptions." Not quite sure where they're going, Wes, Eva, Colin, Theanna, and Jason take off across the country and end up buying a run-down farm house on 135 walnut-studded acres near Springfield, Missouri.

The land supports cows, chickens, several gregarious hound dogs, and the three kids, who thrive. When my son Tim and I stop by in 1978 (on the same trip to visit my cousin Phoebe), Wes is doing graphics for the local utility company.

Before Pop dies, a kind of peace has been achieved. Eva has just read *One For My Baby* and comments on it. Pop replies:

12 July 1980—HAPPY BASTILLE DAY!

Now, love, I am mildly amazed by your question, "Why do you have an attraction to sad people . . . the cast-out, the abused and used of the world . . ." YOU are the Christian in this family and I am only an unaffiliated Communist but another of my major influences as a MAN as well as a writer, was none other than Jesus of Nazareth who also had "an attraction to . . . the cast-out, the abused . . . etc." Am I wrong?

In a friendly reply, Eva writes that the kids are "nuts about the poster and the pictures you sent," then adds that the cattle they're raising have enabled them to buy a twenty-five-hundred-dollar bull, and now, a tractor. "If our plans go the way they should, we will achieve self-sufficiency within five years. An artist needs to be self-sufficient."

Helen Clare is another matter. "She never writes any more and thinks the Salvation Army is after her. She will end up on the news . . . exposed as an example of evil." Slipping deeper and deeper into paranoia and refusing help from Eva, Helen Clare endures a five-year-long bout with lung and bone cancer, then dies. (Like Alvah, she was a heavy smoker.)

Eva has slowly been putting the pieces together. She returns to graduate school and obtains a doctorate in psychology. As I write, she's been a practicing psychologist for several years. We're using e-mail now, and when I ask for her impressions of the sixties, she zips back a reply: It was the perfect time, she says, for a young person wanting to experiment with life to "test the limits." Drugs, plus multiple sex partners, she feels (from the vantage of thirty years), don't work. And she's grateful that she didn't fall into the lethal traps so many of her contemporaries did. Still, the "quest for truth [during the sixties] led to the spiritual paths now so prevalent in health care, psychology, and holistic medicine."

For Wes, the sixties were swept by a "brilliant tidal wave of insight . . . a step up on the ladder of progress [that] lit up the popular American mindscape with the thunder, flash and determination of lightning." Some of America, he feels, is still reeling from that shock, "and the wave moves ever onward."

Hunkered down on his cozy Ozark farm, Wes returns to posters. Anything from the early San Francisco days is wildly collectible; so collectible that for a time he publishes *Off the Wall,* a poster journal aimed at aficionados. Something of the commercial entrepreneur Eva wasn't sympathetic to twenty years earlier, he also turns out handsome new graphics (as well as paintings) and for three years, promotes a Rock Poster Expo in San Francisco's Golden Gate Park. At last word, he has just completed a new poster, an ad for French's Mustard, designed to sit on school lunch counters. In his classic sixties style, a woman is pictured, meditating with a fork and spoon. The slogan: "Make Lunch, Not War."

Perhaps, like so many in my family, Wes and Eva have simply been lucky. Maybe they've simply blundered through two decades of disjointed connections and a search for understanding, to come out on the other side whole, happy, and productive. Or maybe the experiences they lived through helped them to discover what most people never do—that there are innumerable paths to success.

Probably, both are true.

FOURTEEN

the distinguished publisher

*We would not be publishing books if we didn't want to
play a role in the development of the ideas and insights
which aim to make life more intelligible and more
beautiful as well as more enjoyable.*

SIMON MICHAEL BESSIE,
IN A SPEECH BEFORE THE
ASSOCIATION OF AMERICAN PUBLISHERS

When Pop's cousin Mike Bessie was new at Harper's during
the late 1940s, it suddenly occurred to him that Harry Truman ought
to be able to do a wonderful book, *Precinct to President.* So he went to
his boss, Cass Canfield, and asked what he thought.

"I think it's terrific," said Canfield, "Why don't you go after it?"

"*Me*? Go after Harry Truman?" replied Mike.

"Sure."

"*Me,* write to Truman?"

"Yes. Do it on Harper's stationery."

"Well," said Mike, "I wrote to Truman, told him about the
notion, and said I'd like to talk to him about it. To my absolute
astonishment, I was invited to come see him in the White House.
And after the conversation, I couldn't help saying, 'Mr. President,
this has been one of the big moments of my life, I can't resist asking
you; a young editor writes you, someone you've never heard of, and
you actually invite him in for a meeting—why?'"

Truman's response was simple and straightforward; and it also
said something about the magic name of the old-line publishing firm

Mike had hired on with: "For two reasons. One, I liked the idea. Second, when I was a boy at home in Missouri, we used to take *Harper's Monthly Magazine*."

As I skirted Washington Square Park that muggy September evening (I couldn't cut directly through because New York's Finest, their red lights flashing, had sealed the entrances), I was thinking back to 1940, when Mom, David, and I lived in Greenwich Village for half a year after leaving Pennsylvania. Then, young matrons strolled the pathways, gossiping, as they pushed gurgling infants in plush carriages. David and I splashed in the big central fountain, while Grandma Addie sat on a bench puffing a Camel and catching up on the latest ax murder in the *Daily News*.

But this was 1990, and as I rounded a corner, I spotted Mike Bessie and his wife Cornelia watching the latest drug bust from the stoop of the big, landmark 1830 house where they'd rented a comfortably old fashioned one-bedroom flat for the past twenty-two years. They looked more like a couple fretting about the changing neighborhood than like the jet-setting publishers they were. Even though he was nearing seventy-five, I imagined that Mike, five-foot-eight and wiry, could probably hold his own against a local mugger. At fourteen years younger, Cornelia's solid, "Sunday gardener" appearance masked a sophistication backed by quiet competence.

More thoughts popped into my head: would it be hard to pry anecdotes out of Mike about Alice B. Toklas, Anwar Sadat, and the other big names whose books he'd published? Probably not, because the Bessies are compulsive storytellers, heirs to an infectious verbosity incubated in generations long gone. Indeed, Adolphe probably wove many more elaborate tales than the slim tidbits sifting down through oral tradition. How much should I talk to Mike and Cornelia about my book? A little, perhaps? That made me think of Pop and about his irritated grumbling whenever Mike's name came up:

> He [Mike] was in town recently but he did not call me. He never will again, I'm sure, since the last time he wrote and asked how we were doing and I told him and asked him to lend me $1,000 on account for a future manuscript and/or translation. He never

replied, but sends little messages whenever he meets someone who knows me, asking how I am.

Pop's sarcastic reference to Mike as "The Distinguished Publisher" became so caustic because Mike never published his work. It didn't take long, once I got to know Mike, to understand that he selected books he felt were well crafted and exciting—and, with luck, profitable. Pop's later work rarely suited the market Mike published for. But such practical thinking would have infringed on Pop's conviction that as family, Mike owed him.

Though Mike felt the resentment, he never mentioned it, for he had a genuine fondness for his cousin. He had seen Pop off to Spain, he told me in a taped interview I conducted that same evening with him and Cornelia: "He'd put up for the night in a hotel on Lexington Avenue and Thirty-seventh Street," he said. "It was an interesting evening, a long evening. He was an influential person in my life in a lot of ways, aside from the fact that he was the first person who told me that Santa Claus didn't exist."

I confess to an ounce of resentment that Pop's sour grapes kept me from getting to know this witty relative much earlier. When I did, I discovered the same engaging zest common to Pop, Uncle Everett, and Grandma Addie. In his eighties now, Mike is still on the loud side and filled with enthusiasm, but that's balanced with a gentle concern and with an informed sensibility on a broad range of subjects and interests.

Although Mike and I had had occasional contact, it was usually for an hour or less. That September was different. I spent a long evening over a wonderful dinner prepared by Cornelia, as the three of us, along with Cornelia's then ninety-two-year-old German mother (she's one hundred as I write), reminisced about Pop, Mike's career, and about the eccentric ramblings of the Bessie family.

I vaguely recall visiting my great uncle Abe, Mike's father, when I was about five. I remember rich, dark furniture and comfortable smells, maybe from the cigars he smoked. (Mike and his sister Helena were under strict orders to remove the stogie from Papa's mouth if he fell asleep on the couch.) Or perhaps the smells were lingering ghosts of the thick gravies created by the family cook, for Abe's wife, Ella Breinin, born to a European sensibility, couldn't be without one. (Some in the family called her an "effete Easterner.") Abe's medical practice was well established, so they could afford a household *chargé d'affairs*, while Ella busied herself with music, literature, and the education of her children.

Mike adored his charming, gregarious father. But he also recalls Abe being so popular when he visited during his first summer at Camp Yukon on Maine's Lake Cabbossee, that when Mike (called by his first name, Simon, then) arrived the next year, the first greeting was invariably, "Hi, Sy, when's your father coming?" This affection extended to Abe's practice, and as time went on, his relationships with his female patients were, according to Mike, "perhaps not always purely medical." If Ella knew, she didn't let on. Opera was her diversion, every Monday night, and Abe didn't accompany her.

Although he practiced in uptown Manhattan, Abe was the model of an old-fashioned small-town doctor, a simple man who genuinely loved his work and whose great joy was delivering babies. He delivered thousands and never stopped being fascinated by the miracle in which he was called upon to participate.

Mike expected to follow in his father's footsteps, but even before his sophomore year at Harvard, he was beginning to feel that he wasn't cut out to be a physician. Laboratory work bored him. His hands weren't agile: "My frog never had a nervous system, at least not by the time I got through with it."

Mainly, other things were on his mind. America had "entered the world" during his childhood and adolescence. "Just as, at first theater, then literature (after snakes) came to your father, politics, socialism, the world, came to my generation," he told me. To Mike, the foreign correspondent was a "glamorous, almost mythic figure," always present at great events. "It represented . . . a form of historical keyhole peeping," and this fascinated him.

Just out of college, he took a staff job on the *Newark Star Eagle*, whose owner had announced that if FDR were reelected in 1936, the Depression would return in full force. "Well," said Mike, "when Roosevelt got reelected, he did the best he could to return the Depression; he fired a lot of people—including me."

There followed two years with RKO-Radio Pictures, then a stint with a market research firm. But journalism stuck. Years later, when the Library of Congress conducted a broad survey among people in all walks of life, asking the question, "Was there a book which changed your life and if so what was the book?" Mike could answer without hesitation, "Vincent Sheean's *Personal History*." It was a book, said Mike, "which caused a lot of people of my generation to buy a trench coat and head for Europe."

By 1938, Pop was returning from Spain, where he'd spent his last night with a bunch of other Lincoln Brigade vets, plastered on champagne supplied by Sheean, who had been covering the war for the *New York Herald Tribune*. By this time, Mike had written a book of his own, *Jazz Journalism*, a history of the tabloid press. It came out in September. Immediately after, he was off to Paris—forever, he thought.

At this point, Cornelia entered from the kitchen with one of those rich *gâteaux*, which are the downfall of even the most well-intentioned diet. Between mouthfuls, conversation drifted back to Abe and Ella Bessie's table of seventy years before. Alvah, his brother Everett, and their parents were guests at dinner one night, and the cook had produced an immense chocolate confection drowning in whipped cream and had set it before my grandfather Daniel. He seized a knife and boldly cut into the cake, which promptly *exploded*—all over Alvah!

As Cornelia's cake went about its artery-clogging business, I was thinking about Pop's three months in Paris in 1928, about his decision to become a writer, and was contrasting that with Mike's expectations ten years later, when Mike picked up the thread: "In the late autumn of 1939, after the war broke out, I came back."

In Europe, he had done some freelance writing and a bit of translating as he moved from modest hotel to modest hotel through France, Portugal, Italy, and into Morocco and Algeria. Back in the States, he took off for Iowa and a job with *Look* magazine. On a lean staff, Mike was soon put in charge of war coverage.

When America got into the fight, Mike, classified as a correspondent (bum eyesight kept him out of combat), bought the obligatory trench coat, and was getting ready to leave for England.

But in September of 1942, based on his experiences abroad (especially North Africa), the Office of War Information asked him to help set up in Algiers what was at first a news department for the BBC and the Voice of America, but which soon became a division of the OWI's Psychological Warfare Branch, churning out material for broadcasts, leaflets, and newspapers supporting the coming Allied invasions of North Africa and Europe. As director of the division, Mike had a box seat for history in the making. In his middle twenties, he had the good fortune to rarely be shot at and was at the absolute center of two theaters of combat. "I was," he says, "very, very, very lucky. I had a marvelous war."

As the Allies advanced, so did Mike—from Algiers, to Italy, Egypt, and then to France—while hopping over to London every now and then. He was in on the war in Tunisia, formation of the first De Gaulle government in Algiers, the invasion and final surrender of Italy. Always busy preparing materials coordinated to precede and augment the landings and occupation, by D-Day Mike was in charge of an operation involving more than three thousand people, supplying news and propaganda for the entire Mediterranean.

Back in Danbury, and later in Poughkeepsie, I was collecting scrap metal to help build bombs and watching Humphrey Bogart or Alan Ladd tussle with spies and saboteurs. If Mike's war didn't match my celluloid version, it was nonetheless an exciting one: there were strategy meetings with General Walter Bedell Smith, preparation of false propaganda designed to mislead the Axis, a Mata Hari discovered in the ranks, coordinated actions with the OSS and MI-5, and a memorable broadcast just before the landings in Sicily. With Mike's entire staff gathered at 4 A.M., the announcement was made that "the next voice you hear will be that of the Commander in Chief of the Allied Force Headquarters, General Dwight D. Eisenhower." The engineer put the recording on at the wrong speed, "and out came Donald Duck!"

Mike came back from the war in the fall of 1946, married to Connie Ernst, a fellow OWI and Voice of America worker he'd met on a brief return to New York in 1945. He had also been awarded the Medal of Freedom and had made a flock of new, influential friends in radio, publishing, and other media. His options were unlimited: he had to decide whether to go back to *Look,* accept a job as director of news at CBS, become managing director of the *New Republic,* or go into book publishing.

When I commented, "So you chose publishing," Mike added that in a sense, it also chose him. Edward R. Murrow helped him make the decision. Mike had met CBS head William Paley during the war and was terribly tempted by his offer. Paley enlisted Murrow to persuade him to take the job. "I had two lunches with Murrow, in the course of which he persuaded me that I shouldn't take it." Murrow didn't feel that Mike had "the kind of personality that's needed in this." Television was coming on, he said, "and television is going to be entertainment and big money. This is an advertising business. These people are sharks. I'm going to survive in it as best I can, doing what I want to do, and I'm going to have a hard time at that." "And God knows he did," Mike went on; then he added, "He did me a real favor."

The *New Republic* was out because FDR's former vice-president, Henry Wallace, had been hired as editor, and though Mike (along with Theodore H. White, also invited aboard) admired Wallace, he felt he'd do a poor job editing a magazine. Cass Canfield, Mike's immediate superior toward the end of the war, had suggested he might try book publishing, something that hadn't occurred to him but something that had been very much on the mind of people like Canfield and Paley, in broadcasting, who, even before peace broke out, were looking for bright young men to recruit.

By the fall of 1946, Mike was hired as an associate editor at Harper's and was on his way to becoming "The Distinguished Publisher" of my father's jibes. He lost little time mining the wealth of material being churned out by people he'd met during the war. By the end of 1947, he'd published two titles and was hot on the trail of more authors. And he'd learned that the magic words, "book publisher" and "Harper's," opened almost any door.

This was how he signed Louis Fisher, with his biography of Gandhi, then the contact with Truman for a book (Harry never found time to write it). He brought in John Cheever's *The Wapshot Chronicle* for a twenty-five-hundred-dollar advance. Cheever warned Mike that if the book contained "too many smells . . . my wife thinks it does," it was too bad; he wasn't going to take them out, "for I am a very olfactory fellow." Smells and all, the book was a best seller.

Tallulah Bankhead's autobiography, *Tallulah,* was cobbled together (with Mike's editing) by Broadway press agent Richard Maney, from answers to questions the flamboyant actress supplied on audiotape. The first question, "What's your first memory?" brought a rather stilted "probably true story about a barn fire or something like that." When it became obvious to Tallulah that she was putting on a performance, she completely broke up and said, "I can't go on with this fucking goddamn thing!" "Then," added Mike, "she staged a whole scene on the tape . . . and she went on and on, ending up with hysterics . . . and then there was a moment's silence, and then, in a completely controlled, direct, honest voice, she said, 'Well, now, let's see. Where were we?'"

Working with Jan de Hartog on half a dozen books (de Hartog also authored the Broadway hit, *The Fourposter*) sometimes meant spending two or three days on the novelist's boat in Florida, for de Hartog insisted on reading each completed work aloud to Mike. One novel presented especially severe problems, and they turned in that night depressed. By morning, de Hartog said he'd fixed the problem. "What did you do?" asked Mike. "I cut out the first thirty-five thousand words," replied the author.

Through all Mike's recollections, there run not only copious anecdotes but also an eclectic intellectual curiosity, reflected in the wide range of books he chose to bring out.

Dr. Alfred Kinsey was "a complex, multifaceted man [who] was enormously interested in painting, and believed that in painting you could find all sorts of clues to the sexual nature or temperament of the painter." After his first two books were issued by a medical publisher, Mike convinced Kinsey to bring these (and others) out through Harper's in popular editions; and he noted that along with his research into human sexual activity, the man had a sense of humor, "one manifestation of which was a capacity to concoct cocktails that would put most of his guests flat on their backs in very little time at all." A devotee of the theory that if rum was sufficiently disguised by fruit juice, you could give people a great deal more than they thought they were absorbing, Mike added, "I can testify that it worked."

All through dinner, Mike and Cornelia had been plying me with copious amounts of a mellow wine, and I was fairly mellow myself, so the parade of authors Mike had brought to Harper's marched by all too quickly: Art Buchwald, Leo Rosten, Kenneth Tynan, General James Gavin, Ignazio Silone, and dozens of others. Grandma Moses decided on Mike for *My Life's History,* because as a child she'd begun to draw by copying illustrations from *Harper's Weekly.*

And then, there was Alice B. Toklas: "To start out with, nobody ever looked like Alice Toklas except Alice. Her clothes looked as if they were on a hanger, on a clothes rack, rather than on a human body. She was always seen in a hat that looked like monkey fur. She by this time had a wealth of hair on her face, a mustache and wisps of hair elsewhere. She was a most extraordinary looking person. And out of this small frame—her face was almost like the smile on a Cheshire cat—came a stream of absolutely fascinating conversation, characterized by extraordinary recall. She seemed to remember everything that had ever passed before her eyes—and a lot had."

Mike had briefly met Gertrude Stein and Alice Toklas in 1938 and again right after the war. In the early 1950s, he was in Paris, scouting for Harper's, and approached Toklas with the notion of writing a book on her life. Stein had died by then, and Alice told Mike that Gertrude had already done her biography. But she thought maybe she could turn out something partly autobiographical. "Maybe a cookbook, because she was a passionate cook." Toklas produced the book "in bits and pieces, and I went over it with her . . . [even though Mike was no expert in cookery] but one didn't have to be. And that's how that book came about."

Stories about Stein and Toklas are legend, so Mike is sometimes unsure if an incident he recalls actually happened to him or to someone else. He recalled the day he sat in their apartment looking at a tiny painting of three small apples. Toklas observed that the painting interested him, told him there was a story with it, and asked what he thought of it.

"Well," said Mike, "It looks like Cézanne, and at the same time it looks like Picasso."

Toklas continued: " 'There is a very good reason for it. When we,'—she always said 'we' when she meant she and Gertrude— 'When we broke up with Gertrude's brother Leo,'—they had all lived together, and when they decided to separate there came the terrible problem of how to divide up the paintings, which they had really collected together . . .

"At any rate it came down to several very painful sorts of decisions, and one of them was that they had Cézanne's three apples, and that was one of the paintings I guess that went to Leo. And a little while later their friend Pablo Picasso came along to have supper with them, and they seemed sad and he commented on this. Well, they had lost Cézanne's three apples!

"So a month or so later Picasso came for supper again and he had a small canvas which he gave them and he said, 'Here, I have painted Cézanne's three apples for you.'"

Though his job was secure, by the late 1950s Mike began to feel he wasn't "a member of the club" at Harper's. Coincidentally, his good friend Alfred A. (Pat) Knopf Jr. was feeling stifled at the House of Knopf, where every decision was made by his aging, strong-willed parents. After Pat's attempt to recruit Mike was squelched by the elder Knopfs, Mike and Pat decided (with a third partner, Hiram Haydn) to begin their own company. Friends put up the necessary capital. They called the new firm Atheneum.

Cornelia, free at last of culinary duties, cut in at this point to recall that "they started with one million dollars and the ill will of three major publishers."

Despite the ill will, Mike and his partners built Atheneum into a thriving independent firm. (A children's line became their most successful division.) A new, small house was attractive to up-and-coming authors. Established ones came on board because Atheneum had enough capital to offer respectable advances.

One of their first titles, *The Last of the Just*, by Andre Schwarz-Bart, became an immediate best-seller. Mike had heard about the book on a trip to France in 1959. Reading the proofs in one night, he told his partners he'd just read a book, not yet published in France, that started in a pogrom in thirteenth-century England and ended in the gas chambers of Auschwitz, "but which we absolutely must publish." "Of course," said his partners.

I, too, read the book, soon after it came out in 1960. While I was enormously moved, family misconnections being what they were, I

Mike and his first wife, Connie Ernst, with one of his authors, Anna Mary Robertson ("Grandma" Moses).

had no idea that a Bessie was responsible for its publication; and it would be twelve more years before Mike and I made contact.

Within the next year, Atheneum had two more huge hits, *The Rothschilds,* by Frederic Morton, and the first in Theodore H. (Teddy) White's series, *The Making of the President,* which had been turned down by other publishers (perhaps because White had been describing it as a textbook). A vigorous, colorful writer who "couldn't write a textbook if he tried," White described how power in American politics was captured by putting a single national election under the microscope.

Immediately after JFK's assassination, Lyndon Johnson's *A Time for Action,* basically a collection of speeches, put together by Mike and George Reedy of the White House press office, came out because Johnson felt he wasn't well-enough known and so had to have a book. In 1964, Mike contracted for Fidel Castro's autobiography. Though he received a huge bundle of pages, like Truman's book it ultimately never materialized. Nor were their titles only political. Atheneum brought out everything from poet Dame Edith Sitwell's autobiography to *The Pepperidge Farm Cook Book.*

With money often in short supply, it was a "cliffhanger" business. There was never enough surplus to put something aside for a rainy day, though a big book usually came along to bail them out. It was a busy sixteen years. Pat Knopf was the salesman. Mike, dashing around the world, signing authors, brought in most of the best-sellers. Increasing disagreement between the partners created tensions that led to Hiram Haydn leaving the company. To Mike, the split was something like the breakup of a marriage.

By then, Mike's marriage to his first wife, Connie, was also faltering. In 1965, it ended. But the books kept rolling in: Janet Flanner's *Paris Journals,* Edward Albee's *Who's Afraid of Virginia Woolf,* Giorgio Bassani's *The Garden of the Finzi-Continis,* Robert Ardrey's *African Genesis,* and work by Ruth Gordon and Eric Ambler. The list goes on and on. Some big ones got away: Eudora Welty's *Losing Battles,* and, unable to afford the million-dollar advance he eventually got, Herman Wouk's *The Winds of War.* Still, they found continuing success with Teddy White's *Making of the President,* 1964, 1968 and 1972. *Breach of Faith,* his study of Richard Nixon, was Atheneum's last title while Mike was there.

By 1970, publishing was in a slump. And in a development similar to that in movies, the emphasis was shifting to big commercial titles. Small independent houses were having a rough time. CBS had gobbled up Holt. Little, Brown went to Time, Inc. Alfred A. Knopf sold itself to Random House. They decided to "get under somebody's umbrella." "And also I thought that I'd had ten very good, very lucky years, and I wasn't at all sure I could keep it up." During the next three years, they tried hard to develop their bottom line on a rising curve, so to be more attractive to a purchaser. But by 1974, they were beginning to be concerned. They were making a profit, "but it was by a succession of miracles. If we hadn't had this best-seller or that, if we hadn't gotten Teddy White's book at that moment, or James Clavell's book at that moment . . . it would have been serious trouble."

Although the financial handwriting was on the wall, "the world had changed and the suitors were less ardent." Finally, Harper's (by then, Harper and Row), which had been wooing Mike again, made an offer, but it was so low that Pat Knopf and the other stockholders were unwilling to sell. So the Atheneum directors bought Mike's stock, and in August of 1975, he returned to Harper and Row as a senior vice-president, member of the board of directors, and publisher of his own small list of books.

By 1981, Mike and his second wife had their own imprint within Harper's, Cornelia & Michael Bessie Books. Though I'd met Cornelia, I didn't have much sense of her until that 1990 dinner.

Shortly after she finished college (Barnard, the Sorbonne, Oxford) she had entered a writing competition sponsored by *Mademoiselle* magazine. At a cocktail party for the winners, a woman approached her and asked, "What can we do for you?"

> CORNELIA: I had the bad taste to say, "Well, as it happens I need a job." So she gave me a list . . . and the first name on the list happened to be Harper's.
>
> MIKE: Well, it's a delicious little story. The woman who then ran the reading department at Harper's, Amy Flaschner, was the perfect New York spinster; she was a woman who never went out without gloves and a hat, she was very proper, and she came into my office one day and she said, "You know that German book that you've been looking for someone to read?" and I said, "Yes," and she said, "Well, there's a young woman here and she reads German, and I was wondering whether you thought I should give it to her." I said, "If it's the kind of book that interests her, fine." She said, "Well she's very young." I said, "How young?" and she said, "She's really a very young person; she's just out of college." And I said, "So?" And Amy said, "But Mike, it's about *Casanova*!"

Mike assured Amy Flaschner that Casanova's peccadilloes were unlikely to debauch a modern college graduate, so the book was assigned, and the report Cornelia handed in was impressive. More books then arrived, at ten dollars for each read, and she thought, "They'll be paying me to eat candy next." Then one day, Amy Flaschner decided Cornelia should meet the man she worked for.

Intriguing as she found her work, Cornelia saw Mike as a "noisy, dynamic, terrifying character," and found any excuse she could to do the work at home. But "since the phone is his art form," she decided to go someplace where the phones didn't work. That meant either Russia or Africa. After a trip to Leningrad with her parents (her father wanted to see the Hermitage), she returned to find Mike worried that she was never coming back.

Somehow, Cornelia overcame her initial trepidations, and by 1968, while Mike was still at Atheneum, they had married. Not surprising—an evening with this effervescent pair makes their commonality of interests easy to understand.

Until Harper and Row became HarperCollins and was swallowed by Robert Murdoch's media empire, Cornelia and Michael Bessie Books published more than a hundred titles, including authors such as Peter Brook, Romain Gary, Doris Lessing, and Aleksandr Solzhenitsyn.

And there were others. When Harper's bid successfully on the biography of Egyptian President Anwar Sadat, one condition was that in addition to publishing the book, Mike was also to serve as editor. So off he went to Egypt. On that first trip, Mike spent hours talking with Sadat about everything from the Nasser regime, which preceded him, to the prospects for peace in the Middle East, to Egypt's internal political situation, to his feelings that Muammar Qaddafi of Libya was a "mental case":

> I think Anwar Sadat was one of the most interesting people I've ever met. . . . He said, "In a couple of months, we're going to take back the Sinai, and we are going to have a ceremony at the foot of the mountain. We would like you to come as our guests."

From here on, Mike and Cornelia had a captive audience as I sat, fascinated, listening to them recall experiences few of us have in the course of a lifetime:

> MIKE: When we came back [to Egypt] after the publication of the book . . . the first thing he said to me was, "You have made me the most happiest man in the world." I said, "That's wonderful, how did we do that?" He said, "Your check has been converted into twenty farmers' houses in my village of Mit Abul-Kum, and those houses are the first in our village to have two water faucets, one for cold—and one for *hot*.

277

Sadat then added that the second check would build forty more houses; among them, the first homes in Egypt with solar heating:

> MIKE: One of the most exciting days we've ever had was that day. We went all the way back to Cairo, and the day after we got there, we were summoned at four o'clock in the morning to the airport.
> CORNELIA: We go in an armored plane.
> MIKE: He was taking back the Sinai region and declaring what they were going to do at the foot of the mountain, which was to build a three-religion sanctuary, Moslem, Christian, Jewish.
> CORNELIA: We get into this plane, which contains his family, the Cabinet of Egypt, the lady who gave him his Nobel Prize . . . and a film goes on.
> MIKE: A little screen.
> CORNELIA: And what is on the screen is an old Laurel and Hardy film, which has nothing in it but plane crashes!

"This is the life," I think to myself. "This is Jack London, Nellie Bly, Robert Cappa."

> CORNELIA: I'm having hysterics. All the Egyptians are sitting there absolutely serious.
> MIKE: This is a plane without windows.
> CORNELIA: And you've got nothing to look at but the screen, which is one plane crash after another. So we get to the airport, and the entire party then gets into three helicopters, and we realize with pleasure and relief that . . . they've put him [Sadat] into the middle helicopter. In other words,

anyone who is gunning for these helicopters would think he's in the first one.

By now, I'm thinking about how I can finagle my way into the publishing business (but without the armored airplanes).

> CORNELIA: Also, the helicopters have windows, so you look down at the road leading through the desert.
> MIKE: And . . . laid out before us were six to eight thousand Bedouin tribesman.
> CORNELIA: On camels.
> MIKE: Mounted and armed.
> CORNELIA: [And you realize that] they've all come over the mountain . . . they're dressed as Bedouins, which means you could have a sub-machine gun under those tunics.

The helicopters eventually land and they are ushered to a large tent, where, along with the Egyptian Cabinet and dignitaries from other governments, they watch the proceedings.

> CORNELIA: And after the ceremony [we are going to be] taken up to St. Catherine's. The Burning Bush is there, the oldest bible is there.
> MIKE: Mount Sinai, where Moses came down from.
> CORNELIA: And nothing works. The cars and jeeps which are supposed to take the distinguished party up to the monastery where the monks are waiting are being commandeered by press people, and it's . . . the common garden variety Egyptian chaos.
> MIKE: It also gave us a foreboding of what could happen during one of those speeches, because we suddenly realized—one shot was all it would take.
> CORNELIA: He was totally unprotected.
> MIKE: This was all six months before he was killed.

The after-dinner drinks were beginning to wear off, but the stories continued. When they set out for the Moscow book fair in 1987, they had some hint about a book that might soon be available—a book by Mikhail Gorbachev.

> CORNELIA: We got off the plane and there was a man there who

Michael knew, a mid-level bureaucrat, leaning against the
ramp, and he said, "Come with me."

Well aware that Harper's was one of the more appropriate publishers for the book, *Perestroika: New Thinking for Our Country and the
World*, the Soviets also knew that an important book warranted an
important advance. Negotiations went on and on, every morning:

MIKE: Bureaucrats were negotiating for the boss.

CORNELIA: So, there was a lot of display because . . . there were a
lot of publishers around, and I think they were quite uncertain . . . who to give this to, and so I think part of the length of
these endless negotiations was that a lot of people had to lay
eyes on us.

DAN BESSIE: They were checking you out.

CORNELIA: Exactly. And then there finally came the day when
one of the people close to Gorbachev said, "Well, he's still in
the south. He's finished the book, and it's left on a plane an
hour ago, and it will be in Moscow tonight, and we'll put it
into translation. Today is Wednesday, and you'll have it next
Wednesday."

Mike and Cornelia had counted on taking the book home, having it translated, then taking a leisurely few weeks to look it over.

MIKE: The manuscript was delivered to us in English in a hotel in
Leningrad, and we had to decide yes or no, if we were going
to take it and publish it, and if we said yes, we were going to
have to pay half a million dollars for it. And if we said no, I
was worried we would be thrown in jail. Cornelia wasn't.

CORNELIA: I thought we were going to get run over by a taxi.

MIKE: It was an awkward situation.

CORNELIA: But having to say no to the General Secretary of the
Soviet Union from your desk at 10 East Fifty-third Street is
somewhat different than doing it in the middle of the Soviet
Union, to a bunch of bureaucrats whose careers you suspect
will either fly or fail.

MIKE: We didn't know what we were going to get, and when
Isachenko showed up with two copies of it at nine o'clock that
morning . . . Cornelia took one copy into the bedroom and I
sat at the table in the sitting room, and after I'd read about

thirty pages, I went in and looked at her lying there on the bed, and I said, "Ummm?" and she said, "I think it's a book," and I said, "I do, too."

CORNELIA: He [Gorbachev] was really interested in one thing, which was not a discussion about money, but he wanted the book published by the seventieth anniversary of the revolution.

MIKE: Which was five weeks hence! You can't do a book in that time.

CORNELIA: Not in America.

MIKE: But we did it.

They did it. And they did it because they felt that despite the huge advance, the interest in the person as well as the book, and their strong feeling that "this man was on the level," would make of its publication a world-class *event*. And an event it became.

The "historical keyhole peeping" that first attracted Mike to journalism has gone far beyond the world of books. In a 1985 appearance at Stanford University, a series of challenging questions to potential future publishers made it clear that Mike's interest in exciting authors and provocative titles has as much to do with making people *think* as with anything else. Would the students, he wanted to know, have been willing to publish Hitler's diaries or *Mein Kampf* in 1935? Would they bring out a title by a famous scientist and Nobel Prize winner whose thesis was that white people are smarter than black people? Would they want to be known as Charles Manson's publisher or be willing to issue a diet book likely to make a lot of money, even if they knew in advance the diet's effectiveness was unknown?

To Mike, questions such as these have to do with First Amendment issues. "Actually, the purpose of the First Amendment is not so much to protect the rights of the writer but to protect the *reader*, to keep the marketplace of ideas as open as possible."

Still, I found his answers to his own questions something of a contradiction. Representing Harper and Row, he would have published Hitler's diaries, but in terms of Bessie Books, he *wouldn't* want to be listed as the publisher. (I keep forgetting to ask him about that.)

Listening to Mike that September evening gave me a clearer picture of Pop's cousin. I began to see that going after Toklas or

(Left) Cornelia, on the Connecticut River, 1994. (Below) Mike at
the helm of his sloop.

Truman, Castro or Rockefeller, was no mere celebrity hopping. It had to do with offering nourishment vital to the human spirit.

Then, too, there are perks: the world travel, hobnobbing with intellectual giants, the rambling old farmhouse Mike and Cornelia have maintained for almost thirty years, the peaceful cove in the Connecticut River where, as a kid, Mike went boating with his father and where he now sails his own thirty-eight-foot sloop.

It's clear that Mike takes after his father in other ways. There's the same small-town quality but tempered with a big city sophistication. Just as Abe delivered thousands of babies, Mike has been midwife to an immense nursery of literary children.

There were so many others that Mike had worked with and been fascinated by: Freeman Dyson, Aldous Huxley, Saul Steinberg. And there were some who he could never convince to write a book. "When I was first in publishing," he added, "I wanted very much to get Toscanini's autobiography, but he said he couldn't do it, he wasn't a writer, and—"

But the hour was late. As I thanked them both for the evening of delicious memories, and Cornelia for the memorable dinner, talk drifted back to the Bessie family, with Mike recalling the wonderful dinners his Aunt Lena cooked, and we could have gone on into the small hours if I hadn't hugged my goodnight hugs, then hurried down the steps and across Washington Square, deserted now, except for several benches where homeless lay asleep under newspapers. Driving along Fourteenth Street, then uptown to the Parkway, I reflected on the evening and thought more about the Bessie family and its quirky fortunes.

Like Pop, who didn't become the lawyer his father insisted he would, Mike didn't become the doctor his father imagined; but then, Abe, who loved doctoring, never became the army officer his father Adolphe had in mind. And Adolphe, who stowed away on a boat to America, didn't become the tradesman *his* father, Daniel Nathan Cohen Bessie, probably thought *he* would.

$\asymp$

There is the same incestuousness in publishing as in the movie business, with executives switching companies, forming their own, hiring friends away from rival firms, then at some point returning to the company they originally worked for; a never-ending game of

The Distinguished Publisher.

musical chairs. So it wasn't surprising that three years later, Mike and Cornelia came to a parting of the ways with HarperCollins and took the Bessie Books imprint to Random House, the same company Mike and Pat Knopf had lured Hiram Haydn away from when they started Atheneum.

By then, Helen and I had completed *Turnabout*, the video on Uncle Harry and Forman Brown. I sent it to Mike, knowing he'd enjoy it and also because he was on the advisory board of New York's public TV station, WNET. I was sure he'd pass it on to the right people. The station called a few weeks later. They'd fallen in love with the show, wanted to run it, and offered a modest sum for the privilege. Helen and I accepted immediately, and almost as immediately I called Mike, who was immensely pleased.

"You know," he said, "in somewhere close to seventy-five projects I've suggested or pitched to the station in all these years, this is the first one they've bought!"

I believe that even Pop, perhaps grumping a bit, would have doffed his beret.

FIFTEEN

gifts

I can trace my ancestry back to a proto-plasmal primordial atomic globule. Consequently, my family pride is something inconceivable. I can't help it. I was born sneering.

FROM *THE MIKADO*, W.S. GILBERT

The man who has nothing to boast of but his illustrious ancestry is like the potato—the best part is underground.

THOMAS OVERBURY

Rare Birds. These have been some of mine. I could have written about others in this odd and energetic family, folks whose eclectic ramblings would double the page count: one who has scaled Aconcagua's twenty-three thousand feet and reached the top of Mount McKinley, despite a storm that killed seven and trapped her for ten days; the leading restorer of Lotus automobiles in the world; a recluse painter who had his first one-man show at seventy; and a doctor who operated on wounded GIs aboard a hospital ship on the storm-tossed Pacific during World War II.

Most families, I believe, have rare birds, a nest of often fascinating and sometimes maddening characters whose stories soar with rhetorical eloquence, inviting skeptical yawns or sarcastic brickbats—or which leave those within earshot rolling on the floor because the lies are so delightfully outrageous. Perhaps the big difference between my family and others is simply that I developed a curious genealogical itch that needed scratching.

Having explored their history in musty archives, torn most of my remaining hair out in an effort to decipher barely legible scrawls on yellowed documents, and sifted through old photos for too many hours, I feel I'm just beginning to know them. Recreating them on paper accelerates the process. It's like sitting down with a roomful of strangers and uncovering a wealth of commonality you didn't realize existed. For me, the larger discovery has been that the multi-colored quilt of family is more than the patchwork of fragments handed down in the stories. Cut from the same sturdy cloth, then woven together, these Bessies and Burnetts and their kin seem like a durable overcoat that gets passed from generation to generation.

In every family, something is handed down. Sometimes the hand-me-down brings with it great sorrow or maybe bragging rights (or a skeleton we keep in the closet). Some view these hand-me-downs as a curse, a huge cross to be dragged along the pathway of life, like Jesus on his way to Calvary.

I like to see these hand-me-downs as gifts, even those that don't come wrapped in fancy paper. In this sense, the rare birds have never really been gone. Each leaves something of his or herself behind (in addition to Adolphe's tarnished Civil War sword). They've all passed on something, adding to who I've become; from the Old Gentleman with his great compassion and unquenchable need to help others, to Uncle Leo's spunky entrepreneurship, to Pop's infectious gift of gab—inherited from Grandma Addie—to his willingness to stand up for what he believed in. Pop's gregarious imagination has been a wonderful gift as well, as has been Uncle Harry's (and even Harold's). So, too, has been Harold's humanity and caring, qualities that transcended his own pain.

Others, like Forman and Phoebe, modeled patience for me as well as emotional balance and the courage to chart an artistic direction in my own life. Eva and Wes helped me understand that it matters less what road we take than that we get there. Seeing Mike, the Distinguished Publisher, through my own eyes instead of through Pop's subjective vision helped me learn to always go to the source to discover who a person is.

Mostly it was from Mom, whose focus and attention to and concern for each living creature, that I learned lessons I had not even known needed to be learned: how not to be afraid to make mistakes, how to look at every experience as an opportunity for potential growth, and how to see each day as a new beginning. (No, I can't honestly say I knew all this growing up. Hindsight and trial-and-error are gifts too.)

Looking at hand-me-downs as gifts, I believe, offers the possibility of seeing the world in a vital and creative way. No matter how difficult it may have been to live within, no matter how famous or infamous its members, family can be a treasure trove of experience on which to draw. With a clear vision of where we came from and how that affects who we are, we have the opportunity to shuck negativity—and invite inspiration.

Ultimately, family comes down to people. Individuals. One-on-one relationships. This has been brought home to me more immediately than ever during the past many months. Taking a long, hard look at my own life, and deciding that even though I've been fortunate enough to do mainly what I've wanted to do, somehow, the pressures of simple existence seem greater than they need to be, the days too short. So, deciding to change that, to live more simply, I bought a small house in the Sierra foothills. Perched on a gentle knoll in a pine-covered river valley, flooded with sunlight and deer, these two and a half acres hold the promise of a peaceful place to write more books, to putter, and to have good friends visit or come to get away when they need a break.

It feels like a reconnection with my birthplace in Vermont, with the Landgrove valley of the two streams that my parents fell in love with before I was born. A reconnection with the past, it's also a reconnection with my brother, David. Though David and I were close as kids, we each went our own way during and after high school, seeing one another only off and on. Busy with separate lives, raising our families, often living hundreds of miles apart through many years, we also seemed (to me) to share little commonality in terms of life goals or "ways of being." David seemed more goal-oriented, more concerned with the need for financial security. I was almost *unconcerned* with that, highly political for a long time, and driven toward involvement in the arts.

But all along, there has been an intense loyalty toward me on David's part, a depth of concern that I never felt I matched. Whenever I needed him, he was always there, offering emotional support or practical help, from driving miles to tow an old car home that some people I trusted had run off with, to calling me almost daily to see how I was doing after the hard breakup of a long-term relationship. The times he's showed that compassion have been too numerous to mention and would only embarrass him if I wrote about them. And initially, it was David who, sensing, I think, that I "belonged" in a peaceful country setting, kept urging me to look for a place with the tranquility of the green foothills where I'm now living. (Of course, he saw it as security for me, too.) It's been David who (often using his own funds) volunteered to build a porch on the little house, build a deck, paint the house, trim the weeds, and help me create a plan for how to live equitably in this lovely spot.

This is a part of what comes from being family. It's part of the heritage that David, too, has received from all those Bessies and Burnetts. We return to the roots we always had. Too often we forget that these lie just below the surface. In the process, I've begun rediscovering a brother I always loved but whose soul I had rarely touched, until recently. New gifts keep arriving.

Enough. I've done my job; and in the doing, I hope that like those who came before, those who gave so much to me, I've given something to those coming up, mine and yours. Each person who passes this way has their own story to tell, and if life leads them in that direction, maybe their own book to write. And these will add to the rich continuum of family that is, in turn, a part of the broad human experience.

Or maybe those who come after us will simply live their lives, and be happy people, and pass on some of that happiness to the others they love and care about—which, after all, is plenty.

Cast of Characters

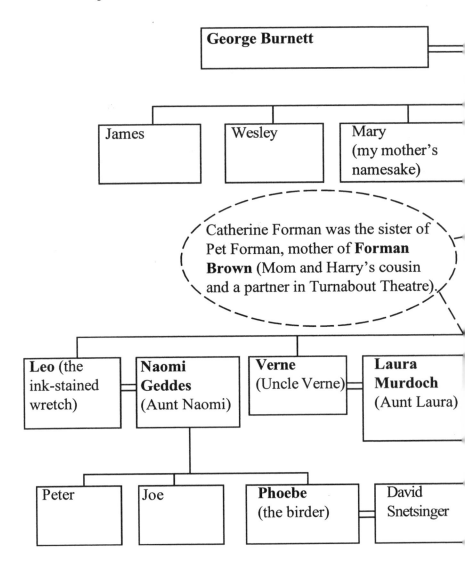

George Burnett

James | Wesley | Mary (my mother's namesake)

*Catherine Forman was the sister of Pet Forman, mother of **Forman Brown** (Mom and Harry's cousin and a partner in Turnabout Theatre).*

Leo (the ink-stained wretch) | **Naomi Geddes** (Aunt Naomi) | **Verne** (Uncle Verne) | **Laura Murdoch** (Aunt Laura)

Peter | Joe | **Phoebe** (the birder) | David Snetsinger